The Irish-American Almanac
and Green Pages

To NOREEN ——————

THE MOST BEAUTIFUL IRISH!!!!!!
ROSE TO BE PRESENTED ......

To JIM ——————

THE GREATEST FLORIST THAT
EVER LIVED ——————— DOES HE
KNOW HIS ROSES? YES SIREE!!

Betty + Jim Atkinson

1990

The

IRISH-

AMERICAN

ALMANAC

And

Green Pages

REVISED AND EXPANDED

Edited by

Brian E. Cooper

PERENNIAL LIBRARY

HARPER & ROW, PUBLISHERS, New York
Grand Rapids, Philadelphia, St. Louis, San Francisco
London, Singapore, Sydney, Tokyo, Toronto

Grateful acknowledgment is made for permission to reprint the map on page xi from *Of Irish Ways* by Mary Murray Delaney, © 1973, Dillon Press, Inc., 242 Portland Avenue South, Minneapolis, MN 55415.

REVISED EDITION

Designer: Cassandra J. Pappas

Library of Congress Cataloging-in-Publication Data
The Irish-American Almanac and Green Pages/Edited by Brian E. Cooper.
  p. cm.
  Includes index.
  ISBN 0-06-096410-3
  1. Irish Americans—Handbooks, manuals, etc. 2. Irish Americans—Directories.
I. Cooper, Brian, 1946–
E184.I6I64 1989
973'.049162—dc20   89-45137

90 91 92 93 94 DT/HC 10 9 8 7 6 5 4 3 2 1

Contents

~~~~~~~~~~~~~~~

Acknowledgments

▄▄▄▄▄▄▄▄▄▄▄▄

R are is the publication that results from solitary effort. Far from being one of these, *The Irish-American Almanac and Green Pages* could not have become a reality without the interest and contributions of many individuals, both in America and in Ireland.

I am particularly grateful for the efforts of six individuals who contributed information for use in the first edition, most of which remains in this revised and expanded edition. These contributing editors were: Martha Moore Battles, New York, N.Y.; Anne K. Bradley, New York, N.Y.; John Vincent Cody, San Francisco, Calif.; Karen S. Daugherty, Greenwich, Conn.; Joan Moody, San Antonio, Tex.; and Timothy Rogus, Chicago, Ill.

The staff of the New York offices of the Irish Export Board also merits special thanks. Jim Mongey, Maureen Frawley, Patricia Sheridan, Eileen McGrath, John McGrath and Maeve O'Malley-O'Reilly were particularly helpful in our efforts to update and expand *The Green Pages*.

Hundreds of other individuals offered information and assistance along the way. We wish, particularly, to acknowledge the following—and we profoundly regret the omission of any name that we may have forgotten to include:

Bediah Baird, Celtic Folkworks, Newfield, N.J.
Anne Barrington, Consulate General of Ireland, New York, N.Y.
Tom Bayne and Bill Cressler, American Irish Historical Society,
     New York, N.Y.
Bob Burns, Editor, *The Irish American News,* Chicago, Ill.
Patrick Campbell, Jersey City, N.J.

Angela Carter, Irish Books and Graphics, New York, N.Y.

Drew Crosby, Alicorn/Irish Books & Things, San Francisco, Calif.

Rev. John Daly, St. Patrick's Church, San Francisco, Calif.

Donn Devine, C.G.I., Consulting Genealogist, Wilmington, Del., and Genealogical Columnist, *The Irish Edition,* Philadelphia, Penn.

Patrick Dowling, Library Director, United Irish Cultural Center, San Francisco, Calif.

Dennis Doyle, *The Southern California Irish Calendar,* Glendale, Calif.

Jim Ford, Boston Public Library, Boston, Mass.

Claire Grimes, Publisher, *The Irish Echo,* New York, N.Y.—and her husband and predecessor, the late John Grimes

A. G. Haworth, Department of Geography, Trinity College, Dublin

Ethna McKiernan and Gigi Schneider, Irish Books & Media, Minneapolis, Minn.

Rev. Kevin O'Brien, St. James Church, New York, N.Y.

Orla MacCurtain, Irish Tourist Board, New York, N.Y.

Patricia O'Callaghan, Project Irish Outreach, New York, N.Y.

Niall O'Dowd, Publisher, *Irish America* magazine and *The Irish Voice,* New York, N.Y.

Denise O'Meara, (formerly of) The Irish Arts Center, New York, N.Y.

Michael O'Shea, Baltimore, Md.

Coilin Owens, The Gaelic League, Washington, D.C.

George Ryan, Editor, *The Pilot,* Boston, Mass.

John Clement Ryan, Irish Distillers International, Dublin

In addition to information provided by those above, we benefited from editorial suggestions, proofreading and other assistance from several individuals, including, most notably:

Nancy C. Aldrich, New York, N.Y.

Josephine Danna, Palomino Press, Briarwood, N.Y.

Arnold Davis, Manager of Port Promotion, The Port Authority of New York & New Jersey, New York, N.Y.

Henry Doolan, Bellerose, N.Y.

Betty Dornheim, Bronxville, N.Y.

Gerard McKeon, Director of Advertising, *Irish America* magazine, New York, N.Y.

Loren Moss, RSW Concept & Design, New York, N.Y.

Terrence O'Neill, Rye, N.Y.

Edward O. Raynolds, Short Hills, N.J.

Steven M. Roffwarg, New York, N.Y.
Leslie Safford Spiro, Waltham, Mass.
Mary Whittell, New York, N.Y.
Charles and Sally (Cooper) Wyman, Lexington, Mass.

For helping guide me in preparing this second edition for publication by Harper & Row, I am particularly indebted to Eamon Dolan, my editor there, and to my literary agent, Hiroko Kiiffner.

Finally, I would like to acknowledge the support of those companies and organizations who advertised in the first edition; and that of my parents, James and Virginia (Daugherty) Cooper. Without their material assistance, the results of so many other efforts might never have come to publication.

BRIAN E. COOPER
Chapel Hill, N.C.

Introduction

▲▲▲▲▲▲▲▲▲▲▲

Great Ireland," the writer and sociologist Rev. Andrew Greeley
has called the United States. It is, in many ways, an apt description.

The 1980 U.S. Census found that over 40 million Americans claim Irish
ancestry, either wholly or in part. (Some have questioned this figure, but
there's little doubt that there are tens of millions of Irish Americans.) By
comparison, the 32 counties of Ireland support a population estimated in
1981 at slightly over five million people. A relative few in the Irish-American community have come to the United States in recent years, notwithstanding the influx of perhaps 100,000 to 200,000 young people seeking the
employment opportunities Ireland has not been able to offer in the last
decade or so. Some Irish Americans are descended from forebears who left
Ireland two to three centuries ago, including the so-called Scots-Irish. Most
Irish Americans probably trace their roots to immigrants who arrived
sometime between the 1820s and the 1920s.

But the significance of Irish America goes far beyond its size, for much
that is characteristic of Irish culture has been perpetuated or recreated in
America.

Indeed, at a time when the use of the Irish language seems to be declining
in Ireland itself, growing thousands of Irish Americans enthusiastically em-
brace the chance to learn the tongue of their forefathers. Irish-American
folk festivals, some of them decades old, grow larger each year, and rare is
the year that doesn't see more festivals launched than discontinued. On the
material side, new businesses emerge to feed Irish America's hunger for
tangible expressions of its heritage, offering a surprising variety of traditional Irish crafts and other products—some made in the United States,

others in Ireland. Students of all ages flock to courses in Irish and Irish-American history, literature, genealogy and the like, spawning an Irish studies association that numbers over 1,500 scholars and teachers, plus hundreds of others. Traditional Irish music becomes more popular in America every year, reckoning among its devotees many who have no Irish heritage whatsoever.

In short, traditional Irish culture is alive and well in America. Hence the occasion for this two-in-one book, now in its second edition.

The idea for *The Green Pages* first came to us about five years ago. Reviewing copies of several Irish-American newspapers, we noticed repeated cases where Irish-related products or services were advertised in only one or two local or regional publications. This made sense, of course, for pubs, restaurants, businesses and organizations designed to serve only members of local Irish-American communities. Often, however, we encountered products and services that clearly had appeal to a national Irish-American audience—and many of these were available through the mail, by telephone and by other means.

We soon concluded that there was a need to be met by bringing together in a systematic, easily accessible way information about the surprising range of "things Irish" available here in the United States.

The idea for *The Irish-American Almanac* followed. As we researched *The Green Pages,* we came upon countless bits of cultural and historical lore that were as novel as they were fascinating. By and large, the information we were uncovering proved as new and as interesting to other Irish Americans as it had to us. Indeed, as we began digging for more information in such categories as traditional Irish drinking toasts, proverbs, Irish-American historical landmarks and the like, we discovered just how difficult it was to find such information. No one seemed to have pulled together in one place anything approaching the wealth of information we were finding traces of. We concluded that a wide audience would welcome such an effort.

While both parts of the book break new ground, we do not pretend they are the final word. This revised edition is bigger and, we feel confident, better than the first edition, which was itself reviewed enthusiastically in scores of newspapers and magazines in early 1987. We look forward to future editions that will keep the "perishable" information in the book up-to-date, while adding new topics and information of broad interest and appeal.

We welcome your comments, suggestions, corrections and additions. Please direct these to us in writing, in care of our publisher, Harper & Row.

Meanwhile, we hope you will find the book informative, entertaining and useful—and as enjoyable to read as we have found it to research and write.

The Irish-American Almanac

Irish Grace: A Toast for Nearly Every Occasion

▬▬▬▬▬▬

B ack in the 1500s, historians tell us, drinkers began to garnish their beer or wine with bits of spiced, toasted bread to add more flavor. Eventually, they found that some well-chosen words often added more to a drink than crumbs of overcooked bread. Even though they stopped putting toast into their drinks, however, this word stuck and has been used ever since to mean a special sentiment expressed before a drink.

Toasting special occasions is a routine custom today. With their love of words, the Irish have developed the art of toasting to a higher level than perhaps anyone else. In fact, we think you'll agree that toasts such as the following might add a special touch to even the most commonplace drink.

We have reprinted some of these toasts with the kind cooperation of Irish Distillers International, Dublin.

For Good Wishes (General)

> *Health and life to you.*
> *The wife (or husband) of your choice to you.*
> *Land without rent to you.*

And may you be half-an-hour in heaven before the Devil knows you're dead. Slainte!

May you live as long as you want, and never want as long as you live!

May the frost never afflict your spuds. May the outside leaves of your cabbage always be free from worms. May the crows never pick your haystack, and may your donkey always be in foal.

For a Wedding

A generation of children on the children of your children.

May you have as many children
and may they grow as mature in taste
and healthy in color
and as sought after
as the contents of this glass.

For an Anniversary

I have known many,
liked not a few,
loved only one.
I drink to you.

For Good Health

The health of the salmon to you:
a long life,
a full heart
and a wet mouth!

I drink to your coffin. May it be built from the wood of a 100-year-old oak tree—that I shall plant tomorrow!

For a Birthday

May you live as long as you want, and never want as long as you live!

May you die in bed at 95 years, shot by a jealous husband (or wife).

May you live to be a hundred years—with one extra year to repent.

For a Retirement, a Promotion or a Farewell

May the road rise to meet you.
May the wind be always at your back,
the sun shine warm upon your face,
the rain fall soft upon your fields,
and until we meet again
may God hold you in the hollow of His hand.

May your doctor never earn a dollar out of you
and may your heart never give out.
May the ten toes of your feet steer you clear of
all misfortune, and, before you're much older,
may you hear much better toasts than this.

May good fortune follow you all your life—
and never catch up with you!

Holiday Toasts

May you have warm words on a cold evening,
a full moon on a dark night,
and a smooth road all the way to your door.

In the New Year, may your right hand always be stretched out in
*   friendship and never in want.*

May peace and plenty be the first to lift the latch on your door, and
*   happiness be guided to your home by the candle of Christmas.* ★

For the Bachelor

May you have nicer legs than your own under the table before the
*   new spuds are up.*

★ This toast refers to the traditional custom of leaving the door unlatched, and a lighted candle in the window, on Christmas Eve.

May you be poor in misfortune,
rich in blessings,
slow to make enemies,
quick to make friends.
But rich or poor, quick or slow,
may you know nothing but happiness
from this day forward.

For a Wake

May every hair on your head turn into a candle to light your way to
Heaven, and may God and His Holy Mother take the harm of the
years away from you.

For No Particular Occasion

May the grass grow long on the road to Hell for want of use.

May you have the hindsight to know where you've been,
the foresight to know where you're going,
and the insight to know when you're going too far.

Here's to you, as good as you are.
Here's to me, as bad as I am.
As good as you are and as bad as I am,
I'm as good as you are, as bad as I am.

May the roof above us never fall in, and may we friends gathered
below never fall out.

Here's to every day I see you—and to every day I don't!

May we never want a friend in need—or a bottle to give him!

Did You Know . . .

. . . That County Mayo boasts a village with the longest place-name in Ireland: Cooneenashkirroogohifrinn. For the record, it means "the little harbor sliding to hell." But please don't ask us how it's pronounced.

Irish Proverbs: An Evergreen Selection*

~~~~~~~~~~~~~~

*I*reland, like most cultures, has a tradition of proverbs—pithy and concise sayings that express ideas and beliefs commonly held among its people. In Ireland's case, most proverbs have one of two origins. Some were originally Gaelic and were ultimately translated into English as that language grew in dominance. Others are English in origin—brought across the Irish Sea by soldiers and settlers and, over time, assimilated into Irish culture.

Comfort is not known if poverty does not come before it.

Every invalid is a physician.

Where the tongue slips, it speaks the truth.

It's almost as good as bringing good news not to bring bad.

Keep a thing for seven years and you'll find a use for it.

* Quoted in: Patricia Houghton, *A World of Proverbs* (Poole, Dorset: Blandford Press, 1981); Mary M. Delaney, *Of Irish Ways* (New York: Barnes & Noble, 1973); *The Irishman,* San Francisco, October 1985; Sean Gaffney and Seamus Cashman, eds., *Proverbs & Sayings of Ireland* (Dublin: Wolfhound Press, 1974); and Selwyn G. Champion, M.D., ed., *Racial Proverbs* (New York: Barnes & Noble, 1950).

A new broom sweeps clean, but the old brush knows all the corners.

There is pain in prohibition.

He who is bad at giving lodgings is good at showing the way.

One person with a plan helps as much as two people can.

Nearest the heart comes first out.

What's got badly, goes badly.

However long the road there comes a turning.

The devil is good to his own in this world and bad to them in the next.

While the cat is out the mouse will dance.

Better the fighting than the loneliness.

If you want praise, die. If you want blame, marry.

The thing that often occurs is never much appreciated.

A blessing does not fill the belly.

Always touch a newborn baby, or when it grows up it will lift its hand against you.

The worst, most damaging witness is a former friend.

A constant beggar gets a constant refusal.

A dimple in the chin, a devil within.

He who can follow his own will is a king.

It's the first drop that destroyed me; there's no harm at all in the last.

Neither make nor break a custom.

Beauty won't make the pot boil.

A little help is better than a deal of pity.

God never closes one door but He opens another.

Sickness is the physician's feast.

Pity him who makes his opinion a certainty.

Don't say everything you want to lest you hear something you would not like to hear.

Where there's love, there's enough.

The thing that often occurs is never appreciated.

Better an ass that carries you than a horse that throws you.

He is like a bagpipe; he never makes a noise till his belly's full.

In the world of the blind the one-eyed man is king.

The heaviest ear of corn is the one that lowliest hangs its head.

Unwillingness easily finds an excuse.

Three kinds of men fail to understand women—young men, old men and middle-aged men.

The greatest war had peace at last.

Hunger is the best sauce.

The nearer the bone, the sweeter the meat.

Did You Know . . .

. . . That James Shields (1806?–1879), a County Tyrone man, is the only person ever to have represented three states in the United States Senate. A hero of the Mexican-American War, in which he served as a brevet major-general, Shields was subsequently appointed governor of the Oregon Territory. Illinois elected him a senator first, and following Civil War service with the Army of the Potomac, he went on to win election as senator for Minnesota and Missouri, respectively.

Some Traditional Superstitions

▄▄▄▄▄▄▄▄▄▄

*L*ike most peoples, the Irish have developed over the centuries a rich folklore reflecting their closeness to the land and nature. Belief in supernatural forces and beings—fairies, leprechauns, banshees and the like—helped them explain the "why" behind many events of everyday life.

Today, phenomena that might once have been attributed to "bad luck" incurred by offending some spirit have been explained by modern science. Still, in the rural West of Ireland, particularly, some superstitions linger. Even where a person doesn't really "believe" seriously that a certain act may bring bad luck, he will often avoid doing it "just in case" there is some truth to an ancient belief.

We offer here a small selection of traditional superstitions, some of which still have a following, however small:

Carrying a wizened potato in your hip pocket will help relieve your rheumatism.

While butter is being churned, there must be no bad words, no arguing and no drinking or singing. Otherwise the butter will not come on the cream.

Even today, fishermen in the north of Ireland avoid directly using certain words, including pig, priest and rat.

On a Monday morning, fishermen will refuse, with a laugh, to give you a light for your pipe, lest they be giving away their luck for the week.

Never tear down an old house, or the spirits of those who once lived in it will never rest.

When moving to a new home, take a bucketful of turf embers from the hearth of the old house to kindle the fire in the new home. (Note: As in most cultures, fire had a special, primeval value in Irish tradition. It was not uncommon for families to have kept fires burning continuously in their hearths for 200 years or longer. The embers would be banked up at night and stoked with fresh turf in the morning. This extreme care in keeping fires alight may be related to an old Gaelic proverb from the days of the Druids: "The wee people [fairies] will go off with the fire if it goes out.")

Green is considered, ironically, to be an unlucky color.

Crosses woven from straw or rushes should be hung over the doors inside a house on the eve of St. Brigid's Day, both to honor the saint and to ward off ill fortune and evil.

The farmyard rooster's crowing is a welcome sign that a new day has dawned, but to hear him crow during the night is very unlucky.

It is an omen of *good* luck for a black cat to cross your path.

Did You Know . . .

. . . That Halloween, as it is observed in the United States, is based on the ancient Celtic celebration, Samhain.

Irish Words That Have Enriched the
English Language

▄▄▄▲▲▲▄▄▄

Banshee—In Irish tradition, a female spirit believed to foretell a death in the family by appearing to family members or wailing outside their house. (From Irish *bean sidhe,* woman of the fairies.)

Bard—A member of an ancient Celtic order of poets who wrote and performed verses in song recalling the legends and histories of their tribes. The word has come to refer, more generally, to any poet, but especially a revered national poet, such as Shakespeare. (From Irish *bard,* and Welsh *bardd.*)

Blarney—Words intended to flatter, beguile or cajole. (From the *Blarney* stone, located at Blarney Castle near Cork, which, tradition says, gives those who kiss it the skill of flattery.)

Bog—Waterlogged and spongy ground, whose soil consists mainly of decayed vegetable matter. The word also refers to an area of such ground, such as a marsh or swamp and, as a verb, "To be *bogged* down," means to be hindered, slowed or impeded, as if in a bog. (From Irish *bogach,* meaning soft ground.)

Bother—To disturb, annoy or irritate, especially with petty actions. (Perhaps from Irish *buaidhrim,* I vex, in turn from Old Irish *buadrim.*)

Brogue—A marked dialectal accent in pronouncing English, especially a heavy Irish accent. This use of the word derives from the older meaning of *brogue,* i.e., a heavy shoe made of untanned leather such as was formerly worn by Irish and Scottish peasants. The word has sometimes been used in a derogatory sense, particularly among some English people, who wished to believe that their pronunciation of the language was the only correct one, and implied that they were superior. (From Irish *brog,* meaning shoe.)

Carrageen (Also, *carragheen, carageen*)—A purplish-brown North Atlantic seaweed, also called Irish Moss, which yields a gelatin-like extract used in medicine and cooking. (From *Carragheen,* near Waterford, where the plant is found in particular abundance.)

Colleen—An Irish girl, especially a young one. (From Irish *cailin,* roughly, little countrywoman.)

Cosher—To coddle or pamper. (Probably from Irish *coisir,* meaning feast.)

Donnybrook—A brawl or free-for-all; an unusually wild and uncontrollable fight. (From *Donnybrook,* County Dublin, where a fair held annually until 1855 was noted for large and riotous altercations.)

Galore—Occurring or available in abundant or plentiful amounts, or great numbers. (From Irish *go leor,* meaning, roughly, to sufficiency.)

Hooligan—A young ruffian or hoodlum. (Generally thought to derive from an Irish family, the *Houlihans,* some of whom, justly or unjustly, became associated in the common mind with rowdy, violent behavior.)

Hubbub—A noisy tumult of voices and other sounds; din; uproar. (From Irish *hooboobbes,* related to Old Irish *abu!,* a war cry derived from Old Irish *buide,* victory.)

Keen—A wailing lament for the deceased, or the act of so wailing. (From Irish *caoine,* meaning lament.)

Limerick—A distinctive form of humorous or nonsensical verse consisting of five lines. The first, second and fifth lines rhyme with one another, while the shorter third and fourth lines form a separate rhyming pattern. (From *Limerick,* North Munster, where the verse form was first practiced. At a social gathering, tradition says, each member of the party would invent a set of verses, after which the rest of the group sang, "Won't you come up to Limerick?")

Lynch—To execute without benefit of due process, especially by hanging. (There are two theories about the origin of this term. According to one, it goes back several centuries to a lord mayor of Galway named Lynch, who was obliged by duty to hang his own son as a criminal. The second theory derives the term from Charles Lynch, an eighteenth-century Virginia planter and justice of the peace, who gained a wide reputation as a "hanging judge.")

Orrery—A mechanical model of the solar system. (After Charles Boyle [1676–1731], 4th Earl of *Orrery,* who had one made for himself.)

Shanty—A crudely built, rickety cabin; a shack. (Probably from Irish *sean tig,* old house.)

Shillelagh—A wooden cudgel or club, customarily made of blackthorn or oak. (From *Shillelagh,* County Wicklow, where these weapons were first made.)

Smithereens—Small pieces or bits of a larger object, usually one that has been violently broken. (From Irish *smidireen,* diminutive of *smoidar,* small fragment.)

Tory—A member or supporter of one of Britain's two major political parties, known since 1832 as the Conservative Party. The word has also come to mean, more generally, any extreme conservative, particularly in political and economic matters. (The term seems to have derived, in roundabout fashion, from Irish *toraidhe,* fugitive or robber, which came in turn from Middle Irish *toir,* pursuit. Tory initially meant an Irish papist or royalist outlaw, which were often one and the same during the last decade of the 1600s. When William of Orange was invited by Parliament to assume the throne of England in 1689, supplanting his father-in-law, the Catholic James II (Stuart), those in Parliament who invited him were determined that his powers be limited, and Parliament's increased. They were called Whigs after a Scottish word meaning, roughly, anti-royalist. The remaining members of Parliament favored keeping the Stuarts in power, and later supported royal authority in general against the encroachments of Parliament. As the pro-royalist and more conservative party, they were dubbed Tories.)

Whiskey—A liquor distilled from barley, rye, corn or other grain and typically containing from 40 to 50 percent alcohol by volume. (From *whiskybae,* derived in turn from Gaelic *uisgebeatha* or *usquebaugh,* water of life. *Note:* Whiskey is the usual spelling in the United States and Ireland, especially when referring to American or Irish liquor. The Scottish and Canadian liquors are generally spelled whisky, especially in their homelands.)

Did You Know . . .

. . . That, according to some estimates, as many as two thirds of the forces fighting for the North during the Civil War were of Irish birth or descent. In the South, the comparable figure was one third. The North claimed several generals of Irish birth or heritage, including Philip Sheridan, Philip Kearny, Thomas F. Meagher, Michael Corcoran, C. C. Sullivan, George Croghan, John Logan and Robert Patterson. Generals Patrick Cleburne and Patrick Finnegan led Confederate troops.

Symbols of Ireland

~~~~~~~~~~~~~

THE SHAMROCK

This is, without a doubt, the most familiar emblem of Ireland. For centuries, every March 17, Irishmen have worn shamrock sprigs in their hats to honor their patron saint, Patrick. The three-leaf, clover-like plant has traditionally been associated with the Welsh-born missionary saint.

While trying to convert a group of Irish people, we are told, St. Patrick had trouble explaining the concept of the Trinity. Seeing some shamrocks close by, he plucked one of the familiar plants. Holding it up for all to see, he explained that the three persons of the Trinity were like the three leaves of the shamrock—held together in one unit by the stem, which he used as a symbol of the godhead.

According to tradition, shamrocks never flower, nor will they grow, anywhere outside Ireland. But just what species of plant are they? According to botanists, there is, in fact, no distinct plant called a shamrock. Nathaniel Colgan, a nineteenth-century botanist, for example, collected samples from various counties of what "competent local authorities" had certified as authentic "shamrocks" gathered for St. Patrick's Day. Of 35 specimens he examined on one

16

occasion, all but two proved to be clover of various species, and the remaining two were black medick, a plant almost indistinguishable from clover during March. A shamrock, then, may be any of several plant species—usually clover, black medick, or wood sorrel—each of which has three leaves and appear similar without careful examination.

THE HARP

Though not as popular as the shamrock, the harp is the oldest official symbol of Ireland. The instrument in question is, of course, not the concert harp used in today's orchestras, but the smaller, portable harp traditionally played by Celtic bards, or minstrels.

Before it was adopted as a symbol of Ireland as a whole, the harp had been used for centuries in the arms of Leinster, the ancient Irish kingdom that endures as one of the island's four provinces. It seems first to have appeared in the heraldic arms of Ireland during the reign of the Tudor king, Henry VIII. Here it was depicted in gold on a field of St. Patrick's blue, the color associated with Ireland until the early 1800s.

When it is used today, as it is quite widely despite not being constitutionally recognized, the harp emblem is modelled on the so-called Harp of Brian Boru housed in Trinity College, Dublin. It appears on Irish coins, the unofficial Irish state arms, the presidential flag, state seals, uniforms and official printed documents and stationery. But the harp is perhaps most often seen in connection with Guinness, the quasi-national brewery that adopted it as a trademark in 1862.

THE IRISH TRICOLOR

If the flag of present-day Ireland reminds you of the French tricolor, it's no coincidence.

Throughout most of the last century, the official flag of British-ruled Ireland retained the gold emblem of Brian Boru's harp. By then, the traditional background of St. Patrick's blue had been replaced by a darkish olive green. This was not yet the vivid green of the modern Irish banner, however, but a shade said to have been

produced by combining the original blue with the orange that symbolized the Protestants of the north.

According to most accounts, the Irish tricolor made its debut in
1848, a year of revolution throughout most of Europe. The Young
Ireland movement, which was particularly sympathetic to the revolution that established the Second Republic in France, sent a delegation to Paris. There the Irish nationalists were urged to adopt a
tricolor of their own.

The model flag brought home by the delegation was based on the
French flag, comprising three vertical bands of solid color and of
equal width. The colors, of course, were appropriately Irish. Far-
thest from the flagstaff came a band of green, the color that had by
now become a popular national symbol among the Catholic majority. On the innermost side, a band of orange symbolized the Protestant minority. Between the two, as Thomas F. Meagher explained
in unveiling the flag, a band of white was inserted to symbolize a
peaceful union between the two chief elements of the Irish population.

Since this flag was revolutionary and thus illegal, displaying it
carried risks. It soon fell into obscurity. During the first two decades
of the century, the design was revived by Sinn Fein, the movement
that was in the process of adopting armed force as a means of winning independence. The flag was first flown on the General Post
Office during the Easter Rising of 1916.

No one yet looked to this as a national flag—it was flown as the
ensign of "E" Company, 4th Dublin Battalion, Irish Volunteers,
Patrick Pearse commanding. Still, the flag had now (or certainly by
1920) assumed its current form, with the colors reversed from their
positions on the 1848 design: green was now nearest the flagpole and
orange on the outer edge. As sympathy for Sinn Fein and its aims
grew, more and more Irishmen came to regard this banner as a
symbol of their solidarity with the militant nationalist group. The
Irish constitution of 1937 recognized the tricolor as the official flag
of the Republic.

The flag of the President of Ireland resembles not the tricolor, but
the quartering for Ireland in the Royal Arms of the United Kingdom, and the former Royal Arms of Ireland. It consists of a golden
harp on a field of blue. The harp, however, is not the one used in
the British arms or in Northern Ireland, but the model traditionally
associated with King Brian Boru.

SYMBOLS OF THE FOUR PROVINCES

For centuries before 1002 A.D., when Ireland was first united under King Brian Boru, the island had been divided into four rival kingdoms: Connacht, Leinster, Munster and Ulster. In general, a single, powerful family or clan dominated each kingdom. At times, however, this family fought with rival families for domination, occasionally having to share dominion or even losing out entirely. When they weren't fighting local rivals for control of their own lands, the rulers of each province were often trying to expand at one another's expense.

In time, the arms or heraldic symbols of each kingdom's dominant family came to be linked with the kingdom it ruled. Thus, the Red Hand of the O'Neills came to symbolize Ulster, and was combined with the red cross of the De Burgos (Burke) family in the provincial arms. The family origins of the other three provinces' arms seem to have been lost. At various times, however, the arms of Leinster (a silver-stringed golden harp), Munster (three antique gold crowns), and Connacht (a black eagle combined with an upright arm bearing a sword) have all served as the national arms of Ireland.

With Ireland's unification under King Brian and its gradual conquest by the Normans and English, the four kingdoms eventually disappeared as meaningful political or administrative units. But these centuries-old divisions had become ingrained. Even today, while they have little practical significance, Ireland's traditional kingdoms live on in the island's four provinces. Leinster, Munster and Connacht lie entirely within the Republic. Ulster's nine counties are divided between the Republic, which includes three, and Northern Ireland, which contains the remaining six.

The traditional arms of the four provinces live on in the official arms of the Republic, where they are quartered together on a shield.

THE WOLFHOUND

The wolfhound figures in some of Ireland's oldest sagas. The hero Fionn, for example, had a favorite hound named Bran, and another called Sceolaing. During the first centuries A.D., the island exported choice specimens to imperial Rome, which prized the dogs for "solemn shows and games." St. Patrick himself is said to have escaped from his boyhood enslavement in Ireland by hiding among a shipment of wolfhounds bound for the Continent.

Given their size, strength and noble bearing, we can easily imagine how these peculiarly Irish beasts came to be valued all across Europe. They were superbly suited for hunting wolves and deer, and probably ranked as status symbols as well. By the eighteenth century, however, wolves had become extinct in Ireland. No longer needed in their homeland, their numbers thinned by shipments abroad, wolfhounds themselves had nearly died out by the early decades of the last century.

Fortunately, an English dog-lover rescued the breed, crossing some of the few remaining specimens with Scottish deerhounds. By 1885, the newly formed Irish Wolfhound Club had compiled pedigrees for 300 of the dogs. Interest in the dog grew as the Irish rediscovered their past traditions in the so-called Celtic Revival. Artists began depicting the dog as an emblem of Ireland, usually grouped with a figure of Erin or Hibernia or in a trio with a round tower and shamrock. It also appeared on the sixpenny coin and was adopted by Belleek, the prestigious chinaware maker, as part of its company trademark.

Today, though the wolfhound remains a symbol among the Irish, it is mainly a token of a heroic past. Racing of greyhounds and hunting with foxhounds seem to monopolize Irish canine interests. It is in London, ironically, that the wolfhound endures as a living symbol of Ireland. There the Irish Guards, one of Britain's most distinguished regiments, keep one of the dogs as an official mascot and sometimes take it on ceremonial parade.

THE ROUND TOWER

The round towers of Ireland have been a familiar sight for centuries. Seventy of the structures dot the island, some in ruins, others well preserved. Nearly all stand next to churches, often amid the ruins of monasteries. Normally rising to between 90 and 110 feet, the towers are typically some 15 feet in diameter and are topped with conical caps. Particularly puzzling, until fairly recently, was the placement of their doors, which were generally set several feet above the ground, seemingly beyond reach of normal humans.

The questions of who had built the towers, when and for what purpose remained subjects of unending speculation until the nineteenth century. Many bizarre theories were put forth, including the proposition that the towers were giant phallic symbols once worshipped by some ancient fertility cult.

Today scholars agree that their origins are much more straightforward. All the towers have been dated between the ninth and twelfth centuries, and their proximity to early Christian monastic sites has given a further clue. They were, we now believe, nothing more than bell towers designed to double as places of refuge in time of danger. Given warning of a Viking raid, a common enough experience for monastic communities during this period, monks and other inhabitants could flee to the local tower, climbing up a ladder that was pulled up behind them.

Like wolfhounds, round towers are a distinctively Irish phenomenon. Outside Ireland, only a handful exist, and these are in the west of Scotland, an area the Irish had much contact with during the period in question. Therefore, the structures were a natural choice to symbolize Ireland.

Did You Know . . .

. . . That Beethoven was fond of Irish music. He prepared arrangements of several traditional Irish tunes, including "Kitty of Coleraine." And those who know the tune of "The Sash My Father Wore" will recognize snatches of it in the master's first piano concerto. Beethoven's composition "Three Variations on an Irish Air," Opus 105 No. 4, was based on the melody, "The Last Rose of Summer."

Digging Up Your Irish Roots

✳✳✳✳✳✳✳✳✳

Genealogy has been an Irish pastime for many hundreds of years. In the past, it was mainly a concern of clan chieftains and members of families with claims to royal blood, who might be called upon to prove their entitlement to rule by right of descent. *Shanachies,* learned men with prodigious memories, were employed by the island's leading Gaelic families to serve as storytellers and keepers of oral traditions. They were also expected to memorize their patrons' genealogies, and to recite them on request.

Today Americans of Irish descent usually have different reasons for pursuing their "roots." And most, of course, do not have ready-made genealogies showing their descent. This can be a blessing, on the one hand, because researching your roots can be a fascinating, challenging and very personal "detective game." For those, however, who undertake the search with preconceptions of what they're going to find, however, it can be frustrating, time-consuming and only marginally productive.

We have space here only for some general observations about how to—and how not to—go about this research, and to point out some of the problems you might encounter.

Two major obstacles come immediately to mind:

• Many records you may need to trace your Irish family tree
  may be difficult to find, if they in fact exist. During the last
  century and the first decades of this one, census records,
  most parish registers and many wills were collected and
  placed in a central repository, the Public Records Office in
  Dublin. In 1922, however, the Four Courts Building that
  housed the PRO was deliberately destroyed in the civil
  war that followed the establishment of the Irish Free State.
  Few records were left to salvage, although there are ways
  of getting around these losses in some cases. The moral
  is, don't embark on your research with unrealistically
  high hopes. If you're able to trace a branch of your
  family back three or four generations, you're doing as
  well as most people. If you can find more, thank your
  Irish luck.

• Irish family names, as we have discussed in another chapter, often changed over the course of several generations—
  sometimes more than once. So you can rarely be certain, as
  you work your way back through earlier generations,
  which of several possible spellings of a surname—or even
  which surname—you're looking for. An ancestor's Gaelic
  surname may have been anglicized several generations back
  —for example, from O Ceallaigh to O'Keily, Kelly,
  Queally, or MacKelly. Or, at the least, the "O" or "Mac/
  Mc" prefix that a surname carried for centuries may have
  been dropped more recently, especially since the late 1800s.
  Since then, many Irish have re-gaelicized their names,
  either by adding a missing "O" or "Mac/Mc," or readopt-
  ing the Gaelic spelling. Part of the surname problem stems
  from the fact that standardized spellings were adopted only
  after most people had learned to read and write English.
  Before that, someone who could write might spell your
  ancestor's surname in any of several ways, each justifiable.
  To take just one case, MacGrath has several common variations: Magrath (the "th" isn't pronounced in this spelling
  or the previous one), Magraw, MacGra, and MacGraw. It
  takes digging, imagination and more than a bit of luck to
  tell how closely a John McGrath who was born in a partic-

ular parish and townland in 1760 might be related to a Vincent Macgraw who was born in the same area in 1791.

You shouldn't be discouraged, however. You won't know what you're going to find until you start digging. And if you run up against a blank wall, you may find that a professional records searcher or genealogist can get you beyond it. In any event, genealogical research can be an enjoyable way of getting to know one or more parts of Ireland, rediscovering distant cousins, and making new friends—regardless of what information you may turn up in the end.

Still interested? Here are some general suggestions and guidelines on how to start:

1. **Start Immediately**—Some of the best clues—sometimes indispensable ones—can come from older members of your family and their close friends. By next week, next month, next year—God alone knows—one or more of them may have passed on, and with them, information that you'll never get otherwise. So, starting with yourself, of course, proceed to "interview" all living relatives you can manage to. Make up a questionnaire to help guide you, and get information that is as complete and as specific as possible. Where were they born? (e.g., not just which province or county in Ireland, but which townland, barony and/or parish)? When were they born? Where and when did they grow up, go to school, work, serve in the armed forces? What information of this type can they give about their parents and grandparents? Where and of what did they die, and where are they buried? (*Note:* Many people find that they can record a lot more information if they interview a relative using a tape recorder, and transcribe the information later. Make sure, before doing this, though, that the relative in question will feel comfortable being recorded. You want to be considerate first of all, and many people clam up in the presence of a tape recorder or video camera.

2. **Document Everything You Can**—People's memories are often faulty. While you can probably accept a good

deal of what you are told, write it down as soon as you can, recording the source, date and circumstances. For example, "Information from telephone interview with John O'Connor, my maternal uncle, on February 14, 1988." Whenever you can, try to find what genealogists call primary records for various facts. These are essentially records that were made at the time of an event, and include birth and baptismal certificates, medical records, school and college diplomas, marriage certificates, armed forces discharge papers, death certificates, census records, and so on. Also ask to see family bibles, old photographs and letters, and various other memorabilia. They can often fill in a missing link in the chain. If you can't find or keep original copies of these documents, have photocopies or photostats made.

3. **Work from the Known to the Unknown, from More Recent to More Distant People, Events and Facts**— As you collect information profiling yourself, your parents, grandparents, aunts and uncles, and so forth, facts from different sources may contradict each other—or seem to do so. Your grandfather and grandmother may have different memories about which county or town in Ireland your great-grandfather was born in. Record both their versions, and soon you're likely to find further facts that prove one of the two correct. Always remember: you're trying to construct an unbroken "chain" of information stretching back from the present into the past. Some of the links will be weak or tentative at first, but as you explore various hypotheses, you'll be able to eliminate some "facts," and to discover or confirm others.

4. **Organize Your Information**—Keep information about each individual in a separate envelope or file. At some point, sooner rather than later, you'll need to start filling in what genealogists call pedigree sheets. Each sheet normally covers four generations. The first will start, typically, with you or your children and branch back through the three preceding generations. For each individual on the sheet—the number doubles, of course, with each generation you go back—your goal will be to fill in as many

of the following vital dates and places as you can: full
name, date and place of birth, date and place of marriage,
date and place of death, place of burial. (Record the source
of each "fact," referring to primary sources whenever you
can. You'll obviously gather a lot more interesting information about the nitty-gritty of your forebears' lives as
you proceed, but you need to construct this "family tree"
to start with.)

5. **Educate Yourself About Genealogical Techniques**—
    You should be familiar with the basic methods that any-
    one researching their roots would normally use, whatever
    the national origin(s) of their families. This is particularly
    true when you're researching a family line—say, your
    mother's grandfather—whose immigrant forebear came
    from Ireland more than two or three generations ago.
    Some good general introductions to genealogical research
    are:

    Harriet Stryker-Rodda, *How to Climb Your Family Tree*
    (Baltimore: Genealogical Publishing Co., 1983)

    Ethel Williams, *Know Your Ancestors* (Rutland, Vt.:
    Charles E. Tuttle Co., 1960)

    You can probably find them in your local library—and
    your librarian may be able to suggest additional or alter-
    native books. You may also wish to enroll in a course in
    genealogical research. They are often offered by adult
    education programs, Irish-American organizations, and
    other groups.

6. **Do as Much Research as Possible in the United States**
    —Unless you're dealing with family lines that came across
    the Atlantic just one or two generations ago, you'll need
    to research first your family's most recent history here in
    America. This task will probably be fairly straightforward
    —you'll have family recollections or traditions that can be
    easily documented (or sometimes disproven) by consult-
    ing records from the counties and parishes where births,
    baptisms, marriages, deaths and other events presumably

took place. Virtually all of them are set up to provide, for
a small fee, copies of vital documents to individuals such
as yourself.

When you start dealing with the ancestor(s) who
actually immigrated from Ireland, don't rush out to make
your airline reservations! You'll probably be surprised
how much you can find out about your Irish ancestors
without going very far from home. Doing your "home-
work" on this side of the Atlantic will save you time,
money and bother if you decide to continue your research
in Ireland. The Mormon Church (Church of Jesus Christ
of Latter-Day Saints, or LDS for short) has compiled perhaps the most extensive collection of genealogical records
in the world. And you, whatever your religion, may use
them for nominal fees by contacting the nearest branch of
the LDS' nearly 500-unit library system. Chances are that
if registers of parish records and other documents useful
to you exist in Ireland, the LDS has already microfilmed
at least some of them, and perhaps put them in its computer system. There are also published volumes listing the
passengers who arrived in various East Coast ports from
Ireland during particular periods. These passenger lists
often provide other helpful information, such as the
names and ages of other family members traveling with
your ancestor, where in Ireland they were from, and so
on. The point, of course, is that there are a lot of records
available if you know where to look. To find out about
what they are, where you can find them and how they can
help, you'll probably want to take a course in basic genealogical research techniques (many Irish-American organizations run courses or workshops tailored to your needs)
or read some basic genealogy texts. Perhaps the single
most valuable book you'll find is Margaret Dickson Falley's *Irish and Scotch-Irish Family Research*. It was originally
published in 1961–62, but is still available through the
Genealogical Publishing Company, Baltimore. (See the
sections titled Genealogical Publications and Genealogical
Resources in *The Green Pages* section of this book.)

At some point, you may wish to consult a genealogist,

who may help you with a research plan, based on the information you have already gathered, that will help make your own further research easier. Or, if you're not a do-it-yourselfer, you may want to have the genealogist take over the search for you. There are competent genealogists who have no particular credentials beyond their experience. But if you want to be sure that you're using a qualified individual, request a list of professional researchers from:

Board of Certification of Genealogists
1307 Hampshire Avenue, N.W.
Washington, D.C. 20036

Frankly, once you've started delving into your family's past, chances are you're going to want to do the searching yourself. Genealogy can become an addiction—there are always more facts waiting to be discovered.★

Did You Know . . .

. . . That Irish-Americans still make up 25 percent of the seminarians studying for the Roman Catholic priesthood in the United States—more than any other ethnic group. But that's down from 34 percent in 1966, according to a survey presented to the National Catholic Education Association in 1986. (*USA Today,* April 3, 1986)

★We are indebted for help in preparing this chapter to Donn Devine, a professional genealogist and Certified Genealogical Instructor who specializes in Irish family research. He writes a monthly column for *The Irish Edition,* Philadelphia, and can be contacted by consulting the listing under "Genealogists" in *The Green Pages*.

Irish Surnames—And How
They Came to Be

༈

There's an old saying that is supposed to answer quite neatly the question of which Irish surnames are "genuinely Irish" —that is, originally adopted by families of Irish Gaelic origin. It ends thus:

> . . . and if he lack both O and Mac no Irishman is he.

There is also a widespread belief outside Ireland that the prefix Mc denotes an Irish Gaelic name, while Mac ultimately indicates Scots Gaelic descent.

In fact, these are both fallacies—or generalizations at best. The subject of Irish surnames is a complex one, largely because Irish history itself has been complex, marked by successive influxes of "foreigners"—from Vikings to Anglo-Normans, from "Old English" (Catholics) to Protestant English and Lowland Scots, with further leavening by gallowglasses (Scots mercenaries), Welsh, French Huguenots (Protestants), Palatine Germans and others.

Surnames that were adopted by the "native" Irish or brought from across the sea often did not remain unchanged for long. At various points in time, individuals or families who had come from England before Tudor times tended to adopt Gaelic culture, and changed their names accordingly. Later, as England's political dominion in Ireland expanded, many "genuine" Irish names were anglicized. They were either rendered into English by government clerks who usually had no feel for the Irish language, or changed by the holders themselves to gain economic advantage in an increasingly anglicized society.

The story of Irish surnames must thus be painted with broad brush-strokes. We shall here attempt to summarize some of the more common types of changes that occurred in names, and important events or forces that lay behind these changes.

Brian Boru (926–1014 A.D.), the first and only "high king" to unite the various petty kingdoms of Ireland into a single realm, is often credited with ordering the general adoption of hereditary surnames that seems to have occurred in the eleventh century. This claim has never been proven to be more than legend.

In any case, about the time of Brian's reign, subjects who had hitherto used no surname beyond the name of their clan or tribe began to adopt patronymic surnames. These were names based on the Christian name of their father, on the one hand, or the name of their grandfather or one of his paternal forebears, on the other.

A man, for example, whose father was named Niall could, if he wished, honor his father by adding the prefix Mac (or its shortened form, Mc) to his father's Christian name. Hence, he would be known as so-and-so Mac Niall—and his descendants might come to use a variant spelling such as MacNeill, McNeil or McNeal, in some cases dropping the Mc or Mac prefix.

If this same man wished to name himself for his grandfather, Donnchadh, or perhaps Donnchadh's father, Conchur (= Conchobair), he would prefix "Ua" to one of their names. (*Note:* The "Ua" soon evolved into "O," though at first without the apostrophe, which came about later under English influence.) Hence, Ua Donnchadha or O Donnchadha, "grandson [or descendant] of Donnchadh," and Ua Conchur or O Conchur, which meant "grandson [or descendant] of Conchur." O Donnchadha would eventually be transformed into such anglicized versions as O'Donoghue, Donoghue, Donohoe and Dunphy. From Ua Conchur, we would ultimately derive the Anglicized forms, O'Connor or simply Connor.

Although patronymics were most common, some of the Irish adopted surnames denoting their father's occupation. These, too, were passed down, generation to generation. A man whose father was a bard, or poet (*Bhaird* in Irish) might adopt the surname, Mac an Bhaird, son of the bard, which was later anglicized as Ward or MacWard. Similarly, another might adopt Mac an Ghabhann, (son of the smith), which was later anglicized to MacGowan, and still later sometimes simply translated into its English equivalent, Smith.

At the time of the Battle of Clontarf in 1214, when King Brian had defeated the Danes (Vikings) and their Irish allies, there had already been colonies of Vikings in Ireland for some time. At least after their defeat, if not before, these new Irishmen of Norse roots also adopted patronymics. Hence, an Eric whose father was named Olaf might take the name, Mac Olaf, "Son of Olaf," which eventually came to be spelled McAuliffe.

The Anglo-Normans, who first arrived in 1169, quickly became quite Gaelicized, much to the chagrin of their overlords in England. As the phrase went, they often became "more Irish than the Irish themselves." Many, however, kept their own surnames, which might or might not contain the prefix, Fitz (from the French, *fils,* meaning son of). With the exception of the surname Fitzpatrick, any Irish or English surname that begins with Fitz today (e.g., Fitzwalter, Fitzgibbon, Fitzsimmons) is an almost sure sign of Norman descent in the male line.

Other Anglo-Normans brought names lacking the Fitz prefix that are still quite common in their evolved forms, such as Burke (originally de Burgo), Cusack and Roche. There are a few examples of Anglo-Norman families adopting Gaelicized surnames. In the wake of the Anglo-Normans, "Old English" families came to Ireland, and often, like the Anglo-Normans, tended to adopt Gaelic culture.

During this period, the English crown made periodic attempts to discourage the "Gaelicization" of the recent settlers. One such attempt was the enactment of the famous Statute of Kilkenny (1366). Nonetheless, until the seventeenth century, the Crown enjoyed only limited success in its efforts to force various aspects of English culture on the inhabitants of the Pale, the area centering on Dublin that for several centuries marked the limits of English political control.

The Plantation of Ulster in 1609 marked the beginning of successful attempts to anglicize Ireland. Under rights granted them by James I, several of London's merchant companies recruited English citizens and English-speaking Lowland Scots for settlement in Ulster. William III's victories against the Catholic Irish and their allies at the end of the century secured English rule over the entire island and sealed the fate of Gaelic culture for the next two centuries.

English rule brought pressure to conform to English ways. Social and economic advancement, many Irish concluded, would come a lot easier if they jettisoned relics of Ireland's Gaelic past. One of the major consequences of this pragmatism was a tendency, during the eighteenth and nineteenth centuries, for Irish families to drop the "O" or "Mac" that might be prefixed to their surname.

With English rule also came English bureaucracy. Clerks, who were required to record Irish names for taxation or other purposes, often replaced the names with their English equivalents, or simply with English names that sounded similar. To give just three examples among hundreds, O Mordha was often changed to Moore, Cullane (O Coileain) became Collins, and at least some O'Hagans had their names changed to Hog, which was easily taken for a variant spelling of Hogg, an English surname.

Ever since, a large percentage of the Irish people has had its origins thrown into confusion. Did a family named Collins, for example, descend from Cullanes who had had their Irish name changed to Collins? Or were their forebears Englishmen who had traditionally borne the name and perpetuated it unchanged after settling in Ireland? The case is similar for Moores, Hogs, Smiths and countless other families.

As the British grip on Ireland began to loosen in the late 1800s, interest in traditional Irish culture grew among much of Ireland's population. Many surnames now went through yet another transformation. The trend, which has continued to the present day, was marked by widespread adoption of more traditional (or traditional-sounding) surnames.

Many Dohertys, for example, resumed calling themselves O'Doherty—or even more Gaelicized forms, such as O Doherty or O Dochartaigh. Smiths who believed that their original ancestor of the name had had his surname changed from an Irish form—or Smiths who simply felt themselves to be essentially Irish—abandoned the English name in favor of Mac Gowan, McGowan, Gowan or some other more Irish form.

For the person trying to trace his Irish genealogy, the changes that have affected many surnames over the centuries can be a major stumbling-block. At the very least, it should cause such root-hunters to proceed with great care in drawing conclusions about their family trees.

Did You Know . . .

. . . That the name Patrick, so common among Irish males, may not owe that much of its popularity to the fact that it was borne by Ireland's patron saint. This, at least, is the claim of one scholar, who surveyed the frequency with which the name occurs at various points in Irish history. He found that the name Patrick was relatively uncommon before the end of the seventeenth century. At that point, its popularity seems to have increased markedly. He suggests that the wider use of the name since that time reflected the tremendous esteem Irish Catholics had for Patrick Sarsfield, an Irish general who scored some notable victories for King James II against the forces of William III. After pushing William's forces out of Connacht in 1689, Sarsfield played only a minor role in the Jacobite defeat at the Boyne. Subsequently, however, he ambushed and blew up a convoy of guns and supplies meant for the Protestant forces besieging Limerick, forcing them to abandon the first siege in 1690. King James made Sarsfield Earl of Lucan in 1691. Soon afterward, the Irish hero defended Limerick against a second siege. The Treaty of Limerick, which ended the siege, provided for those Irish troops who wished to leave Ireland to depart without hindrance. Sarsfield and 12,000 of his troops left for France and there joined the Irish Brigade, in whose service he was killed in 1693.

Irish Given Names: Origins, Meanings and Equivalents

~~~~~~~~~~~

MEN'S NAMES	ORIGIN AND/OR MEANING	EQUIVALENTS
Ailbhe	"Gentle one"	Alby, Albert
Ailin	"Of gentle birth"	Allen, Alan
Amhlaoibh	Norse, "Ancestral relic"	Olaf, Humphrey
Aodh	"Fire"	Hugh, Egan
Aonghus	—	Angus, Niece
Art	"Stone" or "bear"	Arthur
Brian	"Strong, sincere"	Bryan, Bernard
Buadhach	"Conqueror"	Victor
Caoimhin	"Sweet offspring"	Kevin

MEN'S NAMES	ORIGIN AND/OR MEANING	EQUIVALENTS
Cathal	"Strong in battle"	Cahal, Charles
Cian	"Ancient"	Kean, Cain
Colm	—	Colum
Conall	"Tall and strong"	Connell
Conchur	"High desire"	Connor, Cornelius
Conn	"Intelligence"	Constantine
Cormac	"Charioteer"	Charles
Criostoir	Greek, "Christ bearing"	Christopher
Deasun	"Of south Munster"	Desmond
Diarmaid	"A freeman"	Dermott, Jeremiah
Donal	"Power of the deep"	Donald, Daniel
Donnchadh	"Brown warrior"	Donogh, Denis, Duncan
Eamonn	Anglo-Saxon, "Blessed protection"	Edmund
Eoin	Hebrew, "Gift of God"	John
Eoghan	"Well-born"	Owen, Eugene

MEN'S NAMES	ORIGIN AND/OR MEANING	EQUIVALENTS
Fearghal	"Bravest of the brave"	Fergal, Virgil
Fearghus	"The choicest one"	Fergus, Ferdinand
Fionn	"Bright" (like the sun god)	Finn
Flann	"Blood red"	Florence
Liam	Germanic, "Strong protector"	William
Niall	"Champion"	Neil
Padraig	Latin, "Noble"	Patrick
Peadar	Greek, "Rock"	Peter
Piras	Norman form of Peter	Piers, Pierce, Pearse
Ruairi	Norse, "Famous ruler"	Rory, Roger, Roderick
Seamus	Spanish name, "Jaime," from Hebrew, "Supplanter"	James
Sean	Norman French, from Hebrew, "Gift of God"	John
Traolach, Tarlach	"Incarnation of the thunder"	Turlogh, Terence

WOMEN'S NAMES	ORIGIN AND/OR MEANING	EQUIVALENTS
Aine	"Beauty" (a quality of the moon)	Anne
Aisling	"An epiphany; manifestation of the Divine"	Esther
Aoibheann	"Lovely shape"	Eavan
Blathnaid	"Little flower"	Florence
Brighid	"Strength"	Brigid, Bridie
Caitrin, Cait, Caitilin	Greek, "Pure"	Katherine, Kate, Catriona
Ciara	"The dark one"	Keary
Damhnait	"Little poet"	Devnet, Dymphna
Eibhlin	Greek, "Sunlight"	Eileen, Evelyn, Helen
Eilis	Hebrew, "Word of God"	Elizabeth
Eithne	"Kernel"	Ethna, Edna
Fionnuala	"Bright shoulder" (an attribute of the moon)	Finola, Nuala
Gobnait	"Small mouth"	Abigail, Deborah

WOMEN'S NAMES	ORIGIN AND/OR MEANING	EQUIVALENTS
Gormfhlaith	"The stranger lady"	Barbara
Grainne	"Perfect," "virginal" (attributes of the moon)	Grania, Grace, Gertrude
Ide	"Thirst"	Ida, Ita
Mairead	Greek, "A pearl"	Margaret, Marjorie
Muire, Maire	Hebrew, "Of the sea," "bitterness"	Mary, Maria, Maura, Miriam, Moya, May
Nora	Latin, "Honorable"	Norah, Honor
Orfhlaith	"The golden lady"	Orla
Proinnseas	Latin, "French, frank"	Frances, Fanny
Sile	Latin, "Blind"	Sheila, Cecily, Julia
Siobhan, Siun	Norman French, from Hebrew, "Gift of God" (feminine of Sean)	Joan, Joanna, Jeanne, Hannah
Sorcha	"Bright"	Sarah
Una	"The white one" (an attribute of the moon)	Agnes, Winifred, Freda

The Irish Language: Yesterday, Today and Tomorrow

~~~~~~~~~~~~~

To speak of "the Irish language" can be ambiguous. To the cynic or realist, the "Irish language" is English, since this is the language in everyday use among the great majority of the Irish people. Here, however, we use the term *Irish language* in its literal sense—the Irish form of Gaelic—since *Gaelic* applies also to the related tongue still spoken by some thousands of Gaels in the northwest of Scotland, and Irish Gaelic seems redundant to some.

Irish is a difficult language for most nonnative speakers to learn. Yet it lends itself to expression so well that it has been called "the language for your prayers, your curses and your lovemaking." John Millington Synge, the Irish playwright, believed there was ". . . no language like the Irish for soothing and quieting." With qualities such as these, it is indeed sad that the language is so little spoken today.

Irish is one of the oldest languages in Europe, and the fact that it is still spoken at all might seem a wonder to many. It is a tongue with a glorious past, inasmuch as Christianity was brought to much of northwestern Europe by Irish-speaking monks who had kept the faith alive in their far-flung island while barbarian invasions had extinguished Christian learning on much of the Continent. To be sure, the Irish spoken by St. Columcille and his brethren is not the same as that used today. Irish, like most languages, has gone through an evolutionary process—from Old Irish (600–900 A.D.) to Middle Irish (900–1200), Early Modern Irish (1200–1650) and Modern Irish (1650–   ). According to Dr. Douglas Hyde's *Literary History of Ireland,* during the Old Irish period the Irish brought rhyme to a perfection undreamt of, even to this day, by other nations. He goes on to show how Irish writers passed along the concept of rhymed verse to other peoples, including the English and Germans.

Until the establishment of the Irish Free State in 1921, and more recently, the Republic of Ireland, Ireland had been ruled, wholly or in part, for more than 750 years by the Anglo-Normans and their English successors. Like most conquerors, the English crown wished to impose its own "superior" culture on the conquered—in this case, the Irish. Yet so alluring was much of native Irish culture that the Anglo-Normans themselves, and most of the English Catholics who came in their wake, readily adopted many of its facets. The Anglo-Normans, in particular, were said to have become "more Irish than the Irish themselves."

Despite numerous legal measures and penalties intended to discourage these settlers from "going native," officials in England could only look on in frustration as Gaelic culture persisted, and even expanded, in Ireland. It was only in the seventeenth century that the situation began to change, and then, only because of the subjugation of all of Ireland, in varying degrees, by the Protestant forces of Oliver Cromwell, and four decades later, those of William III.

Under the Protestant Ascendancy, penal laws were enacted to discourage the practice of Catholicism and the Gaelic culture that usually went hand-in-hand with it. Under such pressure, the Irish began in increasing numbers to adopt English, sometimes to avoid penalties for speaking Irish, sometimes to "get ahead," especially in the cities and other areas of strong English influence. The Irish language was least affected in the rural areas of the West and South.

Even so, some five million of the estimated eight million people who inhabited the island in the early 1800s still spoke Irish. In 1831, the establishment of a national school system with English as the language of instruction further spurred the use of English. When the Great Famine of the mid-1840s brought death and misery to much of the island, it was precisely the counties where Irish was still most widely spoken that lost the greatest share of their population to starvation and emigration. The 1851 census found that Irish was spoken by only one-fourth of the population; by 1911, that fraction had fallen to one-eighth.

Toward the end of the century, interest in Gaelic culture began to revive and reassert itself in language, music, sports, art, literature and other forms. In 1893, Douglas Hyde, a Protestant scholar of Gaelic who later became first President of Ireland (1937–1945), and Eoin MacNeill, a historian who was to become Chief of Staff of the Irish Volunteers, took the lead in establishing the Gaelic League. Their aim was to encourage the perpetuation of the Irish language where it was still spoken, and to encourage its revival among the people at large.

The Gaelic League, which had started as a nonsectarian, nonpolitical organization, eventually developed ties with the more advanced elements of the movement for political independence. With the establishment of the Irish Free State in 1921, it could count on the new government to further much of its nationalist cultural agenda.

The new state did, indeed, make the survival of Irish part of its official policy. In 1925 it established the Gaeltacht Commission, whose mandate was to study conditions in the remaining Irish-speaking areas. Preserving the vitality of the Gaeltachts, the only areas where sizeable numbers of native Irish speakers lived, became a priority. It was furthered with the use of special subsidies to inhabitants as well as provision of other government services.

The other arm of the government's language policy involved using the state's powers to encourage study and use of Irish among the rest of the population. To these ends, at various points, students in state schools were required to demonstrate a certain level of proficiency in Gaelic to advance from the intermediate to the advanced level; and later, as a condition of receiving a diploma. In addition, some knowledge of Gaelic was made a prerequisite for civil service positions. (This requirement was dropped in 1974.)

The Irish Constitution of 1937 pronounced Irish the official language of the Republic. It "recognized" English as its second language. This dual approach to the language issue—both idealistic and pragmatic—is seen to this day in bilingual road signs, bilingual publication of parliamentary legislation, and in other manifestations.

So what of the present—and the future—of Irish? There is no

doubt that the Irish people, on average, have a better appreciation of their ancestral language than they did in, say, 1910. At the same time, the movement to make Irish an everyday language outside the Gaeltachts has had, at best, very limited results. The population of the Gaeltachts themselves seems to be slowly shrinking. But then, Ireland itself has been experiencing a net outflow between emigrants and immigrants.

At the same time, it seems apparent from numerous polls and interviews over the years that most of the Irish would feel sad indeed to see the Irish language, a central part of Irish culture, die. The question is, are they willing to personally help assure its survival? They know from experience how difficult a language it is to master. Many also ask themselves how Ireland's trade and tourism with the rest of Europe would be affected if Irish were spoken generally.

As plans for far-reaching integration of the Common Market countries await implementation in the 1990s, the fate of Irish may hang in the balance. As they come into greater contact with Germans, French, Italians and others, the Irish could *conceivably* react by turning inward culturally and sparking a meaningful revival of Irish. However, as native speakers of English, they enjoy an advantage over most of their European partners, inasmuch as English shows no signs of relinquishing its role as the de facto international language.

Chances are, we will see Irish survive as a second language among some of the Irish people into the next century. Although it will come as little consolation to those who have worked so hard to foster Irish in this century, the death of Irish should occasion neither blame nor shame if it comes. It has survived thus far against often formidable odds. And the Irish have shown, through their colorful everyday brand of English—and the works of their great writers—that they have mastered English as well as the English, or anyone else.

Did You Know . . .

. . . That Limerick-born John Sullivan, a New England schoolmaster during the mid-18th century, was the father of two state governors, two state attorneys general, a major-general in the Continental Army, the first judge appointed by George Washington in New Hampshire, and four other sons who served as officers in the Continental Army.

Sports in Ireland

^^^^^^^^^^^

*I*reland offers an array of sports broad enough to suit the taste and purse of nearly any participant or spectator. Some of these sports are Irish in origin, others are imports. For many Irish people, this distinction is more than a casual one.

The last decades of the nineteenth century saw a great revival of interest in traditional, "authentic" Irish culture—including language, literature, art, music and other pursuits that tend to go hand-in-hand with the independent nationhood toward which the Irish were working. The year 1884 saw the founding at Thurles, County Tipperary, of the Gaelic Athletic Association, an organization whose future influence could scarcely have been predicted by the seven men who met to establish it. Its founders, who secured the patronage of Dr. Thomas Croke, Archbishop of Cashel, aimed "to preserve and to popularize native Irish pastimes and thereby to reawaken national pride and self-reliance."

Though its aims were broader, the GAA was interested, first and foremost, in sports. Looking around them, its founders saw thousands of their fellow Irish playing rugby, cricket and soccer, among other games. These sports, if not all English in origin, had been introduced to Ireland by the English. In any event, as popular as they were, the GAA and many Irish people saw these sports as alien,

43

irrelevant to traditional Irish culture, and too closely associated with the British garrison in Ireland. They also seemed to be gaining in popularity, while the old Irish sports seemed endangered.

The reason for the popularity of English sport was not just pressure to conform to English ways. The 1798 Rebellion and the deaths and emigration following the Great Famine of the mid-1840s had depleted Irish-games playership in Wexford, Limerick, Cork, Kilkenny, Galway and Waterford, some of the strongest hurling counties.

Today, more than 100,000 people participate in hurling, Gaelic football, and camogie (the women's version of hurling) under the auspices of the GAA. All players, at whatever level, are amateurs. Experts have estimated that about one-third of Ireland's population attends and follows some of the hundreds of games played each summer, the championship season. Outside Ireland—in Britain, the United States, Canada, Australia, New Zealand and parts of Africa —many thousands more play these ages-old Irish games.

HURLING

Hurling, picturesquely described as "the clash of the ash," is a thrilling spectacle to watch. It is generally considered the fastest field sport anywhere. Under today's rules, two teams of 15 players each (formerly 17, and before that, 21) vie with each other to drive a fist-sized leather ball, the sliothar, through their opponent's H-shaped goalposts using their hurleys, or camans. These are ashwood sticks that resemble hockey sticks. (*Note:* In North American GAA games, each team fields only 13 players.)

Points in hurling may be scored in two ways. A full goal, worth three points, is scored when the ball is driven *under* the crossbar of the goalpost and past the defending goalkeeper into the net. Getting the ball *over* the post is good for one point. Games are played nonstop to their conclusion, except for a break between the two halves, which run 30 minutes each in normal play but are extended to 35 in Finals matches. Up to three substitutions are permitted for injured players—it can be a rough game. Deft stickwork combines with virtuoso footwork to make hurling a sport requiring brains as well as brawn.

Hurling is the object of fierce rivalry among Irish counties. A dozen counties have compiled records that place them in the first echelon. Until about 1890, competition normally pitted neighboring parishes or baronies against one another, with no limit on the number of players per team.

GAELIC FOOTBALL

Gaelic football seems, at first glance, to be a combination of soccer and rugby. In fact, football "under Irish rules" was popular in Dublin, Louth, Meath and Cork for more than a century before these English variants made their Irish debuts. Some scholars believe, however, that Gaelic football, and today's English football variants, had a common ancestor between 800 and 900 years ago.

Like hurling, Gaelic football was once played with enormous numbers of men on each side. Town would play town, or parish play parish, with anywhere from 25 to 100 players per side. There were attempts to keep the numbers even, but in practice one side might easily have 5 to 30 more players than its opponent.

The rules in those earlier centuries did not provide for a fixed playing field with measured boundaries. Quite the contrary. If two parishes were competing, for example, the game would normally start at a point about halfway between the two. The boundary line of each parish might be as little as two miles away, or as many as ten. Whichever team managed to get the ball over the parish boundary line of its rival was the winner. Time-outs were not permitted.

In today's game, each side fields 15 players—13 in North American games. They compete on a flat, rectangular field 140 to 160 yards long and 84 to 100 yards wide. At each end of the field sits a goal net framed by an H-shaped goalpost. The vertical posts sit 21 feet apart and rise 16 feet into the air, with a horizontal bar eight feet above the ground that forms the upper limit of the goal-scoring zone.

Gaelic football features exceptional long kicking, grueling body contact and players jumping high into the air to catch the ball. A player may not advance the ball by throwing it, but dribbling, kicking it along the ground, punting it and punching it are all allowed.

Scoring is similar to that in hurling. Getting the ball past the goalkeeper and into the goal net earns a three-point goal. Getting it over the horizontal bar earns a single point. A game is normally divided into two 30-minute halves—extended to 35 minutes in Finals matches. There are no time-outs, and whoever is ahead when the clock runs out is the winner. Ties are not resolved with further play.

The climax of the football year comes in September, when the counties with the best season records send their teams to compete in the All-Ireland Finals. These championship matches, held in Dublin's famous Croke Park, are Ireland's biggest sporting event. The park is almost invariably filled to its capacity of 65,000 spectators.

HANDBALL

Handball, the third partner in the GAA trinity, is a sport whose "Irishness" may come as a surprise to some. In fact, it was once much more popular than it is today.

In handball's earlier form, the ball was hit against a single wall. By about 1800, today's more elaborate alleys (courts, in American parlance), with three walls, had become fairly common. The ball is hit with bare hands. In the hard-ball variety, played only in Ireland, an "alley-cracker," traveling at lightning speeds, is used.

A handball game has traditionally consisted of 21 "aces," with the best of three or five games needed to win a match. In recent years, "time-based" matches have increased in popularity for nonchampionship play. The player who is leading at the end of a prescribed period, normally 30 minutes, is the winner.

Handball is played today around the world—though not with the hard ball sometimes used in Ireland. An Irish-born American, Phil Casey, brought the world championship title briefly to the United States when he emigrated to Brooklyn in 1889.

Soon after the Irish Free State was established in 1921, however, handball seemed to be dying as hurling and Gaelic football increased their followings. Valuing it for its traditional importance, the GAA took control of the sport. It substituted a type of amateur title for the semi-professional title for which players had formerly competed. With GAA sponsorship and more limited following, chances are that this sport will survive, but without the mass support its Irish rivals enjoy.

ROAD BOWLING

Another ancient Irish sport, road bowling (it is sometimes pronounced to rhyme with *growling*), is played almost exclusively in the northern county of Armagh and in the southernmost, Cork. Even in these counties, the game is confined to rural areas, for it must be played on quiet country roads that are relatively free of traffic. (It is not illegal, as some people suppose, but you can be ticketed if you obstruct traffic in the course of play.) Games normally pit two two-man teams against each other.

As in golf, to which it may be distantly related, the object in bowling is to move a ball along a fixed course several miles long using as few throws as possible. In this case, the "ball" is a 28-ounce iron sphere. Like golf, road bowling presents the player with a series of obstacles. The road itself will generally run up and down slopes and around bends. Sometimes there are streams and rail bridges to contend with. Players use a good deal of body English to give the "bullet" the spin it needs to follow the course and keep clear of obstacles.

POPULAR SPORTS OF FOREIGN ORIGIN

Other sports, foreign in origin, remain popular, the GAA notwithstanding. In addition to soccer, rugby and cricket, these include golf. Ireland boasts several world-class golf courses, and has, in fact, more golf courses per square mile than any other nation.

EQUESTRIAN SPORTS

Among the sports closest to Irish hearts are those involving horses. Ireland's lush greenlands make the island an ideal venue for horse-related activities. Irish equestrian sports, and racing in particular, are among the most classless in the world. Spectators and participants are drawn from every social and economic level.

Irish equestrian activities start with the breeding and training of some of the finest horses in the world. At the National Stud in the Curragh of County Kildare, and the stables of such renowned trainers as Dermot Weld, Vincent O'Brien and Paddy Prendergast, thoroughbreds are prepared to compete one day in the world's classic racing events. In fact, the breeding, training, racing and export of horses constitute one of Ireland's most important industries.

Ireland has nearly 30 race courses—including two in the North— and a schedule that offers races on 250 days throughout the year. The best-known flat races are the Irish Derby, held at the Curragh in late June or early July, the Irish Oaks and the Irish St. Leger. For steeplechase enthusiasts, who outnumber flat-racing fans, the Irish Grand National, run at Fairyhouse near Dublin during Easter week, is a must. Betting is a major feature of both the flat-racing and steeplechase scenes.

The famous Royal Dublin Society Horse Show, held in Dublin in August, marks the height of the Dublin social season. It draws spectators and contestants from around the world.

Throughout Ireland, thousands of people enjoy riding to the hounds in search of foxes, a sport the Irish wit Oscar Wilde once dubbed ". . . the unspeakable in pursuit of the inedible." An estimated 85 packs of hounds are scattered throughout the island, used by such well-known groups as the Galway Blazers and the Limerick County Hunt. Hunting draws people from a broader spectrum of the population than it does in England. A given hunting event may include farmers, professional men, jet-setters and even priests. In County Cork, the Dulhallow Hunt still hunts regularly as it has done since 1745, when it is said to have inaugurated modern fox hunting on a regular basis. Visitors to Ireland will normally have no problem joining a local hunt, though only experienced riders should seek out this potentially dangerous sport.

No discussion of Irish horses would be complete without mention of the island's Connemara ponies. These are native to Ireland and most closely associated with County Galway. They no longer run wild, but are kept and systematically bred under the auspices of the Connemara Pony Breeders Society. They are particularly popular for use with children, and can often be seen in jumping competitions at local agricultural fairs.

OTHER POPULAR SPORTS

For those whose interests are not satisfied by the sports we have discussed, there are many more to choose among. Coarse and game fishing are popular throughout the island. Salmon and trout are taken in fresh water, and a variety of saltwater fish are caught off the east and south coasts, in particular. Cricket, hockey, soccer (also called association football in Ireland) and rugby are still tremendously popular, and rowing and canoeing, long-distance running and cycling, track and field sports, tennis, greyhound racing, yachting, wind-surfing, and boxing are just a few examples from the remaining repertoire.

In the past, as we have noted, many of Ireland's people have been concerned by the growth of "English" sports at the expense of native Gaelic competitions. Soon, however, the threat may come from a different quarter. Over the last decade or two, American sports have come to many European countries, and Ireland seems to be following the trend, however belatedly. Semi-professional basketball has been played in Europe for years, with teams often enjoying corporate sponsorship. More recently, a basketball program for young people has been started in Ireland.

Baseball, that most American of sports, is now played not only in Japan and Latin America but also in several European countries, including France, a nation generally guarded against foreign cultural influence. Now, in the wake of exhibition games in Britain by American professional football teams—and a Fall 1988 game in Dublin between two American college football teams, Army and Boston College—it doesn't seem farfetched to ask how soon, not whether, America's major team sports will come to Ireland in a big way. International telecasting of American games via satellite to Europe only hastens the day.

Ironically, the Irish government itself encouraged the Army versus Boston College event—dubbed The Emerald Isle Classic—as a way of attracting Irish-American tourists. In this they were successful, but many Irish citizens also attended and came away with enthusiastic comments about the American institution.

You may be able to take the "Irishness" out of Irish sports, but you're not likely to take sports out of the Irish. When and if American sports come to Ireland in a meaningful way, the Irish are likely to play them with all the skill, vigor and enthusiasm they now put into their own games—and to add some special touches of their own.

Irish Food . . .

A century and a half after the Great Famine brought starvation and death to perhaps a million Irish people, and forced a similar number to emigrate, the Irish are, ironically, perhaps the best-fed nation in the world.

The average Irishman now consumes between 3,000 and 3,500 calories a day—more than the average citizen of any other nation. Among more than 100 countries surveyed in 1980, Ireland ranked tenth in per capita meat consumption, sixth in daily protein consumption and seventh in milk consumption.

Irish meals are not only substantial, they're frequent. From waking, when a cup of tea is the rule, until bedtime, many families consume as many as six meals or snacks.

Irish breakfasts are famous for their size and quality. They are also more leisurely than their American counterpart. Hot cereal, usually porridge or stirabout (oatmeal), is the usual starter, perhaps with milk, which in country homes may be straight from the cow and still warm. (Monica Sheridan, who has written one of the best Irish cookbooks, notes that the little boys in her family had little use for porridge, but would eat it ". . . so they would have the strength and stamina to be good footballers.") Then come eggs—freshly laid —and slices of lean Irish bacon, which many consider the finest in the world. Finally, there's fresh bread, thickly sliced and slathered with butter and marmalade or other jam. To wash things down, there's tea, which is excellent in Ireland—or coffee, which is improving but still not up to the standards Americans are used to.

About 11 a.m., most people will take a break for a bit of pastry with coffee or tea. The day's main meal, dinner, is typically eaten around one in the afternoon, especially in the country, where the menfolk have been working up an appetite in the fields. Though people who work in Dublin, Cork, Belfast and other major cities are turning more to pubs and restaurants for their midday meal, most people still head for home, where a six-course affair is not uncommon.

At dinner, the centerpiece may be roast beef, steak, roast pork, ham (especially Limerick ham), lamb chops, mutton or roast baby lamb, or it may feature Irish stew, corned beef and carrots, boiled bacon and cabbage, or black or white meat pudding (an acquired taste for most). You may find fish or other seafood—perhaps superb trout or salmon from Ireland's rivers and streams, or, less often, shellfish. What you won't find is corned beef and cabbage. While considered quintessentially Irish fare in the United States, this combination is virtually unknown in Ireland, though bacon and cabbage is a popular dish.

No Irish dinner would be complete without potatoes in some form. In fact, it's not considered odd to serve as many as four potato dishes at the same meal. Irish potatoes are a lot tastier, to begin with, than those grown elsewhere—or so, at least, many Irish people are convinced. And Irish cooks have invented countless ways to prepare the nutritious tuber since it was first brought from the New World by Sir Walter Raleigh in the late 1500s. Monica Sheridan recalls some of the picturesque names under which Irish potatoes have been marketed: Golden Wonders, Ulster Chieftains, Aran Banners, Irish Queens, Dunbar Rovers, Skerry Champions, and so on—rather reminiscent of athletic team names.

Colcannon—potatoes cooked with cabbage, onions, cream and butter—is among the most popular of choices. So, too, is champ— potatoes mashed with milk, to which chives, peas or parsley may be added for variety. Other traditional potato dishes include potato cakes, cooked on a griddle; potato soup; potato flounces, a pie of layered potatoes and onions; and boxty, a bread of sorts made from raw potatoes, mashed potatoes, whole wheat flour, butter and bacon grease, which are kneaded, rolled and baked until golden brown.

As far as many people are concerned, though, nothing can beat a plain Irish potato, boiled or roasted in its skin and served with a generous dollop of butter. This often forms a course by itself.

Freshly baked bread will also be on the table. It may be soda bread, which has been leavened with baking soda, not yeast, and which may or may not contain carraway seeds, currants and other additions. Or, perhaps, brown bread, made with stone-ground whole-wheat flour. Irish cooks are proud of their baking skills, and Irish breadmaking is one of the great traditions in Irish cooking. A good housewife, according to Sheridan, "wouldn't dream of offering a visitor" anything less than three distinct types of her own bread, various scones, and two or three cakes—all baked especially for the occasion.

Like other people throughout the British Isles, the Irish seem to be born with well-developed sweet tooths. Plum puddings, trifle, sultana (seedless yellow raisin) cake and apple tarts are among the most popular desserts.

Strong, sweet tea is served with most meals, but milk and buttermilk are drunk as well. For every cup of coffee they drink, the Irish consume three or four cups of tea. Wine is still not an everyday drink for many, though as more Irish people travel abroad on business or on vacation, wine and other Continental touches are becoming more popular among some parts of the population.

There are a number of dishes that are local specialties—and perhaps an acquired taste even where they are served. Drisheens, a County Cork specialty, are made by combining strained sheep's blood with milk, water, mutton suet, breadcrumbs and seasonings. Boiled crubeens are also chiefly a Cork dish. They're the hind trotters of a pig, which have succulent meat hidden between the bones. Dublin coddle is a meat stew, made primarily of Irish sausage, bacon, onions and potatoes. It is virtually unknown outside the capital, and even there is eaten mainly by families that have lived in Dublin for many generations. Dean (Jonathan) Swift ate Dublin coddle in the eighteenth century; today it is served particularly on Saturday nights after the menfolk have returned from the pub.

Few people would describe typical Irish fare as haute cuisine. Given the quality and freshness of the meat, dairy products and vegetables the Irish countryside yields, there's little need for fancy sauces, seasonings and cooking methods. Irish cuisine, as one authority has put it, is simply "good, honest food."

Some claim that good conversation and good company—not the food itself—are the elements that make an Irish meal memorable. Yet Irish food is good—indeed, has long been outstanding in some of its aspects—and it seems, on the whole, to be getting even better.

Did You Know . . .

. . . That the Declaration of Independence was written in the hand of an Irish-born patriot, Charles Thomson; first read to the people, outside the hall where it was drafted, by John Nixon, another native of Ireland; first printed by an Irish-born Philadelphian, John Dunlap; and signed by at least three Americans of Irish birth: James Smith of Pennsylvania (a native of Dublin), George Taylor (another representative of Pennsylvania) and Derry-born Matthew Thornton (who represented New Hampshire). At least five other signers had Irish-born parents or grandparents: Thomas McKean, George Read, Robert Treat Paine, Thomas Lynch, Jr. and Charles Carroll of Carrollton.

. . . And Drink

~~~~~~~~~~~

The Irish have been stereotyped, since the last century at least, for their reputed fondness for alcohol. In this there is, in fact, some truth. But, while drinking has long been, and remains today, an important social pastime among the Irish and their cousins abroad, Ireland also boasts one of the highest percentage of teetotalers in the world.

Those Irish who do indulge have two world-class native drinks for which their enthusiasm may be excused—Guinness stout and Irish whiskey. According to one survey, these and other drinks account for as much as 14 percent of the average drinker's disposable income. That figure, however accurate, is still misleading, in that a good share of what the Irish pay to drink goes to the government in taxes.

Stout, a strong, dark beer with an extremely malty taste, is Ireland's most popular drink. And Guinness, a brand name virtually synonymous with stout, is by far the most popular. Traditionally considered a man's drink, Guinness has a bitterness that makes it an acquired taste even for many men. Guinness has been brewed along the banks of Dublin's Liffey River since 1759, when the Guinness family first launched its business.

Today the Guinness Brewery in St. James's Gate sprawls over a one-square-mile area, and even boasts its own railroad. Guinness accounts for about 60 percent of the beer sold in Ireland, and the drink is exported to more than 100 countries, having been popularized by Irish soldiers, sailors and merchants since the 1800s. Indeed, in Africa, Guinness is often prescribed by doctors and is considered an aphrodisiac by many people.

Some Guinness fanciers insist that the drink at its best can only be had in Ireland. It doesn't travel well, they claim. Furthermore, a pint drawn in a pub is far superior to the bottled version. And it takes an expert bartender to "pull a pint" just right, so that it finishes off with a head of creamy foam so thick you can carve your initials in it.

Irish whiskey has traditionally come in several brands, each with a distinct "personality" and taste. If you're a regular whiskey drinker, you're probably loyal to a particular brand: Jameson's, Paddy, Dunphy's, Power's, Murphy's, Tullamore Dew or Old Bushmill's. The last is distilled in the North, at the world's oldest licensed distillery (1609), and tastes rather closer to Scotch. All are (or were) made by the Irish Distillers Group, which brought virtually all production of distilled spirits in Ireland under its umbrella in the 1930s. (*Editor's note:* Within the last year, as you may have already discovered, Irish Distillers has stopped making Paddy, Dunphy's, Murphy's, Tullamore Dew, and Power's.)

An English historian and scribe who visited Ireland in the sixteenth century came home praising the virtues of Irish whiskey:

> It sloweth age; it strengtheneth youth; it helpeth digestion; it cutteth fleume; it abandoneth melancholie; it relisheth the harte; it lighteneth the mind; it quickeneth the spirites; it cureth the hydropsie; it puffeth away ventrositie . . . and trulie it is a soveraign liquor if it be orderlie taken . . .

Unlike its American and Canadian cousins, "Irish" starts with barley rather than corn or rye. The barley is malted (permitted to sprout) and then dried and mashed with water. The malt mixture is then distilled—not once, as Scotch normally is, but three times. Triple distillation gives Irish whiskey (note that it's spelled with an "e") a taste that's smoother and milder than Scotch. Scotch whisky is distilled only once—and also takes on a smoky taste from the peat that fuels the open malting ovens. The grain in "Irish" is cured in a closed oven heated by smokeless anthracite coal. Once distilled, the liquor is still clear, but after at least seven years in an oaken cask—the required period for maturing "Irish"—it takes on an amber shade from the wood in the casks.

Irish whiskey is 86 proof—that is, 43 percent alcohol by volume. Some drink it neat (straight or undiluted), others add some water. Experts, however, frown on adding soda or ice.

There are three other drinks, all based on Irish whiskey, that have popular followings, even if their origins are fairly recent. Irish cream liqueur can be a particularly habit-forming aperitif, blending whiskey, cream and chocolate. Irish Mist liqueur, a proprietary brand, weds the sweetness of honey with the smooth "punch" of Irish whiskey.

Best known of all, perhaps, is Irish coffee, which may have been invented in the United States, or in Ireland, depending on whom you listen to. In any case, it seems to be more popular among visitors to Ireland than among the natives. This internationally known brew is made as follows: first, warm an eight-ounce goblet or an Irish coffee glass in very hot or boiling water. Next, pour in a measure of whiskey. Then add five or six ounces of fresh, hot black coffee, followed by a teaspoon of sugar. After you stir the contents until the sugar is dissolved, a generous dollop of sweetened whipped cream is floated on top. The resulting concoction is usually irresistible, especially on a cold or rainy day.

Poteen or poitin (pronounced "pot-cheen"), named for the "little pot" in which it is normally made, is Ireland's version of "moonshine"—an illegal, home-brewed liquor. Poteen is more a vodka than a whiskey. In the past, it was usually distilled from potato mash, but grain, a less expensive substitute, is the rule nowadays.

Poteen is not easily come by today. For one thing, many expert poteen-makers, disliking the attention of the gardai (Irish police), emigrated to America during Prohibition, where many used their know-how to make enormous fortunes. Still, when economic times are bad in the rural districts of the West and South, there's usually an upsurge in poteen distilling. In any event, even when poteen is available, it is a well-kept secret to outsiders. That's probably all for the best, since—as the initiated know from experience—it produces some of the worst hangovers imaginable.

Did You Know . . .

. . . That Briarwood Beach, Ohio, is currently the only community in the United States that observes a legal holiday on St. Patrick's Day, March 17th. And Mayor Leonard English (of Irish descent despite his name) has also proclaimed John Jameson Irish whiskey as Briarwood Beach's official drink! (*National Hibernian Digest,* March/April 1984)

. . . That the United States once had a ship named the U.S.S. *Shamrock.* Launched at the Brooklyn Navy Yard on St. Patrick's Day, 1863, she was christened with a bottle of Irish whiskey and presented with a souvenir wreath of shamrocks. The 240-foot steam vessel carried eight guns, which she used during blockade duty with other Union ships along the Carolina coast.

ULSTER

Derry
DERRY
ANTRIM
DONEGAL
TYRONE
Belfast
Donegal
FERMANAGH
MONAGHAN
ARMAGH
DOWN
Armagh
CONNACHT
Sligo
Dundalk
SLIGO
LEITRIM
CAVAN
LOUTH
MAYO
ROSCOMMON
LONGFORD
MEATH
WESTMEATH
Dublin
Athlone
DUBLIN
GALWAY
OFFALY
KILDARE
LEINSTER
Galway
Kildare
WICKLOW
LAOIS
Wicklow
CLARE
Carlow
Kilkenny
CARLOW
TIPPERARY
KILKENNY
Limerick
Cashel
WEXFORD
LIMERICK
Clonmel
Tralee
Wexford
Waterford
KERRY
WATERFORD
CORK
Cork

MUNSTER

IRELAND

The Old 32: Profiles of Ireland's Counties

*I*f you're an American, you're not just an American, of course. You're also a Texan, a Californian, a Minnesotan, a Vermonter or whatever. And so, too, if your roots lie in Ireland—or almost anywhere else.

Nations are usually too large and abstract to monopolize our loyalties. For many of Irish heritage, traditional family ties remain important, as do links to the native towns or villages of parents or grandparents. But the Irish have a special place in their hearts for their home counties—one or more of the 32 traditional territorial divisions that have existed on the island for centuries.

Traditional county ties remain strong among many Irish Americans. Wherever there are large numbers of Americans with Irish roots, there are likely to be one or more local county clubs or societies. In some larger U.S. cities, such as New York, Boston, Chicago and Los Angeles, virtually all of Ireland's 32 counties are represented by local organizations under an umbrella group called The United Irish Counties Association or a similar name.

Considering the importance of county associations, we have brought together here—for the first time, we believe—sketches of all 32 counties, grouped alphabetically under their respective provinces. **Please note:**

1. The lists of "notable natives" under each county have
   been compiled using a variety of secondary sources, but
   mainly from Henry Boylan, *The Dictionary of Irish Biography* (New York: Barnes & Noble, 1978) and Brian de
   Breffny, General Editor, *Ireland: A Cultural Encyclopedia*
   (New York: Facts on File, 1983). We found several cases
   in which an individual was claimed by more than one
   county, and have tried conscientiously to resolve such
   conflicts where possible.

2. Similarly, listings of annual events and festivals in each
   county have been compiled from official information supplied by the Irish Tourist Board, and supplemented by
   other sources. In a few cases we found conflicting information on the timing or location of a given event.
   Although we have tried to list only events that are held in
   the same place and at approximately the same time each
   year, the dates and locations are always subject to change.
   In some cases, moreover, an event may be cancelled, especially if it has been running regular deficits for some time.
   So we strongly urge you to contact the Irish Tourist
   Board for up-to-date details before you make travel plans
   around an event listed here.

3. For readers who may wish to subscribe to one or more
   Irish national or county newspapers, we have listed the
   main newspapers serving each county as well as the Dublin and Belfast newspapers. The latter are widely read far
   beyond these cities. To obtain a sample issue before subscribing, we suggest you contact one of the sources listed
   in *The Green Pages* section of this book under "Newspapers and Magazines, Imported—News Dealers." If
   your sample issue doesn't contain information for overseas subscribers, request a copy of *Newspapers* (Information Sheet No. 4) from the Irish Tourist Board and then
   write or phone the newspaper for details. Information on
   newspapers from all 32 counties is included in *Benn's Press
   Directory*, available in many libraries. Last, you may call
   one of the several U.S. consular offices maintained by Ireland or the United Kingdom, depending on where the
   paper you're interested in is published.

PROVINCE OF CONNACHT (CONNAUGHT)
GALWAY
County town: Galway
Area: 2,293 sq. mi.

Notable natives: Lady Augusta Gregory (1852–1932), writer, dramatist and nationalist, who was a leader of the Irish Revival and the Irish theatre movement; Padraic O'Conaire (1883–1928), a leading short-story writer of the early twentieth-century Irish literary revival; Father Tom Burke (1830–1883), Irish civil rights champion; Liam O'Flaherty (1896–1984), novelist whose works include *Thy Neighbor's Wife* (1923), the prize-winning *The Informer* (1925), which was made into the classic film of the same name, and *Insurrection* (1950); Robert O'Hara Burke (1820–1861), first white man to cross Australia from south to north; Colonel Thomas Blood (1618–1680), adventurer who succeeded in stealing the Crown Jewels from the Tower of London in 1671 and, after his capture, was pardoned by Charles II out of admiration for his daring; Patrick Ford (1837–1913), founder of the recently defunct Irish-American newspaper, *Irish World,* who in his day was, according to Michael Davitt, "the most powerful support on the American continent of the struggle in Ireland"; Edward Martyn (1859–1924), dramatist and co-founder of the Irish Literary Theatre (now the Abbey Theatre), which produced his best play, *The Heather Field,* in 1899.

Places of interest: Galway Town, a port that still retains a certain Mediterranean flavor, a legacy of centuries of trading with Italy, Spain and other countries since the Middle Ages; the Church of St. Nicholas, Galway, where Columbus is said to have prayed during a supposed stopover at Galway on his first voyage of discovery; Galway City Museum; the Aran Islands, 30 miles offshore and home to Gaelic-speaking fisherfolk and weavers; the Brown and Alcock monument, which marks the landing site of the first transatlantic flight in 1919, eight years before Lindbergh's 1927 solo; Connemara, a district that is home to Connemara ponies, Ireland's only native horse breed, and to the Connemara Gaeltacht, one of Ireland's largest Gaelic-speaking areas; Coole Park, Gort, where Lady Gregory once hosted such literary stars as Shaw, Synge, O'Casey and Yeats in her grand house, now destroyed—and whose wooded glens figure in many Yeats poems; Kilkieran, a pretty Gaelic-speaking harbor village whose main industry is seaweed harvesting; the fishing village of Claddagh, where the famous rings of this name were first made; Connemara Marble Factory, Moycullen, where you can watch craftsmen cutting, grinding and polishing marble quarried nearby.

Events: Clarinbridge Oyster Festival, Clarinbridge (September); Connemara Pony Show (August); Galway International Motor Rally (February); Galway Races (July); Great October Fair, Ballinasloe, said to be the world's oldest horse fair; the Claddagh Festival (August); Galway Horse Show (June/July); Feis Ceoil an Iarthair (autumn), a festival of traditional song, dance and storytelling; the Galway Salmon Run (June-July), when you can see the noble fish lining up to jump Galway Town's salmon weir on their way to upstream spawning grounds.

Newspapers: Connacht Sentinel (weekly); *Connacht Tribune* (weekly); *Herald & Western Advertiser* (weekly).

LEITRIM
County town: Carrick-on-Shannon
Area: 589 sq. mi.

Notable natives: Sean McDiarmada (1886–1916), leader of the 1916 Easter Rebellion; Wilhemina Geddes (1887–1955), stained-glass designer, who created notable windows in England, Canada and Belgium as well as Ireland; Susan Langstaff Mitchell (1866–1926), writer remembered for her religious poetry *(The Living Chalice and Other Poems)* and her verses satirizing notable Irish literary and public figures, many of whom she entertained as one of Dublin's leading hostesses; Thomas H. Parke (1857–1893), surgeon who accompanied Henry M. Stanley on his Congo basin explorations and was credited with keeping the expedition from disaster.

Places of interest: Carrick-on-Shannon, a center for river cruising and coarse fishing; O'Rourke's Table, a rock plateau that offers memorable views of Lough Gill and its islands, including Innisfree, which W. B. Yeats immortalized in verse; Prince Connell's Grave, the name given locally to a splendid prehistoric gallery grave dating from 2000 to 1500 B.C.; Sheebeg, a hill overlooking the village of

Keshcarrigan that is topped by a prehistoric mound reputed to contain the grave of the legendary hero, Finn McCool.

Events: Wild Rose Festival (August); Festival of the Shannon (July).

Newspapers: Leitrim Observer (weekly).

Miscellaneous: By the way, the county name is pronounced LEE-trim.

MAYO
County town: Castlebar
Area: 2,084 sq. mi.

Notable natives: Michael Davitt (1846–1906), founder of the Irish Land League; George Moore (1853–1933), playwright, short-story writer and novelist *(The Brook Kerith, Heloise and Abelard)* associated with Yeats, Lady Gregory, and the like in the Irish Literary Revival and founding of the Abbey Theatre; William O'Dwyer (1890–1964), Mayor of New York, 1946–1950, and U.S. Ambassador to Mexico, 1950–1952; Admiral William Brown (1777–1857), who emigrated to South America, where he founded the Argentine navy; Paul O'Dwyer (1907–   ), New York lawyer and politician.

Places of interest: Knock, whose Shrine of Our Lady of Knock rivals Lourdes and Fatima as a pilgrimage site: the village's new basilica, designed to seat 20,000, is Ireland's largest church—and the community has its own international airport as well!; Croagh Patrick, on whose peak St. Patrick is said to have fasted for 40 days, and where he supposedly banished the snakes from Ireland; Cong, the town where *The Quiet Man* was filmed; Westport, Mayo's most attractive town, which was laid out in the eighteenth century and was once a center for linen making; Westport House, Westport, a classical gem filled with collections of portraits, silver and Waterford glass; the Nephin Beg mountains, Ireland's most desolate and least-inhabited area; Ballintober Abbey (thirteenth century), the only royal abbey in Ireland or Britain still operating (over 750 years); Achill, Ireland's largest island, which is worth visiting to take in 2,200-foot Slievemore mountain and awesome oceanside drives above seas that thrash the rocks far below.

Events: Croagh Patrick Pilgrimage (last Sunday in July); International Sea Angling Festival, Westport (June); Castlebar International Song Contest (October); Westport Horse Show (June); Claremorris Ham Fair and Festival (July); Ballina Salmon Festival (July); Rock Music Festival, Castlebar (July); Ballina Agricultural and Industrial Show (August).

Newspapers: Connacht Telegraph (weekly); *Western Journal* (weekly); *Western People* (weekly); *Mayo News* (weekly); *Mayo Post* (weekly).

ROSCOMMON
County town: Roscommon
Area: 951 sq. mi.

Notable natives: Father Edward J. Flanagan (1886–1948), founder of Boys Town, U.S.A., Omaha, Neb.; Douglas Hyde (1860–1949), poet, scholar, playwright, translator, first president of the Gaelic League and first President of Ireland, 1937–1945; John G. Downey (1826–1894), Civil War governor of California and first Los Angeles land developer; Arthur Murphy (1727–1805), actor, journalist and lawyer, best known for the plays he wrote, including comedies and farces such as *Three Weeks After Marriage* and *The Way to Keep Him* as well as tragedies such as *Zenobia* and *The Orphan of China;* Padraig O Caoimh (1897–1964), General Secretary of the Gaelic Athletic Association, 1929–1964, a period during which the GAA became Ireland's largest and most powerful sporting organization; John E. Lawe (1923–   ), International Transport Workers Union president, 1985–   .

Places of interest: Strokestown Craft Centre; Horse Market, Athleague; Clonalis House, Castlerea, a Victorian mansion where state documents, original Irish manuscripts and priceless books are exhibited.

Events: O'Carolan Harp and Traditional Music Festival, Keadue (early August); Boyle Gala Coarse Fishing Festival, Boyle (May).

Newspapers: Roscommon Champion (weekly); *Roscommon Herald* (weekly).

SLIGO
County town: Sligo
Area: 694 sq. mi.

Notable natives: Michael Corcoran (1827–1863), who commanded the "Fighting 69th" New York Militia at the start of the Civil War and later recruited the Irish Brigade; Patrick Collins (1910–   ), self-taught painter of landscapes and figures, whose works are represented in all of Ireland's major collections; Thomas Rice Henn (1901–1974), Yeatsian scholar who organized and subsequently directed the Yeats International Summer School held annually in Sligo Town; William Higgins (1763?–1825), chemist who is said to have first formulated the atomic theory, which refuted the centuries-old phlogistic theory explaining chemical phenomena.

Places of interest: The Yeats Memorial Museum; Yeats' grave, Drumcliff churchyard, and many other places associated with W. B. Yeats and his poetry; the County Museum, Sligo, with its Municipal Art Gallery, which has an excellent collection of modern Irish art; the impressive ruins of Sligo Abbey, a thirteenth-century Dominican friary; flat-topped Ben Bulben, the famous 1,730-foot-high mountain that looms above Yeats' grave at Drumcliff, and on whose summit you will find unusual arctic and alpine plants; Strandhill, a seaside resort whose beaches attract large numbers of surfers; Knockarea, a 1,078-foot hill on whose summit stands a stone cairn reputed to be the burial place of Maeve of Connacht, an ancient Irish warrior-queen; Lough Gill, which can be toured using shoreside roads, or on a three-hour boat cruise that leaves from Doorly Park, Sligo Town; Lissadell House, once home to the Gore-Booth family, with its noted sisters: Eva, the poetess, and Constance—later Countess Markievicz—who played a leading role in the 1916 rising and later in Irish politics.

Events: Yeats International Summer School, Sligo (August); Enniscrone International Sea Angling Festival (August); Sligo Fleadh Cheoil, a traditional music festival and fiddlers' competition (June); Folk Festival, Ballisdare (August); Michael Coleman Commemoration, Riverside, honoring a legendary Sligo-born traditional fiddler (September); Sligo Feisanna, Sligo (March/April); Sligo Midsummer Festival (June); Sligo Triathlon Competition (June).

Newspapers: Sligo Champion (weekly).

PROVINCE OF LEINSTER
CARLOW
County town: Carlow
Area: 346 sq. mi.

Notable natives: Pierce Butler (1744–1822), U.S. senator from South Carolina and signer of the Constitution; Peter F. Collier (1846–1909), American publisher who founded *Collier's* magazine (3.2 million circulation at its peak) and pioneered subscription publishing with *The Harvard Classics* and other series; Patrick F. Moran (1830–1911), Archbishop of Sydney and first Australian cardinal, who championed Australian federation and Irish home rule; William Dargan (1799–1867), who built 600 miles of Irish railway— including Ireland's first line, from Dublin to Port Laoghaire—as well as the Ulster Canal; Myles Keogh (1840–1876), who fought with Papal forces against Garibaldi's army, then emigrated to the United States where he rose to lieutenant colonel in the Union Army, later commanding a troop of the 7th Cavalry at the Battle of the Little Big Horn; Kevin Barry (1902–1920), medical student captured while taking part in an IRA arms raid, whose subsequent execution at age 18 became a cause célèbre that drew scores of fellow students to the outlawed group and inspired a popular ballad.

Places of interest: County Museum, Carlow; Browne's Hill, near Carlow Town, the site of a prehistoric dolmen, or stone structure, which experts claim is up to 5,000 years old and has Ireland's, and perhaps Europe's, largest capstone: 5 feet thick, 20 feet square and 100 tons in weight.

Newspapers: Nationalist & Leinster Times (weekly).

Miscellaneous: One of Ireland's smallest counties, Carlow sent relatively few emigrants to the United States.

DUBLIN
County town: Dublin
Area: 356 sq. mi.

Notable natives: Containing Ireland's largest metropolis and seat of culture, County Dublin has long produced a disproportionately

large number of people who have gone on to play leading roles in
Ireland, the United States, Britain and other countries: Maureen
O'Hara (1921–   ), Irish-American film actress; Victor Herbert
(1859–1924), Irish-American composer of such beloved operettas as
Babes in Toyland and *Naughty Marietta;* John Dowland (1562–1626),
composer and lutenist, the foremost lute player of his day, whose
songs were tremendously popular then and are still performed;
Augustus Saint-Gaudens (1848–1907), world-famous American
sculptor, born of a French father and an Irish mother; Eamonn
Kevin Roche (1922–   ), prolific, distinguished Irish-American
architect; Catherine McAuley (1778–1841), founder of the Order of
Mercy, the largest religious congregation in the English-speaking
world; Edmund Burke (1729–1797), British statesman and political
writer, widely considered the father of modern political conserva-
tism; Robert Emmet (1778–1803), eloquent patriot executed for his
role in the abortive 1803 rising; Henry Grattan (1746–1820), statesman, orator and prophetic champion of Catholic emancipation;
Theobald Wolfe Tone (1763–1798), revolutionary nationalist who
founded the United Irishmen and was executed for his role in aiding the French expedition landed in 1798 to foment an anti-British
rising; Patrick Pearse (1879–1916), poet, president of the 1916 Provisional Government and martyr of the Easter Rising; Arthur Grif-
fith (1872–1922), founder of the *United Irishman* and of Sinn Fein,
and later president of the Dail; Cornelius Ryan (1920–1974), Irish-
American war correspondent who went on to write such best-selling World War II chronicles as *The Longest Day, The Last Battle* and
A Bridge Too Far; Richard Montgomery (1736–1775), American
revolutionary general; the Anglo-Irish cleric and satirist, Jonathan
Swift (1667–1745), author of *Gulliver's Travels;* Brendan Behan
(1923–1964), the noted dramatist and writer; Bram Stoker (1847–
1912), author of the chilling gothic masterpiece, *Dracula;* James
Joyce (1882–1941), author of *The Dubliners, A Portrait of the Artist as
a Young Man* and the monumental *Ulysses;* playwrights Samuel
Beckett (1906–1989), Sean O'Casey (1880–1964), and Richard Brin-
sley Sheridan (1751–1816); Irish-American playwright Dion Bouci-
cault (1820–1890), whose works include *The Colleen Bawn* and *The
Shaughraun;* George Bernard Shaw (1856–1950), whose brilliant
plays typically deal with such themes as war *(Arms and the Man),*
religion *(St. Joan),* prostitution *(Mrs. Warren's Profession)* and eco-

nomics *(Widowers' Houses);* Oscar Wilde (1854–1900), known as much for his general wit as for such plays as *The Importance of Being Earnest* and *Lady Windermere's Fan* and a novel, *The Picture of Dorian Gray;* poet and playwright William Butler Yeats (1865–1939), whose genius and whose love of Ireland are legendary; and dramatist John Millington Synge (1871–1909), whose *Riders to the Sea* and *Shadow of the Glen* are marked by masterly use of the language of Irish fishermen and country folk.

Places of interest: Trinity College, Dublin (TCD)—founded in the 1590s—with its library, which houses the *Book of Kells* and other Irish cultural treasures; Kilmainham Jail Museum; The Royal Hospital (1680s), Kilmainham, which is widely considered the most important seventeenth-century building in Ireland and is certainly its first full-scale example of neoclassical architecture; the National Museum of Ireland, which has opened a new exhibit hall next to its main building devoted to early medieval Dublin and featuring recently unearthed Viking artifacts; Phoenix Park, one of Europe's largest and most beautiful urban green spaces; The Abbey Theatre, most prestigious and important of Dublin theaters; Dublin Castle, dating from the early 1200s, which was once the residence of English viceroys in Ireland as well as housing a prison for important prisoners; Christ Church Cathedral; St. Patrick's Cathedral; The Custom House (1791), Dublin's finest public building—in fact, one of Europe's finest; Martello Tower, Sandycove, James Joyce's workplace-retreat; Dun Laoghaire, the port of Dublin and Ireland's main port-of-entry, with vessels sailing regularly to and from Britain; Guinness Brewery, a 60-acre complex just south of the River Liffey, whose water is wondrously transformed here—where you can also visit the Guinness Museum; Malahide Castle (fourteenth century), which houses much of the National Portrait Collection; Hugh Lane Municipal Gallery of Art; the Chester Beatty Gallery of Oriental Art; National Botanical Gardens, Glasnevin, where 20,000 plant varieties grow indoors and outdoors; Howth Castle, renowned for its rhododendron gardens, which contain more than 2,000 varieties of the flowering shrub.

Events: Dublin Arts Festival (March); Dublin Horse Show, perhaps the year's premier social and sporting occasion (August); All-Ireland Hurling Final (September); All-Ireland Football Final (September); major horse racing events (May through September); Dublin Festival of Twentieth-Century Music (June); An Fleadh Nua: Traditional Music and Dancing (June); Dublin Spring Show and Industries Fair (May); Irish International Boat Show and Fisheries Exhibitions (February); Dublin Theatre Festival (October); Holiday and Leisure Fair (February); Antique Dealers Fair (August); Spring Season of International Grand Opera (April); Dublin Indoor International Horse Show (November); Polo Games, All-Ireland Polo Club, Phoenix Park (three times weekly, May through mid-September).

Newspapers: Evening Herald (daily); *Evening Press* (daily); *Irish Independent* (daily); *The Irish Press* (daily); *The Irish Times* (daily); *The Sunday Independent* (Sunday); *The Sunday World* (Sunday); *The Sunday Press* (Sunday): *Catholic Standard* (weekly); *Inniu/Today* (weekly); *Irish Oifigiuil/Dublin Gazette* (semiweekly); *Bray People* (weekly).

KILDARE
County town: Naas
Area: 654 sq. mi.

Notable natives: Arthur Guinness (1725–1803), founder of the Guinness Brewery; Sir Thomas Dongan (1634–1715), first Roman Catholic governor of (colonial) New York, 1682–1688, during the reigns of Charles II and James II, and later Earl of Limerick; Sir Ernest Shackleton (1874–1922), Antarctic explorer who nearly reached the South Pole in 1907; St. Laurence O'Toole (1132–1180), Archbishop of Dublin, who led resistance to the Anglo-Norman invasion; Richard Power (1928–1970), novelist in English and Gaelic *(Land of Youth, The Hungry Grass);* John Devoy (1842–1928), Fenian organizer, exiled for his activities in Ireland, who settled in the United States where he became the preeminent leader of Clan na Gael and raised considerable sums for the cause of Irish independence.

Places of interest: The National Stud Farm and Irish Horse Museum, Tully; Castletown House, Celbridge, one of Europe's finest Georgian houses and headquarters of the Irish Georgian Society (demonstrations of eighteenth-century dancing are held on

Sundays); Curragh Racecourse, center of Irish horse racing and home of such famed flat races as the Irish Sweeps Derby, the Irish St. Leger and the Irish Oaks; St. Patrick's College, Maynooth, Ireland's premier Roman Catholic seminary, established during the 1790s (the College also houses the Ecclesiastical Museum); Naas and Punchestown, sites of popular racecourses; Cathedral of St. Brigid, Kildare, which has been largely rebuilt but still contains medieval remains; the Canal and Transport Museum, Robertstown; Irish Pewter Ltd., Timolin-Moone, where you can watch pewter being made and buy pewter items at the mill's shop.

Events: Robertstown Grand Canal Fiesta (August); Freshwater Angling Gala Week, Prosperous (May); Festival of Great Irish Houses, Castletown House, Celbridge (June).

Newspapers: Leinster Leader (weekly).

KILKENNY
County town: Kilkenny
Area: 796 sq. mi.

Notable natives: James Hoban (1758–1831), architect of the White House, Washington, D.C.; Edmund Ignatius Rice (1762–1844), founder of the Irish Christian Brothers, a teaching order active in many countries; Michael Cudahy (1841–1910), founder of Cudahy Packing Company, whose innovations revolutionized the U.S. meatpacking industry; George Berkeley (1685–1753), Anglican bishop and religious philosopher, whose ideas have had a major impact on subsequent European philosophers; Mildred Anne Butler (1858–1941), painter known for her watercolors, which were unappreciated for years because they remained in the family's home; Thomas Kilroy (1934–   ), dramatist whose plays include *Death and Resurrection of Mr. Roche, The O'Neill* and *Tea, Sex and Shakespeare;* John O'Donovan (1809–1861), scholar of Irish antiquity, whose greatest achievements were his translations of *The Annals of the Kingdom of Ireland by the Four Masters* and *The Martyrology of Donegal,* and his role in founding the Irish Archaeological Society; James Archer (1550?–1617/1624), Jesuit educator and missionary, who served as first rector of the Irish College at Salamanca, Spain, and also worked as an "underground" missioner in Ireland, narrowly escaping capture by Crown forces on many occasions; Henry Flood (1732–1791), statesman and orator, who led the nationalist opposition in the Irish House of Commons and was judged the finest speaker of his day; John Locke (1847–1889), Irish-American writer of poems and short stories, including "Morning on the Irish Coast," which expresses an exile's feelings on returning to Ireland.

Places of interest: Dunmore Cave, an enormous underground wonder; Edmund Rice Birthplace, Westcourt, Callan; Rothe House Museum, Kilkenny, an Elizabethan town house with a museum displaying archaeological relics from the area; Simon Pearce Glass, Bennettsbridge, where you can watch demonstrations of the ancient craft of glassblowing; Kilkenny Castle, a Butler family stronghold from Anglo-Norman times until 1935, which retains three of its four towers and houses a nicely restored art gallery in one wing; Jerpoint Abbey, built as a Cistercian house in the thirteenth century, which includes a church and a partly restored cloister with impressive, larger-than-life statues of medieval knights and church leaders.

Events: Kilkenny Beer Festival (May); Kilkenny Arts Week (late August/early September); Kilkenny Roots Weekend (April).

Newspapers: Kilkenny People (semiweekly)

LEIX (LAOIS)
County town: Portlaoise
Area: 664 sq. mi.

Notable natives: Richard Milhous (eighteenth century?), great-great-grandfather of President Richard Milhous Nixon; Thomas Prior (1682–1751), founder of the Royal Dublin Society (now the RDS), which works to promote agriculture, manufacturing, the arts and sciences; James Fintan Lalor (1807–1849), United Irishman activist who worked to promote land reform and tenant rights; Frank Power (1858–1884), war correspondent who, as acting British consul, welcomed General Gordon to Khartoum and then filed regular dispatches to *The Times* during the siege of Khartoum before he was killed trying to escape down the Nile; William Robinson (1838–1935), who began his career as a garden boy at Bally-kilcavan and went on to become one of the most influential gardeners and horticultural writers of his time, leading the revolt against Victorian ideas in favor of simpler garden design; William Shoney O'Brien (1825?–1878), one of the so-called Irish-American Big Four or Bonanza Princes who became multimillionaires after paying $10,000 in 1859 for rights to the Comstock Lode, the now-famous silver strike in Nevada that ultimately produced over $500 million in silver.

Places of interest: Portarlington Power Station, Ireland's first turf-fired electrical generating plant; the Slieve Bloom mountains, a scenic range punctuated with green glens, helping enliven the county's generally plain topography; Abbeyleix, a planned village built in the eighteenth century, with modest but charming Georgian houses and the impressive Abbeyleix Gardens; the Irish Steam Museum, Stradbally, with a diverse collection of steam-powered vehicles and machines; the Round Tower, Timahoe, a twelfth-century specimen with an unusual and ornate double doorway.

Events: Stradbally Steam Rally (August); Vintage Car Rally, Portlaoise (July); Portarlington French Festival (July).

Newspapers: Leinster Express (weekly).

Miscellaneous: The name of the county is usually pronounced LEASH or, less often, LEEKS. Until independence, it was called Queen's County, originally in honor of the English queen, Mary Tudor, who tried to restore Catholicism in England after her father, Henry VIII, died.

LONGFORD
County town: Longford
Area: 403 sq. mi.

Notable natives: Poet and playwright Padraic Colum (1881–1972), whose plays were among the first staged at Dublin's Abbey Theatre; Oliver Goldsmith (1728–1774), writer, poet and playwright, whose works include *The Vicar of Wakefield* and *She Stoops to Conquer;* General Sean McEoin (1893–1973), the "blacksmith of Ballinalee," IRA commander, veteran politician and twice a candidate for president; James A. Farrell (1863–1943), Irish-American "steel king," who headed United States Steel, the nation's largest steel-making firm; John Keegan Casey (1846–1870), Fenian and patriotic poet who died in prison at age 24 and is best remembered for his rousing ballad, "The Rising of the Moon"; Frank McCoppin (1834–1897), Mayor of San Francisco after the Civil War, the first Irish-born mayor of a major U.S. city.

Places of interest: Inchmore Island, in Lough Gowna, where remains of a sixth-century church stand on a monastic site founded by St. Columcille; Edgeworthstown, ancestral home of the Edgeworth family, whose talented members included Maria, author of *Castle Rackrent,* a satire on the evils of the nineteenth-century Irish landowning system, and her father, Richard, an inventor of note; Inchlauran, an island-bound monastery site in Lough Ree, with several old churches and many early Christian grave slabs.

Events: Granard Harp Festival and Summer Harp School (August); Irish Hot-Air Balloon Championships, Ballymahon (September).

Newspapers: Longford Leader (weekly); *Longford News* (weekly).

LOUTH
County town: Dundalk
Area: 317 sq. mi. (Ireland's smallest county)

Notable natives: St. Brigid of Kildare (453–523), one of Ireland's three patron saints, who was born at Faughart, according to tradition; internationally famed architect Michael Scott (1905–   ), whose designs include the Irish Pavilion for the New York World's Fair (1939) and the Abbey Theatre, Dublin (1965); Paul Callan (1799–1864), priest, inventor and scientist, known for his pioneering work in electrical science, including invention of the induction coil—which made the modern transformer possible—and his discoveries involving high-tension electricity; John E. Cairnes (1823–1875), economist whose book, *The Slave Power,* did much to sway British opinion toward sympathy for the North during the Civil War; Paul Vincent Carroll (1900–1968), award-winning playwright (*Shadow and Substance, The White Steed),* known for his unsurpassed depictions of clergymen and clerical life; John O'Boyle Reilly

(1844–1890), Irish-American poet, journalist and patriot; William D'Arcy McGee (1825–1868), writer and nationalist who emigrated to Boston, became editor of *The Pilot,* then worked as London correspondent for *The Nation* before breaking with the Young Irelanders over their revolutionary methods and emigrating to Canada. There he entered Parliament, served in the government and played a leading role in promoting Canadian federation before he was assassinated for denouncing a threatened Fenian invasion of Canada from the United States.

Places of interest: The Cooley Peninsula—"Cuchullain Country" —setting for many ancient Irish sagas; Monasterboice, site of a once-great monastic settlement, of which remains a round tower and 17-foot Muiredach's Cross, finest of Ireland's high crosses; ruins of Mellifont Abbey, first and greatest monastic foundation of the Cistercians, who became the most influential Continental order in Ireland; Transport Museum, Dunleer; Shrine of St. Brigid (built in 1933), Faughart, housing a relic of Ireland's patroness-saint.

Events: Dundalk Maytime Festival and Amateur Theatre International (May); Omeath Gala Week (August).

Newspapers: Drogheda Independent (weekly); *The Argus* (weekly); *Dundalk Democrat* (weekly).

MEATH
County town: Navan
Area: 903 sq. mi.

Notable natives: Turlogh O'Carolan (1670–1738), blind composer and harpist, one of the last, and perhaps the greatest, of the Irish bards; Arthur Wellesley (1769–1852), first Duke of Wellington, victor of the Battle of Waterloo and British prime minister; St. Oliver Plunkett (1629–1684), Catholic Archbishop of Armagh, martyred on perjured charges for alleged complicity in the so-called Popish Plot; Sir William Johnson (born MacShane; 1715–1774), Superintendent of Indian Affairs on the New York frontier and British-American hero of the French and Indian War; Rear-Admiral Sir Francis Beaufort (1774–1857), Royal Navy officer and hydrography pioneer, who originated the Beaufort scale of wind velocities and a tabulated system for recording weather, both still used; James Connell (1850?–1929), writer, nationalist and self-taught lawyer, best known as author of "The Red Flag," the socialist anthem; Sir Edward Lovett Pearce (1699–1733), architect of the Irish Houses of Parliament (now Bank of Ireland), which are considered among Europe's finest public buildings; Ambrose O'Higgins (1720?–1801), viceroy of Peru under Spanish rule and father of Bernardo O'Higgins, the Liberator of Chile; Thomas Hussey (1741–1803), first president of Maynooth College, Ireland's premier seminary; Trevor G. McVeagh (1908–1968), lawyer and sportsman extraordinaire, who represented Ireland over 70 times in four different sports, gained international laurels for tennis, hockey, squash and cricket in 1938 and captained Ireland's hockey team to three straight Triple Crown wins.

Places of interest: Trim Castle, largest Anglo-Norman castle in Ireland; the Hill of Tara, containing ruins of the former religious and cultural capital of pre-Norman Ireland and seat of Ireland's High Kings; Newgrange, an important pre-Celtic burial site; the Hill of Slane, where St. Patrick is said to have first lit the Paschal Fire in 433 A.D., in defiance of the pagan Druids.

Events: Moynalty Steam Threshing Festival, Moynalty (August).

Newspapers: Meath Chronicle (weekly).

Miscellaneous: The county is sometimes called "Royal Meath" because of the heritage of Tara and Ireland's High Kings.

OFFALY
County town: Tullamore
Area: 771 sq. mi.

Notable natives: Edward Hand (1744–1802), American military hero and major general during the Revolution; Charles Jervas (1675?–1739), court painter to George I and George II, also known for his portraits of leading Irish figures of his day; Joseph Coyne (1803–1868), playwright, theatrical producer and writer who excelled at writing farcical plays (*How to Settle Accounts with Your Laundress, The Widow Hunt,* etc.) and was one of the founders of *Punch,* the leading English magazine of satirical humor; Jasper Joly

(1819–1892), book collector and philanthropist, whose collection of 23,000 books, prints and other items became the nucleus of the National Library, Dublin.

Places of interest: Birr Castle, with its museum, its impressive gardens and ruins of the Great Telescope, constructed for the 3rd Earl of Rosse in 1845, and which remained the world's largest telescope for 75 years; Clonmacnoise, Shannonside remains of what was perhaps Ireland's most famous monastery; Clogan Castle, Banagher, built in 1120 and one of Ireland's oldest inhabited buildings.

Events: Birr Vintage Week (August); Irish Carriage Driving Championship, Birr Castle, Birr (September); Offaly Grand Canal Boat Rally (May/June); Edenderry Festival, Edenderry (July).

Newspapers: Midland Tribune (weekly); *Tullamore Tribune* (weekly); *Offaly Topic* (weekly).

Miscellaneous: Until independence, Offaly was called King's County, originally in honor of King Philip II of Spain, husband of the English queen, Mary Tudor.

WESTMEATH
County town: Mullingar
Area: 681 sq. mi.

Notable natives: Michael J. Meany, father of George Meany (1894–1979), U.S. labor leader who was the first head of the combined AFL-CIO and American labor's leading spokesman; John McCormack (1884–1945), legendary Irish tenor known for his renditions of popular Irish songs as well as his operatic performances; T. P. O'Connor (1848–1929), journalist, litterateur and Nationalist member of parliament.

Places of interest: Tullynally Castle, Castlepollard, home of the Earls of Longford; Military Museum, St. Columb's Barracks, Mullingar; Athlone Castle Museum, The Castle, Athlone.

Newspapers: Westmeath/Offaly Independent (weekly); *Westmeath Examiner* (weekly); *Midland Topic* (weekly).

WEXFORD
County town: Wexford
Area: 908 sq. mi.

Notable natives: John Barry (1745–1803), U.S. naval officer and "Father of the U.S. Navy"; Patrick Kennedy, immigrant great-grandfather of President John F. Kennedy; Sir Robert McClure (1807–1873), who discovered the Northwest Passage linking the Atlantic and Pacific oceans; Admiral Sir David Beatty (1871–1936), British naval officer who took command of the Grand Fleet in 1916 and successfully countered the U-boat threat, later serving as Admiral of the Fleet and First Sea Lord; Beauchamp Bagenal Harvey (1762–1798), Wexford landowner whose support of Catholic emancipation and parliamentary reform led him to join the United Irishmen, who subsequently elected him commander-in-chief of the rebel forces during the 1798 rising, after whose failure he was executed; Leo Rowsome (1900–1970), "King of Irish Pipers"; John Edward Redmond (1856–1918), nationalist leader who remained loyal to Parnell after the O'Shea affair, later becoming leader of the reunited Irish Parliamentary party where he pushed through the Land Act of 1903, helped found the National University, and secured introduction of the third Home Rule Bill in 1912, before the polarization of opinion between the Ulster Unionist movement and the revolutionary nationalists undermined his moderate, parliamentary approach to independence.

Places of interest: Hook Lighthouse, near Fethard—one of the world's four oldest lighthouses, a thirteenth-century tower on a site where a light is said to have been kept continuously burning since the third century; the Saltee Islands, Ireland's foremost birding spot, where over three million birds flock during warmer months; Wexford Wildfowl Reserve, a wintering spot for Greenland geese; Dunganstown, site of the Kennedy family homestead, from which JFK's paternal great-grandfather emigrated; Johnstown Castle Gardens and Agricultural Museum, Wexford, where you can enjoy an impressive collection of trees set amid lakes and landscaped gardens, and then tour an exhibition illustrating the evolution of Irish agriculture and rural life; Wexford Maritime Museum, The Quay, Wexford; John F. Kennedy Park, New Ross, a 500-acre arboretum containing a wide range of flowers, shrubs and other plants as well as forested areas.

Events: Wexford Opera Festival, featuring little-performed operatic classics (October); Enniscorthy Strawberry Festival (late June/early July); Wexford Mussel and Seafood Festival (August); Tagoat Steam Rally and Agricultural/Horticultural Show, Tagoat (August).

Newspapers: Echo and South Leinster Advertiser (weekly); *Enniscorthy-Gorey Guardian* (weekly); *New Ross Standard* (weekly); *Wexford People* (weekly).

WICKLOW
County town: Wicklow
Area: 782 sq. mi.

Notable natives: Charles Stewart Parnell (1846–1891), champion of Home Rule during the late 1800s who was forced to retire from politics after a scandalous affair with a married woman; Michael O'Dwyer (1771–1826), patriot leader who took part in the abortive risings of 1798 and 1803 and then, after surrendering voluntarily, was transported to Australia where he became high constable of Sydney in 1815; Robert Childers Barton (1881–1975), last surviving signer of the 1921 Anglo-Irish Treaty, who had resigned his commission in the Dublin Fusiliers and joined the Republicans when the 1916 Easter Rising erupted, later winning election as a Sinn Fein MP; Edwin L. Godkin (1831–1902) who, after covering the Crimean War for the *Daily News,* emigrated to America, founding *The Nation,* in which he opposed Tammany Hall, the Boer War, American annexation of Hawaii and the Philippines, and supported Home Rule.

Places of interest: Powerscourt, a 12,500-acre estate whose grand house was destroyed by fire in 1974, but whose gardens remain among Europe's finest, with magnificent Japanese and Italian-style gardens, a 400-foot waterfall, fountains, statuary and a deer park; Avondale House, near Rathdrum: birthplace of Charles Stewart Parnell, which houses the Parnell Museum; the Vale of Avoca, which inspired Thomas Moore's famous verses, "The Meeting of the Waters"; Glendalough, where St. Kevin founded a monastic community in the sixth century that became known as the "Rome of the Western World," and whose remains include the ruins of seven churches and a 100-foot round tower; Glenealy Agricultural Museum; Mount Usher, Ashford, magnificent gardens along the Vartry River where exotic plants from Africa, Sri Lanka and New Zealand flourish in summer; Woodenbridge Trout Farm, near Arklow, where you pay for what you catch using tackle provided free; the Maritime Museum, Arklow; Avoca, a center for distinctive handweaving; Hunter's Hotel, Rathnew, one of Ireland's oldest coaching inns; the Wicklow Way, Ireland's first government-sponsored hiking trail; the Beit Art Collection, Russborough, Blessington, which includes important Spanish, Dutch and Flemish Old Masters.

Events: Arklow Music Festival (March); Melody Fair, the Vale of Avoca, celebrating the popular Irish melodies of Thomas Moore (July); Blessington Horse Show, Blessington (July); Tinahely Agricultural Show, Tinahely (August).

Newspapers: Wicklow People (weekly).

Miscellaneous: Wicklow is known as the Garden of Ireland. Relatively few Wicklow people emigrated to the United States, though a good number settled the Australian island of Tasmania.

PROVINCE OF MUNSTER
CLARE
County town: Ennis
Area: 1,231 sq. mi.

Notable natives: John P. Holland (1841–1914), Irish-American inventor of the submarine; Brian Boru (926–1014), high king and unifier of Ireland; Brian Merriman (ca. 1750–1803), Gaelic poet, schoolmaster, musician and mathematician, best known as the author of "Cuirt an Mhean Oiche" ("The Midnight Court"), one of the greatest poems ever written in Gaelic, and sometimes suppressed because of its ribald content; Willie Clancy (1921–1973), Uillean pipes virtuoso and "godfather" of the Irish traditional music revival who thrilled audiences throughout Europe and the United States as well as Ireland; Michael Cusack (1847–1906), co-founder of the Gaelic Athletic Association (GAA); the Kirby family, a multigeneration dynasty of international handball champions; Harriet Smithson (1800–1854), actress who won the love of French composer Hector Berlioz, whose *Symphonie Fantastique* was dedicated to her, and to whom she was for a time married; Peadar Clancy (18??–1920), vice-commandant of the Dublin Brigade during the War of Independence, who acquired a reputation for springing prisoners from British jails; Austin Hogan (1907–1974), co-founder with Kerryman Mike Quill of the Transport Workers Union of America (TWU); Dr. Patrick Hillery (1923–   ), President of Ireland, 1976–; St. Senan (?–560), who founded 20 monasteries.

Places of interest: Bunratty Castle and Folk Park, which includes Ireland's finest remaining medieval castle as well as reconstructions of turn-of-the-century rural homes and a nineteenth-century village street; Knappogue Castle, one of 42 built by the McNamaras; Ballycasey Craft Workshop; Clare Heritage Centre, Corofin; the Cliffs of Moher, nearly five miles of sheer cliffs towering as high as 700 feet above the sea; Craggaunowen Castle, Quin, whose grounds house a rebuilt crannog, or Bronze Age lake dwelling; the Burren, an enormous limestone area unique in Europe and featuring spectacular caves, underwater streams and plants native to the Arctic thriving next to others native to subtropical regions; Lisdoonvarna, a Burren town renowned as a spa and as a mecca for Irish bachelors and spinsters in search of mates; Lahinch, site of Ireland's oldest golf course, also one of the country's three finest; Shannon International Airport, a major engineering feat when constructed during the 1930s—the first airport built to serve commercial transatlantic air traffic—and the focus of much of Ireland's industrial development effort; Quin Abbey, an excellent example of a medieval Franciscan friary, with well-preserved cloisters.

Events: Lisdoonvarna Folk Festival (July); Matchmaking Festival of Ireland, Lisdoonvarna (September); Willie Clancy School of Irish Music, Miltown Malbay (July); Merriman Summer School, Lisdoonvarna (August); Fleadh Nua, Ennis, celebrating traditional music (May); Ennis Harvest Festival (August); Queen of the Burren Autumn Festival, Lisdoonvarna (October); Burren Landscape Painting School, Lisdoonvarna (May).

Newspapers: Clare Champion (weekly).

CORK
County town: Cork
Area: 2,881 sq. mi. (Ireland's largest county)

Notable natives: Thomas Davis (1814–1845), poet, leader of the Young Ireland movement and a founder of *The Nation;* William R. Grace (1832–1904), U.S. steamship magnate and first Catholic mayor of New York; Sean O'Faolain (1900–   ), versatile writer who produced stories, novels, a play, a travel book, literary criticism, translations, an autobiography and numerous biographies of famous Irishmen; William Penn (1644–1718), Quaker leader who founded Pennsylvania; Michael Collins (1890–1922), veteran of the Easter Rising who later served as commander-in-chief of the Free State Army; Patrick Cleburne (1828–1864), Confederate general known for his bravery and leadership in battle; Jeremiah O'Brien (1740–1818), who captured the British schooner *Margaretta* in what many consider the "first naval action of the American Revolution"; Sir Richard Church (1784–1873), the "Liberator of Greece," a Quaker merchant's son who ran away to join the British army where he became sympathetic to the cause of Greek independence and, after briefly commanding the forces of the King of Naples, accepted an invitation to become commander-in-chief in the struggle that secured Greece's freedom from Turkish rule; James Barry (1741–1806), painter who drew subject matter from ancient Irish history (e.g., *The Conversion by St. Patrick of the King of Cashel*) and later, classical antiquity; writer Frank O'Connor (born Michael O'Donovan; 1903–1966), known for his short stories; Elizabeth Bowen (1899–1973), novelist and short-story writer whose works include the best-selling *Heat of the Day,* as well as *A Summer's Night* —a short story set in Cork and said to be surpassed only by Joyce's *The Dead*—and *The Last September* (1929), a novel describing life in a great house in Cork during "The Troubles"; Timothy M. Healy (1855–1931), nationalist politician and first governor-general of the Irish Free State; Richard Hennessy (1720–1800), French-Irish soldier and distiller whose name is immortalized in world-famous Hennessy's brandy; Archbishop Thomas W. Croke (1824–1902), who worked actively for temperance, the Land League and the Gaelic Athletic Association, and is commemorated for the last in Croke Park, Dublin; Jack Lynch (1917–   ), Prime Minister of Ireland, 1966–1973 and 1977–1979, and President, the European Council, 1977.

Places of interest: Blarney Castle (and its Stone); the port of Kinsale, a center for first-rate deep-sea fishing; Cobh (formerly Queenstown), in Cork Harbor, where transatlantic liners once called; Bantry Bay, widely considered Ireland's most beautiful bay; Castletownbere, with its nightly fish auction; Crawford Municipal School of Art and Gallery, Cork, a showcase for twentieth-century Irish painting; the Opera House, Cork, featuring opera and ballet performances by the Irish Ballet Company; West Cork Regional Museum, Clonakilty; Garinish Island, whose Italian-style garden features plants and shrubs from around the world set among shelter trees, with coastal and mountain vistas as a backdrop; Fota House, Carrigtwohill, a restored Regency great house (early 1800s) containing the nation's finest collection (after the National Gallery's) of Irish landscapes painted between 1750 and 1870; Fota Arboretum, a magnificent collection of trees and shrubs from around the world.

Events: Cork Film Festival (June); Cork International Choral and Folk Dance Festival (May); Guinness Jazz Festival, Cork (October); Cobh International Folk Dance Festival (July); West Cork Drama Festival (March); Midleton Art Fest (April); Cork Western Music Jamboree (March); Macroom Mountain Dew Festival, featuring outdoor concerts (June); Kinsale Gourmet Food Festival (October); Dungannon Horse Fair (August); Cork International Film Festival, Cork (October); Baltimore Sailing Regatta, Baltimore (August).

Newspapers: *Cork Evening Echo* (daily); *Cork Examiner* (daily); *Cork Weekly Examiner* (weekly); *Southern Star* (weekly).

KERRY
County town: Tralee
Area: 1,815 sq. mi.

Notable natives: Daniel O'Connell (1775–1847), "The Liberator," who won election to the British Parliament, where he was instrumental in the 1829 passage of the Catholic Emancipation Bill; St. Brendan the Navigator (484?–577), who is believed by some to have sailed to America nearly one thousand years before Columbus; Horatio Herbert, Lord Kitchener (1850–1916), British soldier, commander-in-chief against the Boers and Secretary for War, 1914; Peig Sayers (1873–1958), traditional Irish storyteller, who preserved hundreds of old Gaelic tales and folksongs that would otherwise have been lost, and whose autobiography is a classic of its kind, recounting a life filled with more than its share of tragedy and sadness, much of it on the bleak Great Blasket Island; Maurice Walsh (1879–1964), novelist and short-story writer whose best-known work, *The Quiet Man,* was made into the popular film.

Places of interest: The Dingle Peninsula, one of Ireland's most picturesque areas; Muckross House, Killarney, with exhibits of Kerry folk life and demonstrations of traditional crafts as well as a variety of gardens worth seeing; Carrantuohill, Ireland's highest mountain (3,414 feet), part of the famed McGillicuddy's Reeks; Derrynane Abbey, Caherdaniel; Waterville, a favorite spot for game fishermen; Gallarus Oratory, Kerry, one of Ireland's earliest churches, a well-preserved structure that is simple in form and built entirely of unmortared stone; the famous Ring of Kerry, a 112-mile route snaking through some of the most scenic country anywhere and offering mountain, lake and seaside vistas.

Events: Puck Fair, Killorglin (August); Fleadh Cheoil na hEireann, traditional music competition (July); Rose of Tralee International Festival (September); Killarney Bach Festival (July); Pan-Celtic Festival, Killarney (May); Kenmare Seafood Festival (September); Siamsa Tire Theatre, home of the National Folk Theatre of Ireland, which performs from mid-June to mid-September; Lamb Festival, Sneem (June); Dingle Races, Dingle, featuring horse and curragh racing (August); Kerry Summer Painting School, Cahirciveen (July); Ballybunion International Bachelor Festival, Ballybunion (June); Rally of the Lakes, Killarney, a motor-sports event (December).

Newspapers: *The Kerryman* (weekly); *Kerry's Eye* (weekly).

Miscellaneous: Kerry lays claim to the mildest climate in Ireland, since its position as the island's most westerly county gives it the benefit of the Gulf Stream's warming effects. Some of its sheltered bays are lined with subtropical plants.

LIMERICK
County town: Limerick
Area: 1,037 sq. mi.

Notable natives: James O'Neill (1847–1920), Irish-American stage actor and father of playwright Eugene O'Neill; Lola Montez (1818–1861), born Maria Dolores Eliza Rosanna Gilbert, the famous adventuress and dancer who, as the favorite of Ludwig I (the "Mad King" of Bavaria), became virtual ruler of that German principality; poet and activist-nationalist Aubrey Thomas de Vere (1814–1902); Philip Embury (1728–1773), the "Father of American Methodism," who established America's first Methodist Episcopal church in New York City; Ada Rehan (born Ada Crehan; 1860–1916), Irish-American comic actress well loved on the stages of New York and London; Francis Bindon (1690?–1765), painter and architect who executed many fine portraits as well as designs for such great Irish houses as Dunsandle (County Galway), New Hall (County Clare) and Bessborough, Woodstock and Castle Morres in County Wicklow; Richard Harris (1933–   ), film and television actor whose film credits include *Camelot, A Man Called Horse, This Sporting Life* and *The Molly Maguires.*

Places of interest: St. Mary's Cathedral, Limerick, built in 1172 by Donal Mor O'Brien, last king of Munster; Lough Gur Stone Age Centre; King John's Castle, Limerick, a massive, reasonably intact Anglo-Norman fortress dating from 1210; The Hunt Collection, National Institute of Higher Education, Plassey, Castleroy; Good Shepherd Convent, Limerick, where the nuns make Limerick lace in the age-old manner.

Events: Limerick Game and Country Fair, Adare (May); Limerick Civic Week (March); Limerick Theatre Festival (March); Church Music International Choral Festival, Limerick (March); Charleville Cheese Festival (June).

Newspaper: Limerick Chronicle (three times weekly); *Limerick Leader* (three times weekly); *Limerick Weekly Echo & Shannon News* (weekly).

TIPPERARY
County town: Clonmel
Area: 1,643 sq. mi.

Notable natives: Laurence Sterne (1713–1768), author of *Tristram Shandy* and other novels; Father Theobald Mathew (1790–1856), the "Apostle of Temperance," who successfully encouraged sobriety among many of Irish heritage in Britain and America as well as Ireland; Brendan R. Bracken, Viscount Bracken (1901–1958), son of a founder of the Gaelic Athletic Association, who entered British publishing, acquired a stable of financial publications and subsequently served as a member of Parliament, Parliamentary Private Secretary and confidante to Winston Churchill, and wartime Minister of Information; Dan Breen (1894–1969), IRA leader during the War of Independence—when he gained a reputation for escaping from tight spots—and for three decades a representative in the Dail for Tipperary; John Burke (1787–1848), genealogist and creator of the two famous handbooks that bear his name: *Burke's Peerage* (once described as "a stud book of humanity") and *Burke's Landed Gentry,* both still published today; Geoffrey Keating (1570?–1650), historian, poet and priest whose narrative *History of Ireland,* written in early Modern Irish between 1620 and 1634, defended Ireland against the criticisms of some English writers.

Places of interest: Holy Cross Abbey; Hayes's Hotel, Thurles, where the Gaelic Athletic Association (GAA) was founded in 1884; Ballyporeen, the birthplace of Ronald Reagan's paternal great-grandfather; the Falconry of Ireland—with one of the world's largest collections of birds of prey—which presents demonstrations of falconry for visitors; the Irish Coursing Club, Clonmel, headquarters of Irish greyhound racing; the Rock of Cashel, one of Ireland's most historic sites, a massive stone outcrop on which stand a ruined twelfth-century cathedral, a 92-foot round tower and other religious structures: Cashel was the ancient capital of the kings of Munster and, in medieval times, Munster's religious center.

Events: Bianconi Days Festival (May); National Coursing Meeting, Clonmel, Ireland's premier greyhound racing event (early February).

Newspapers: The Nationalist & Munster Advertiser (weekly); *Clonmel Express* (weekly); *The Nenagh Guardian* (weekly); *Tipperary Star* (weekly).

WATERFORD
County town: Waterford
Area: 710 sq. mi.

Notable natives: Sir Robert Boyle (1627–1691), Anglo-Irish physicist and first president of The Royal Society; Thomas F. Meagher (1823–1867), Young Ireland leader who escaped prison to distinguish himself as a Union general in the Civil War; actor and comedian William Grattan Tyrone Power (1797–1841), whose great-grandsons included the American film star, Tyrone Power (1913–1958) and the director, Sir Tyrone Guthrie (1900–1971); Charles Kean (1813–1868), a leading actor on the nineteenth-century London stage; William Vincent Wallace (1812–1865), composer of operas and piano music and best known for *Maritana* and *Lurline,* two operas that were quite popular in their time but rarely heard today; General Richard Mulcahy (1886–1971), soldier and politician who fought with the Irish Volunteers in 1916, became commander-in-chief of the Republican Army, General Officer commanding the Provisional government forces during the civil war, and later a Dail member, cabinet minister and leader of the Fine Gael party; Thomas Roberts (1748–1778), artist whose paintings for well-heeled patrons include some of the most inspiring scenery of Ireland ever put on canvas.

Places of interest: Waterford Glass Works; the Theatre Royal (1788), where internationally famed performers have appeared—and professional Irish touring companies still perform; Waterford Maritime Museum, The Quay, Waterford; Municipal Art Gallery, Waterford.

Events: International Festival of Light Opera (late September/early October); Waterford Glass Angling Competition, Dungarvan (June).

Newspapers: Dungarvan Observer & Munster Industrial Advocate (weekly); *Munster Express* (weekly); *Waterford News & Star* (weekly); *East Cork News* (weekly).

PROVINCE OF ULSTER (REPUBLIC OF IRELAND)
CAVAN
County town: Cavan
Area: 730 sq. mi.

Notable natives: Thomas Brady (1752–1827), born a farmer's son, who emigrated to Austria and rose to become a field marshal in the imperial army; Patrick Donahue (1811–1901), founder of *The Boston Pilot,* the leading Irish-American journal of its day; Mary Anne Sadlier (born Mary Madden; 1820–1903), Irish-Canadian author of some 60 popular novels, including *The Red Hand of Ulster* and *The Old House by the Boyne;* Philip H. Sheridan (1831–1888), U.S. soldier renowned for his exploits as a major-general of cavalry during the Civil War, winning the last major battle of the conflict, Five Forks, and later, after serving as military governor of Texas and Louisiana and fighting Indians on the frontier, rising to become U.S. army commander-in-chief.

Places of interest: Cavan Crystal Ireland Ltd., Cavan; Derragara Folk Museum, Butlersbridge; Derragara Inn, Butlersbridge, one of Ireland's oldest inns, with pub food that has won seven national awards; Bellamont Forest, near Cootehill, one of Ireland's finest Palladian-style great houses.

Events: Water Sports Regatta, Lough Sillan (August); Cavan International Song Contest (February); Summer Craft School, Mountnugent (July/August); Belturbet Festival of the Erne, a coarse fishing event (July).

Newspapers: The Anglo-Celt (weekly).

DONEGAL
County town: Lifford
Area: 1,865 sq. mi.

Notable natives: St. Columcille, also called Columba (A.D. 521–597), one of Ireland's three patron saints, who founded the famous monastery of Iona and others in his efforts to convert the tribes of Scotland; Francis Makemie (1658–1708), "Father of American Presbyterianism"; Isaac Butt (1813–1879), "Father of Home Rule," who lost leadership of the movement to Parnell; William Allingham (1824–1889), poet *(Day and Night Songs)* member of the pre-Raphaelite circle and author of *Laurence Bloomfield in Ireland,* which has been called "an epic of Irish philanthropic landlordism"; Michael O'Clery (1575–1643), chronicler of Irish history who compiled a *Martyrologium* of Irish saints, lists of Irish kings and their pedigrees, and was the chief author of the so-called *Annals of the Four Masters,* an indispensable record of Irish history up to 1616.

Places of interest: Lough Derg, site of an annual pilgrimage; Killybegs, a major Irish fishing port; Glencolumbkille, which has a folk museum with a recreation of a traditional country village; Donegal Abbey, where the Four Masters are said to have written their famous *Annals* during the early 1600s; Slieve League, Europe's highest cliffs (1,972 feet); Ardara, a center for the weaving and sale of famous handwoven Donegal tweed; the Donegal Gaeltacht, a traditional Gaelic-speaking district; the Grianan of Aileach, a splendidly preserved circular stone fort built atop Greenan Mountain around 1,700 B.C.; Glenveagh National Park in the Donegal Highlands, with 25,000 acres of memorable views; the Bloody Foreland, a headland between Falcarragh and Gweedore whose rocks turn the color of blood as the sun goes down; Mountcharles, a town that ascends a steep hill whose top offers stunning views of Donegal Bay; Malin Head, Ireland's most northerly point; Falcarragh, a seaside village in the Donegal Gaeltacht, and a good starting point for climbing 2,200-foot Muckish Mountain and 2,460-foot Errigal, which offer rewarding views.

Events: Letterkenny International Folk Dance Festival (August); Donegal International Car Rally, Letterkenny (June); Glengad/Malin Sea Angling Competition, Malin (September); Killybegs Festival, Killybegs (August).

Newspapers: Donegal Democrat (weekly); *Donegal People's Press* (weekly); *Derry People and Donegal News* (weekly).

MONAGHAN
County town: Monaghan
Area: 498 sq. mi.

Notable natives: James Connolly (1870–1916), first active socialist in Irish history and a leader of the Easter Rising of 1916, for which he was executed; Ann Jane Carlile (1775–1864), pioneering Irish temperance leader; John O'Neill (1834–1878), who led the Fenians' raids into Canada from the United States after the Civil War; John Bagenal Bury (1861–1927), classical scholar and historian, whose monumental *History of the Later Roman Empire*—completed at age 28—placed him among the world's foremost historians; Patrick Kavanagh (1907–1967), poet whose works celebrated rural Irish life; John Robert Gregg (1867–1948), Irish-American inventor of Gregg shorthand, which is still used in this age of dictating machines and word processors; Richard Pockrich (1690–1759), inventor of the musical glasses, sometimes called the "glass harmonica"; Sir Charles Gavan Duffy (1816–1903), nationalist cofounder of *The Nation* who, after imprisonment for his role in the abortive 1848 rising, entered Parliament and then, discouraged about reform prospects, emigrated to Australia where he became prime minister of the state of Victoria; Thomas Taggart (1856–1929), Mayor of Indianapolis, Chairman of the Democratic National Committee and U.S. senator from Indiana.

Places of interest: Carrickmacross, a scenic town where the handmaking of lace flourishes; Folk Museum, Iniskeen.

Events: Farney Coarse Fishing Festival, Carrickmacross (April or May); Clones Agricultural Show, Clones (August).

Newspapers: Northern Standard (weekly); *Monaghan Democrat* (weekly).

PROVINCE OF ULSTER (NORTHERN IRELAND)
ANTRIM
County town: Ballymena
Area: 1,122 sq. mi.

Notable natives: James Galway (1939–   ), world-famous concert flutist; Siobhan McKenna (1923–1986), stage and screen actress; Alexander T. Stewart (1803–1876), U.S. department store pioneer; Samuel S. McClure (1857–1949), founder of the first U.S. newspaper syndicate; Sir Hamilton Harty (1879–1941), composer and former conductor of the Hallé Orchestra; James McHenry (1753–1816), private secretary to George Washington, delegate to the Constitutional Convention and Secretary of War, 1796–1800 (Fort McHenry, Baltimore, whose successful stand against a British naval bombardment inspired *The Star-Spangled Banner,* is named for him); Thomas Hunter (1831–1915), Anglican Young Irelander who emigrated to New York, becoming a noted educational reformer—the city's Hunter College commemorates him; C. S. Lewis (1898–1963), noted poet, prose writer and theologian; Sir Roger Casement (1864–1916), British diplomat and Irish patriot, executed on charges of treason for arranging German arms shipments to aid the 1916 Easter Rising; Sir Samuel Ferguson (1810–1886), poet and antiquary known for his translations of Old Irish poems and sagas; James Bryce, Viscount Bryce (1838–1922), historian and diplomat whose masterly *The American Commonwealth* (1888) is considered one of the most perceptive books ever written about the United States, where he later served as British ambassador; James B. Armour (1841–1928), liberal Presbyterian leader who supported Home Rule and opposed Sir Edward Carson and others favoring partition, contending it would tend to exaggerate "racial and religious hatreds"; Field Marshall Sir George White (1835–1925), hero of the Siege of Ladysmith (Boer War), which earned him the Victoria Cross; Sean Lester (1888–1959), last secretary-general of the League of Nations; Timothy Eaton (1834–1907), founder of Eaton's, the Toronto-based department-store chain that ranks among North America's largest; William Thomson Kelvin, first Baron Kelvin (1824–1907), scientist and inventor who, after entering Glasgow University at age 11, went on to discover the Second Law of Thermodynamics, conducted research on electrical currents that assured the success of the Atlantic Cable, invented a variety of nautical and electrical instruments, and is immortalized in the Kelvin Scale for measuring absolute temperature; St. Clair Mulholland (1839–1910), a major general in the American Civil War who won the Medal of Honor and later served as chief of police in Philadelphia.

Places of interest: The Giant's Causeway, a geological wonder of volcanic origin; Old Bushmill's Distillery, the world's oldest, dating from the early 1600s; Carrickfergus Castle, the largest and best-preserved medieval castle in the North; Dunluce Castle; Carrick-a-Rede Rope Bridge, an adventure for the stouthearted, near Ballycastle; Belfast Pottery; Slemish Mountain, where St. Patrick is said to have herded pigs as a boy-slave; Ulster Museum, the Botanic Garden, Belfast, which contains Irish antiquities, treasures from a Spanish Armada wreck, costume and fine arts collections, and exhibits portraying the early industrialization of the province; Belfast Zoo, set in a mountain park above the city; the Glens of Antrim, nine of which open onto the sea, providing panoramas of rocky cliffs, green swatches and cascading waterfalls; the Round Tower, Antrim, one of Ireland's best-preserved; Crown Liquor Saloon, Belfast, a high Victorian pub with elaborate decoration and fine woodwork, glass and tiles; Sixmilewater, where you can board an excursion boat for a cruise on Lough Neagh, the largest lake in the British Isles.

Events: Royal Ulster Agricultural Show, Belfast (May); Belfast Festival, featuring music, drama, opera and film (November); The Lord Mayor's Show, Belfast, a parade featuring scores of bands and floats (May); Slemish Pilgrimage (St. Patrick's Day); Glens of Antrim Feis, Glenariff (July); Oul' Lammas Fair, Ballycastle, the North's oldest and largest (August); Lady Day: Ancient Order of Hibernians Celebrations (August 15); Orangemen's Day (July 12).

Newspapers: Belfast Telegraph *(daily);* Irish News & Belfast Morning News *(daily);* News Letter *(daily);* Sunday News *(weekly);* Ballymena Observer *(weekly);* Ballymena Chronicle & Antrim Observer *(weekly);* Ballymena Guardian *(weekly).*

ARMAGH
County town: Armagh
Area: 489 sq. mi.

Notable natives: George William Russell (1867–1935), poet, essayist and painter who wrote under the pseudonym "AE" and is known for his contributions to the Irish Literary Revival; James Logan (1674–1751), secretary to William Penn, who emigrated with Penn to Pennsylvania, rising to become chief justice of the colony's Supreme Court as well as a scholar of some note: Thomas Cardinal O'Fiaich (1923–   ), Primate of All Ireland; Edward Bunting (1773–1843), who, while not as famous as Thomas Moore, collected and published hundreds of old Irish airs and tunes, many of them set to words by Moore in *Irish Melodies;* Tommy Makem (1932–   ), musician and entertainer known for his lively performances of Irish music.

Places of interest: Armagh Town is the seat of ecclesiastical authority for both the Roman Catholic Church and the (Protestant) Church of Ireland: their respective cathedrals face each other from opposite hills, the latter containing a tablet said to mark the grave of Brian Boru; Navan Fort, hilltop capital of the Conor and other kings of Ulster from about 600 B.C. (also linked with the hero Cuchullain and the Red Branch Knights); Planetarium & Astronomy Centre, Armagh.

Events: Ulster Road Bowls Finals, Armagh (July & August); Lady Day: Ancient Order of Hibernians Celebrations (August 15); Orangemen's Day (July 12); Armagh Apple Blossom Festival (late May/early June).

Newspapers: Armagh Observer (weekly); *Ulster Gazette & Armagh Standard* (weekly).

*DERRY/LONDONDERRY**
County town: Derry/Londonderry*
Area: 804 sq. mi.

Notable natives: The parents of John Cardinal McCloskey (1810–1885), America's first native-born Catholic cardinal; John Mitchel (1815–1875), Presbyterian leader of the Young Ireland movement who wrote *Jail Journal;* George Farquhar (1678–1707), playwright

---

* Note: Irishmen south of the border and nationalists in the North have traditionally called the town and county Derry, its original name. After Scottish and English Protestants settled the area under a charter from James I early in the seventeenth century, they changed the name to Londonderry, in honor of the London company that had organized the so-called Plantation. The newer name is the official one in Northern Ireland and Britain as well as the name recognized by Unionists. In 1984, however, the City Council of Londonderry voted to formally remove *London* from its name. Partly, perhaps, as a result of this, the name Derry seems to be growing in popularity throughout the community.

known for two Restoration comedies, *The Recruiting Officer* and *The Beaux' Strategem;* Charles Thomson (1729–1824), first secretary of the U.S. Continental Congress, a drafter of the Declaration of Independence, and designer of the Great Seal of the United States; Rev. Charles H. McKenna (1835–1917), "Apostle of the Holy Name Society," who emigrated to America where he founded this popular organization for Catholic laymen among his other devotional activities; Oliver Pollock (1737–1823), wealthy American patriot who helped finance George Washington's army; William Ferguson Massey (1856–1925), Prime Minister of New Zealand, 1913–1925, the only premier in the world to continue in office from the pre–World War I period through the end of the war; Matthew Thornton (1714–1803), signer of the Declaration of Independence; Charles Donagh Maginnis (1867–1955), world-renowned architect whose commissions included the National Shrine of the Immaculate Conception, Washington, D.C.

Places of interest: Mussenden Temple, Downhill, an oddity of eighteenth-century classical architecture built by Frederick Hervey, Earl of Bristol and Anglican Bishop of Derry; the Sperrin Mountains, a less-visited area featuring whitewashed cottages and sparsely settled moors crossed by narrow, winding roads; the Guild House, Derry, whose beautiful stained-glass windows depict highlights of the city's history; the City Wall, Derry, a 20-foot-thick, mile-long enclosure that helped the city's Protestant inhabitants withstand the famous 105-day siege by James II's Catholic forces in 1689; Cathedral of St. Columb, Derry, in Gothic style (built 1633) with a chapter house that displays relics of the 1689 siege; Movanagher Fish Farm, Kilrea, where you can see several million trout at various stages of growth.

Events: Portstewart Music Festival (late May/early June); Portstewart Regatta (summer); Relief of Derry Celebration/Apprentice Boys' March (August 12); Lady Day: Ancient Order of Hibernians Celebrations (August 15); Orangemen's Day (July 12).

Newspapers: Derry Journal (semiweekly); *Sentinel* (weekly).

DOWN
County town: Downpatrick
Area: 952 sq. mi.

Notable natives: Rev. Patrick Brontë (born Prunty; 1777–1861), clergyman and writer, better known as the father of the three Brontë sisters—novelists who among them wrote such classics as *Jane Eyre, Wuthering Heights* and *Agnes Grey;* Harry Brogan (1905–1977), who made his stage debut at age 13 with Countess Markievicz, then, after a stint with touring actors, became active in the Abbey Theatre company and appeared in nearly every feature film made in Ireland during his career; Harry B. Ferguson (1884–1960), engineer and inventor who in 1909 became the first person in Ireland to fly (in a monoplane he designed and built), and who later designed a revolutionary tractor manufactured by Ford Motor Company in the only partnership Henry Ford ever entered.

Places of interest: Down Cathedral, Downpatrick, built on the supposed site of St. Patrick's first stone church (tradition holds that the remains of Sts. Patrick, Brigid and Columba lie within the churchyard); St. Patrick Heritage Centre, Downpatrick; Mountstewart Gardens, where a mild climate supports eucalyptus, bamboo and other subtropical plants; Saul, site of Ireland's first Christian church, built by St. Patrick about 432 A.D.; the Mountains of Mourne, ". . . that sweep down to the sea," best explored by foot or pony; Ulster Folk Village and Transport Museum, Cultra Park, Holywood, where traditional life in rural Ulster has been recreated, with cottages, churches, mills and other buildings moved here from throughout the province and restored to their original state (some are centuries old); Ballycopeland Windmill, thought to be Ireland's only working example; the Ards Peninsula, an unspoiled finger of land between Strangford Lough and the sea, dotted with charming shoreside villages, windmill towers and the ruins of ancient hilltop strongholds; Newry Canal, Newry, the first canal in the British Isles, which proved the practicability of canals.

Events: Ulster Harp National Steeplechase, Downpatrick (late February/early March); Lady Day: Ancient Order of Hibernians Celebrations (August 15); Orangemen's Day (July 12).

Newspapers: County Down Spectator (weekly).

FERMANAGH
County town: Enniskillen
Area: 653 sq. mi.

Notable natives: Rev. James MacDonald (late 1700s), great-grand-father of both Rudyard Kipling (1865–1936), the British novelist and "Poet of Empire," and Stanley Baldwin (1867–1947), British prime minister intermittently from 1923 to 1937; Field Marshall Sir Alan Brooke, the Viscount Alanbrooke (1883–1963), leading British commander during World War II; T. P. Flanagan (1929–), artist known for his watercolors of literary and historical landscapes; Shan Bullock (1865–1935), writer whose works include several novels of Fermanagh life *(By Thrasna River, The Squireen, Dan the Dollar* and *The Loughsiders)* as well as poetry and autobiography; Hugh O'Brien (1827–1895), first Irish-American mayor of Boston, who was inaugurated for the first of his three terms in 1885.

Places of interest: The Belleek Pottery, Ltd., home of world-famous chinaware; Upper and Lower Lough Erne, a mecca for fishing and cruising enthusiasts; the Royal School (1777), Portara, where both Oscar Wilde and Samuel Beckett studied; Castlecoole, a magnificent late Georgian house and estate near Enniskillen; Devenish Island, a medieval monastic site, with Ireland's best-preserved round tower as well as church and abbey ruins.

Events: Lady Day: Ancient Order of Hibernians Celebrations (August 15)); Orangemen's Day (July 12); Enniskillen Agricultural and Industrial Show (August).

Newspapers: Fermanagh Herald (weekly).

Miscellaneous: Bountifully blessed with lakes and waterways, Fermanagh is sometimes called the "Lake District of Northern Ireland." The correct pronunciation is fer-MA-na.

TYRONE
County town: Omagh
Area: 1,218 sq. mi.

Notable natives: James Shields (1810–1879), U.S. military officer and statesman, the only person ever elected a U.S. senator by three states; Bernadette Devlin (1947–), now Mrs. Michael McAliskey, the fiery nationalist-socialist who became the youngest member of the House of Commons in 1968; John Joseph Hughes (1797–1864), first Catholic Archbishop of New York and builder of St. Patrick's

Cathedral; John Dunlap (1747–1812), Irish-American printer and publisher who issued America's first daily newspaper, *The Pennsylvania Packet,* and printed the first copies of the Declaration of Independence; Flann O'Brien (1912–1966), popular writer of comic plays, novels and broadcast humor in both English and Gaelic; Brian Friel (1930–   ), dramatist, author of *Philadelphia, Here I Come* and other plays; Jimmy Kennedy (twentieth century), prolific songwriter who produced over 2,000 songs, including "Red Sails in the Sunset," "The Isle of Capri," "South of the Border" and "Did Your Mother Come from Ireland?"

Places of interest: Woodrow Wilson Ancestral Home, near Strabane; Ulster-American Folk Park, outside Omagh, which recreates the rural lifestyle of Ulster emigrants both in Ireland and America; the 18-foot Arboe Cross, Ireland's finest high cross, with sculpted panels depicting biblical scenes; Tullaghoge Fort, near Cookstown, a fine hilltop enclosure that served as headquarters and coronation site for the O'Neills, chiefs of Ulster (twelfth to the seventeenth centuries); Gray's Printing Press, Strabane, an eighteenth-century printing shop where both James Dunlap, printer of the American Declaration of Independence, and President Woodrow Wilson's grandfather, James Wilson, are thought to have learned the trade.

Events: Lady Day: Ancient Order of Hibernians Celebrations (August 15); Orangemen's Day (July 12); Traditional Irish Music Summer School, Benburb (July).

Newspapers: Derry People & Donegal News (Saturday); *Strabane Weekly News* (weekly); *Tyrone Constitution* (weekly).

Did You Know . . .

. . . That the Irish wolfhound is the tallest breed of dog recognized by the American Kennel Club. Despite its size and strength, however, the wolfhound is well-known for its gentle and even-tempered disposition. Other breeds with Emerald Isle roots include the Kerry blue terrier, the Irish terrier, the Irish water spaniel and the Irish setter.

Ireland and Irish America

in the Movies

▲▲▲▲▲▲▲▲▲▲▲

Movies have been made about Ireland, the Irish and their American cousins for nearly as long as there have been movies to make. *How Molly Malone Made Good,* one of the earliest efforts, came to the screen in 1915. A small flood of other silent films followed in the 1920s, including *My Wild Irish Rose* (1922), *Irish Luck* (1925), *The Callahans and the Murphys* (1927) and *Blarney* (1928).

Most of these early releases, like silent-era movies in general, were clearly products of an infant industry undergoing growing pains. The few copies that remain in film archives today are curiosities or grist for scholarly histories. By the 1930s, however, the advent of "talkies" had, by and large, brought with it new actors, better scripts and more sophisticated production techniques.

Though "Irish" films have never been immune to bad directing, bad acting, bad scripts and other ills—even to the present day— many have benefited from the best talent available. *The Informer,* still a television staple around St. Patrick's Day, marked one of the best early efforts by John Ford, the distinguished Irish-American director, bringing him an Oscar in 1935—and a second for its writer, Dudley Nichols.

The Informer and a selection of other films made since the 1930s are summarized in the following pages. Titles that can be rented or bought in videocassette format are indicated with a (V) at the end of an entry.

The Informer (U.S., RKO, 1935, 91 min.) Directed by John Ford; nominated for Best Picture; starring Victor McLaglen. A simple minded hanger-on betrays an IRA leader to earn a payoff that will help him emigrate. He finds that he can escape neither the wrath of his former comrades nor the pangs of his own conscience. (V)

Beloved Enemy (U.S., Samuel Goldwyn/United Artists, 1936, 90 min.) Starring Brian Aherne, Merle Oberon, David Niven. Amid the turmoil of the 1921 Irish rebellion, the rebel leader steals the heart of a British officer's fiancee. (V)

The Plough and the Stars (U.S., RKO, 1936, 72 min.) Directed by John Ford; starring Barbara Stanwyck, Preston Foster, Barry Fitzgerald, Arthur Shields, Una O'Connor, Bonita Granville. Screen version of the Sean O'Casey play but, despite the cast, not a match for the original. In 1916 Dublin, amid "The Troubles," a man's marriage is threatened when he is appointed to command the nationalist forces.

Parnell (U.S., MGM, 1937, 96 min.) Starring Clark Gable, Myrna Loy, Edmund Gwenn, Donald Crisp. Charles Stewart Parnell, the champion of Irish nationalism during the late nineteenth century, finds his career tragically destroyed when he becomes romantically involved with a married woman.

Angels with Dirty Faces (U.S., Warner Brothers, 1938, 97 min.) Starring James Cagney, Pat O'Brien, Humphrey Bogart, Ann Sheridan. Two boyhood friends grow up and lose track of each other. When they meet again as adults, one has become a priest, the other a gangster. Good wins out in the end. (V)

The Fighting 69th (U.S., Warner Brothers, 1940, 89 min.) Starring James Cagney, Pat O'Brien, George Brent, Jeffrey Lynn, Alan Hale, Frank McHugh. Serving with the famous Irish-American regiment in the muddy trenches of World War I France, a cocky recruit surprises his buddies with heroism that costs him his life.

Going My Way (U.S., Paramount, 1940, 130 min.) Awarded Best Picture; starring Bing Crosby, Barry Fitzgerald, Rise Stevens,

Frank McHugh. Bing Crosby plays a young priest sent out to serve a tough New York parish under the watchful eye of its tightwad rector. (V)

Little Nellie Kelly (U.S., MGM, 1940, 100 min.) Starring Judy Garland, George Murphy, Arthur Shields. A sentimental saga about the feuds within an Irish-American family in New York. Garland plays mother and daughter, dying in the former role but turning up 18 years later as the daughter. In the latter role, she makes peace between her father and grandfather, who have been estranged. Some "New York cops" give a rousing rendition of "It's a Great Day for the Irish."

The Sullivans (U.S., 20th Century-Fox, 1944, 111 min.) Alternate title: *The Fighting Sullivans;* starring Anne Baxter, Thomas Mitchell, Selena Royle, and Edward Ryan. For all its homespun sentimentalism, this is a true story about five brothers growing up during the thirties in a working-class neighborhood of an Iowa city. Despite occasional spats among themselves, they are inclined to stick together when any of them is in trouble. When Pearl Harbor jolts the United States into World War II, all five brothers enlist in the navy. All are assigned to the cruiser U.S.S. *Juneau,* and are drowned when the ship is sunk off Guadalcanal. The Navy subsequently named a destroyer the U.S.S. *The Sullivans* in their honor.

A Tree Grows in Brooklyn (U.S., 20th Century-Fox, 1945, 128 min.) Directed by Elia Kazan; starring Dorothy McGuire, Peggy Ann Garner, Ted Donaldson, James Dunn, Joan Blondell. The trials and troubles of a young girl growing up in an Irish-American family in turn-of-the-century Brooklyn. Based on the novel by Betty Smith.

Hungry Hill (Britain, GFD/Two Cities, 1946, 92 min.) Starring Margaret Lockwood, Dennis Price, Cecil Parker, Michael Denison, Siobhan McKenna, Dan O'Herlihy. Three generations of an Irish family are trapped in an ongoing feud.

Captain Boycott (Britain, GFD/Individual/Universal, 1947, 93 min.) Starring Stewart Granger, Kathleen Ryan, Alistair Sim, Robert Donat, Cecil Parker, Noel Purcell, Niall MacGinnis. Hard-pressed Irish tenant farmers, squeezed to the limit and threatened with eviction, organize to resist oppressive landlords and their agents.

My Wild Irish Rose (U.S., Warner Brothers, 1947, 101 min.) Starring Dennis Morgan, Arlene Dahl, Andrea King, Alan Hale, George Tobias. A middling period musical that follows Irish tenor Chauncey Olcott through a roller-coaster relationship with Lillian Russell.

Odd Man Out (Britain, GFD/J. Arthur Rank, 1947, 120 min.) Directed by Carol Reed; starring James Mason, Robert Newton, Kathleen Ryan. An award-winning, moving drama about an Irish rebel, wounded in a hold-up, who must choose between those who might help him escape and others who would turn him over to the police. (V)

The Luck of the Irish (U.S., 20th Century-Fox, 1947/1948, 99 min.) Starring Tyrone Power, Cecil Kellaway, Anne Baxter, Lee J. Cobb, Jayne Meadows. A New York journalist visiting Ireland meets a leprechaun, whose efforts to be helpful only complicate his love life.

Fighting Father Dunne (U.S., Warner Brothers, 1948, 93 min.) Starring Pat O'Brien, Darryl Hickman, Una O'Connor. A priest works to help poor boys amid the squalor and violence of an urban slum.

The Fighting O'Flynn (U.S., United Artists, 1949, 94 min.) Starring Douglas Fairbanks, Jr., Helena Carter, Richard Greene. In the waning years of the eighteenth century, an impoverished young adventurer foils Napoleon's plans to invade Ireland. The premise of this film will occasion understandable ambivalence among many.

Top o' the Morning (U.S., Paramount, 1949, 100 min.) Starring Bing Crosby, Barry Fitzgerald, Anne Blythe, Hume Cronyn. The Blarney Stone disappears, and investigations follow.

The Quiet Man (U.S., Republic/Argosy, 1952, 129 min.) Directed by John Ford; nominated for Best Picture; starring John Wayne, Maureen O'Hara, Barry Fitzgerald, Victor McLaglen, Ward Bond.

A former boxer returns from America to Ireland in search of a peaceful retirement and a wife. A boisterous comedy full of Irish wit and color—and more than its share of blarney. (V)

Captain Lightfoot (U.S., Universal, 1955, 92 min.) Starring Rock Hudson, Barbara Rush, Jeff Morrow, Kathleen Ryan. A rebel struggles against injustice and foreign rule in nineteenth-century Ireland. Not an award winner.

The Search for Bridey Murphy (U.S., Paramount, 1956, 84 min.) Starring Teresa Wright, Louis Hayward, Kenneth Tobey, Richard Anderson. A Colorado businessman, whose hobby is hypnotism, persuades a woman neighbor to let him transport her back into her previous existence as a long-dead Irish peasant. The tension builds when she seems unable to return from her previous life.

The Rising of the Moon (Ireland, Four Province Productions/Warner Brothers, 1957) Directed by John Ford; starring Maureen Connell, Eileen Crowe, Cyril Cusack. Based on the play of the same name by Lady Gregory.

The Last Hurrah (U.S., Columbia, 1958, 125 min.) Directed by John Ford; starring Spencer Tracy, Jeffrey Hunter, Diane Foster, Pat O'Brien, Basil Rathbone, Donald Crisp. As Frank Skeffington, the veteran Irish-American political boss of a New England town, Spencer Tracy takes to the campaign trail in a final reelection bid. Humorous touches and a variety of well-acted characters complement Tracy's performance. (V)

Darby O'Gill and the Little People (U.S., Disney, 1959) Starring Albert Sharpe, Janet Murno, Sean Connery, Jimmy O'Dea. A blend of animation with real characters and sets. An Irish storyteller on the verge of losing his job falls down a well into the realm of the little people. There he ultimately wins the right to have three wishes granted. Blarney-soaked but charming family fare, with good special effects. (V)

Shake Hands with the Devil (Ireland, United Artists/Troy/Pennebaker, 1959, 110 min.) Starring James Cagney, Glynis Johns, Don Murray, Dana Wynter, Michael Redgrave, Sybil Thorndike, Cyril Cusack, Richard Harris. A surgeon in 1921 Dublin leads a double life as a secret leader of the IRA and grows attached to violence for its own sake rather than as a means to an end.

The Night Fighters (Allied Artists, 1960, 90 min.) Original title: *A Terrible Beauty*. Starring Robert Mitchum, Anne Heywood, Dan O'Herlihy, Cyril Cusack, Richard Harris. As World War II erupts, the IRA revives its activities in a northern Irish village.

Studs Lonigan (U.S., 1960, 95 min.) Starring Christopher Knight, Frank Gorshin. A young Irish-American drifter, dissatisfied and without great prospects, grows up amid the fast-paced, sometimes violent surroundings of 1920s Chicago. Based on the trilogy by James T. Farrell. (V)

The Girl with Green Eyes (Britain, United Artists, 1963, 91 min.) Starring Rita Tushingham, Peter Finch, Lynn Redgrave. Incisive drama of a relationship between a naive Dublin shopgirl and a worldly writer. Good location scenes strengthen the film.

Young Cassidy (Britain, MGM/Sextant, 1965, 110 min.) Starring Rod Taylor, Maggie Smith, Edith Evans, Flora Robson, Michael Redgrave, Julie Christie, Jack McGowran, Sian Phillips, T. P. McKenna. The early Dublin years of Irish playwright Sean O'Casey, from his days as a laborer to the opening of his play *The Plough and the Stars* at the Abbey Theatre. Provides an evocative picture of the Irish capital at the turn of the century.

The Fighting Prince of Donegal (Britain, Walt Disney, 1966, 104 min.) Starring Peter McEnery, Susan Hampshire, Tom Adams, Gordon Jackson, Andrew Keir. An Irish chieftain fights the encroachments of Elizabeth I's lieutenants in the sixteenth century. (V)

Ulysses (Britain, Walter Reade, 1967, 132 min.) Starring Maurice Roeves, Milo O'Shea, Barbara Jefford, T. P. McKenna. Based on James Joyce's classic novel, this film follows a young poet and a Jewish journalist through 24 hours of adventures in Dublin. It was considered extreme at the time for its off-color language, and the critics were generally uncharitable. (V)

Finian's Rainbow (U.S., Warner Brothers/Seven Arts, 1968, 140 min.) Starring Fred Astaire, Petula Clark, Tommy Steele, Keenan

Wynn. A leprechaun attempts to find and bring back a pot of gold taken to America by an old Irishman and his daughter. Not up to the standards of the 1947 Broadway hit. (V)

The Molly Maguires (U.S., Paramount/Tamm, 1970, 123 min.) Starring Richard Harris, Sean Connery, Samantha Eggar, Frank Finlay, Anthony Zerbe. A detective infiltrates a secret society, dedicated to fighting the oppressive system imposed on Pennsylvania coal miners in the 1870s, and exposes its leaders. Based on a true story, many of whose participants were Irish-American. (V)

Quackser Fortune Has a Cousin in The Bronx (U.S., UMC Pictures, 1970, 90 min.) Starring Gene Wilder, Margot Kidder, Eileen Colgan, Seamus Ford. An Irish fertilizer salesman strikes up an acquaintance with an American exchange student, who finds she is attracted to this uneducated, but not ignorant, man. (V)

Ryan's Daughter (Britain, MGM/Faraway, 1970, 194 min.) Starring Sarah Miles, Robert Mitchum, John Mills, Trevor Howard, Leo McKern. In 1916 Ireland, a rural schoolmaster's wife falls in love with a British major and is ostracized for betraying her country.

Barry Lyndon (Britain, Stanley Kubrick/Warner Brothers, 1975, 184 min.) Directed by Stanley Kubrick; starring Ryan O'Neal, Marisa Berenson, Patrick Magee, Hardy Kruger. Thackeray's satirical novel brought to life in one of the most visually stunning movies ever made, though it has less to commend it dramatically. A roguish Irish peasant rises from obscurity to wealth and position during the period of the Seven Years War between England and France, but ultimately falls from grace. (V)

Hennessy (Britain, 1975, 103 min.) Starring Rod Steiger, Lee Remick, Eric Porter, Richard Johnson. A Northern Irish Catholic whose politics are neutral becomes unbalanced after his wife and child, innocent onlookers at a street riot, are accidentally killed by British gunfire. Vowing revenge, he sets about a plan to assassinate the Queen of England and members of her government. Colorful but farfetched.

The Outsider (1978/1979) Starring Sterling Hayden, Craig Wasson. A young American Vietnam veteran joins the IRA.

Cal (1984, 104 min.) Starring John Lynch, Helen Mirren. The librarian-widow of a Protestant policeman and a young IRA activist fall in love amid the violence of present-day Northern Ireland. The film won praise for its superior acting and its intelligent handling of a problematic subject. (V)

Danny Boy (Ireland, Motion Picture Company of Ireland, 1984, 92 min.) Originally released in Ireland in 1982 under the title, *Angel*. Starring Stephen Rea. A deaf-mute girl is murdered by extortionists, and a musician finds himself up against the rackets as he sets about trying to track down the murderers before they find out he is on to them. The story is set in south Armagh, and while one might presume that "the bad guys" are the IRA, this isn't clear from the film, which is a first-rate thriller though not a political one. (V)

A Quiet Day in Belfast (Warner Brothers/Goldcrest, 1984, 92 min.) Starring Margot Kidder, Barry Foster. A realistic, tension-filled story set amid the urban war being waged between British soldiers and IRA members in the Northern Irish capital. Centered around the colorful everyday drama of a betting parlor, the action moves the opposing sides to a brutal, bloody climax. (V)

Heaven Help Us (U.S., 1985, 102 min.) Starring Donald Sutherland, John Heard. An irreverent but entertaining comedy about the coming-of-age antics of three boys in a predominantly Irish-American Catholic high school in Brooklyn during the sixties. Though some scenes are overplayed, many will find the film nostalgic. (V)

James Joyce's Women (Ireland, The Rejoycing Co., 1985, 91 min.) Starring Fionnula Flanagan, Timothy O'Grady, Chris O'Neill. This highly rated film presents dramatic portraits of James Joyce's wife and three of his characters, including Molly Bloom. (V)

No Surrender (1985, 100 min.) Starring Michael Angelis, Ray McAnally. Two groups of old-age pensioners, one Orange, the other Green, find themselves booked into the same Liverpool night spot to celebrate New Year's Eve. The resulting confrontation is frequently hilarious. (V)

Da (U.S., Filmdallas Pictures, 1987, 102 min.) Directed by Matt Clark; starring Barnard Hughes, Martin Sheen, William Hickey.

After his father dies, a middle-aged man goes through his belongings. His father's ghost appears to talk with him about life, death and their own relationship while both were alive. Based on the play by Hugh Leonard. (V)

The Dead (Britain, Vestron Pictures/Zenith, 1987, 82 min.) Directed by John Huston (this was his last film); starring Angelica Huston, Donal McCann, Dan O'Herlihy. The screen version of James Joyce's memorable short story from *The Dubliners,* set in turn-of-the-century Dublin.

A Prayer for the Dying (U.S., Peter Snell/Samuel Goldwyn Co., 1987, 104 min.) Starring Bob Hoskins, Mickey Rourke, Alan Bates. An IRA hit man has second thoughts about his violent life only to find that both his fellow nationalists and the police have claims on him. A gripping political drama adapted from the book by Jack Higgins. (V)

Did You Know . . .

. . . That, when the modern Olympic Games were inaugurated in Athens in 1896, the first first-place medal (called a gold medal starting with the 1900 games) went to James Brendan Connolly, a "Southie" from Boston and one of twelve children whose parents were natives of the Aran Islands. Connolly's first place came in the hop, step and jump (now called the triple jump), and he placed second in the high jump and third in the broad jump. At the Paris Olympics four years later, Connolly took the silver medal in the triple jump.

Irish Names upon Our Land

<del>▪▪▪▪▪▪▪▪▪▪</del>

T he Irish were active in settling this country and pushing it westward from the days of the earliest English colonies. So it's not surprising that Irish family- and place-names are common throughout the United States.

In 1914, for example, two scholars estimated that there were 65 places in the United States named after people whose names began with the Irish prefix "O," and more than 1,000 that commemorated the "Mc's."

They claimed they had found 253 counties and about 7,000 other places apparently named after Irish places or family names. Among these were 24 Dublins, 21 Waterfords, 18 Belfasts, 16 Tyrones, 10 Limericks, 9 Antrims, 8 Sligos, 7 Derrys, 6 Corks and 5 Kildares. (Many of these seem to have been swallowed up by other communities since then; only some 13 Dublins remain today, for example.)

Places named for prominent Irishmen and Irish-Americans as well as lesser-known countrymen are beyond counting. The Carrolls of Maryland, for example, live on in the names of many communities, as do the famous Irish-American generals, Philip Kearny and Philip Sheridan. Irish patriots are likewise remembered, as Charles Stewart Parnell is in the name of an Arkansas town.

For good measure, New York claims a community named Erin

and Missouri's towns include one called St. Patrick. Towns named Shamrock can be found in North Carolina and Oklahoma, and Pennsylvania has a Shamrock Station.

The following is an alphabetical listing of thirty-nine states with places that bear the names of places in Ireland. We have not attempted to enumerate the places that bear Irish (family) surnames, in that they are so many and are sometimes difficult to distinguish:

Alabama—Ardmore, Carlowville, Shannon
Arkansas—Avoca, Belfast, Shandon, Shannon
California—Boyle, Dublin, Shandon, Waterford
Colorado—Sligo, Tyrone
Florida—Killarney, Mayo, Ormond Beach
Georgia—Auburn, Dublin, Shannon, Tyrone
Idaho—Dingle, Mullan, Rathdrum
Illinois—Auburn, Munster, Shannon
Indiana—Avoca, Bandon, Clare, Dublin, Greencastle, Munster
Iowa—Avoca, Brandon, Clare, Curlew, Shannon City
Kansas—Boyle, Longford
Kentucky—Boyle County, Dublin
Louisiana—Antrim, Clare, Derry, Sligo
Maine—Belfast, Carlow Island, Clontarf, Limerick
Maryland—Ardmore, Baltimore, Dublin, Dundalk, Mayo
Massachusetts—Auburn
Michigan—Antrim, Boyne City, Clare, Darragh, Dublin, New Baltimore, Roscommon, Wexford County
Minnesota—Avoca, Clontarf, Kilkenny, Lismore
Mississippi—Boyle, Brandon, Dublin, Shannon
Montana—Ennis
New Hampshire—Antrim, Derry, Dublin, Londonderry
New Mexico—Derry, Tyrone
New York—Auburn, Avoca, Belfast, Galway, Tyrone, Ulster County
North Carolina—Colrain, Dublin, Mayo River, Shannon, Sligo
North Dakota—Bantry, Donnybrook, Kenmare
Ohio—Belfast, Dublin, Londonderry
Oklahoma—Ardmore, Bray, Kildare, Tyrone

Oregon—Bandon

Pennsylvania—Antrim, Ardara, Ardmore, Armagh, Avoca, Castle Shannon, Colrain (township), Derry, Donegal, Dublin, Dunmore, Fermanagh (township), Limerick, New Derry, Sligo, Tyrone

South Carolina—Mayo, Shannontown

South Dakota—Ardmore

Tennessee—Ardmore, Belfast

Texas—Donnybrook Place, Dublin, Ennis, Ireland, Kildare, Monahan, Shannon

Vermont—Londonderry

Virginia—Dublin, Dungannon, Dunmore County, Kinsale, Mayo, Stormont

Washington—Curlew, Lake Shannon

West Virginia—Dunmore, Ireland, Killarney, Tralee

Wisconsin—Kildare, New Munster

Wyoming—Tipperary

Did You Know . . .

. . . That, since the Congressional Medal of Honor was first awarded in 1863, 257 Irish-born Americans have earned this recognition for distinguished, courageous military feats. This is more than twice the number of winners born in Germany, the next highest contributor, with 126, and compares with 95 English-born recipients, 52 from Canada, 38 born in Scotland, and so forth. While these figures bear testament to the bravery and fighting abilities of Irish-born Americans, they also reflect the unusually large number of Irish immigrants who fought in the Civil War and later conflicts.

Ireland in the White House:
U.S. Presidents of Irish Heritage

▰▰▰▰▰▰▰▰▰▰

For a people whose Old World forebears had typically lived in humble huts or cottages, Irish-Americans have made it in surprising numbers to the most prestigious address in America. Even for so-called Scots-Irish and other Protestant immigrants who furnished most of the earlier Irish settlers and most of our presidents of Irish heritage, a move into the White House usually marked an almost incredible advance beyond the circumstances of their fathers, or their fathers before them. In all, from John Adams to Ronald Reagan, no fewer than 17 Presidents of the United States have traced all or part of their ancestry to Ireland. Three were sons of immigrants.

Indeed, the very architect of the White House was an Irish-Catholic immigrant. James Hoban (1758–1831), a native of Kilkenny who had settled in Charleston, South Carolina, was chosen for the assignment in competition with a large number of other architects. In planning the home of America's First Families, Hoban is said to have been strongly influenced by the design of Dublin's Leinster House, which serves today as the meeting place for Ireland's parliament.

The roster of U.S. presidents of Irish heritage reads as follows:

1. **John Adams**—His mother, Susanna Boylston Adams, was reportedly descended from a family that had been farmers in Ulster for generations. The family name is thought originally to have been Boyle, embellished to Boylston, as was not uncommonly done.

2. **James Monroe**—Monroe's Irish antecedents are a little hard to pin down, but a direct ancestor named Monroe (or Munro) is said to have been a Scottish officer who married a local woman while serving in Ulster during the late seventeenth or early eighteenth century.

3. **John Quincy Adams**—As the son of John Adams, he naturally had his father's Boylston heritage.

4. **Andrew Jackson**—Both parents came from the village of Boneybefore in Carrickfergus, County Antrim.

5. **James K. Polk**—The family name had originally been Pollock, a common Ulster name since the Plantation. His mother's family was also from Ulster.

6. **James Buchanan**—Both of his father's parents came from County Donegal, after having lived for a time in Larne, County Antrim. His mother's roots seem also to have been in Ulster.

7. **Andrew Johnson**—His Irish ancestors came from County Antrim.

8. **Ulysses S. Grant**—Grant's mother, Hannah Simpson, lived in a small farmhouse at Dergenagh, County Tyrone, before emigrating to America.

9. **Chester A. Arthur**—His father, William Arthur, was born in the Dreen, Cullybackey, County Antrim, in a house that still stands. His mother was reportedly also of Ulster ancestry.

10. **Grover Cleveland**—His mother's father was a Neal (or Neill) who had immigrated from Ulster.

11. **Benjamin Harrison**—Harrison had Ulster roots on his mother's side.

12. **William McKinley**—His father's family had come from Dervock, County Antrim, where the name had been spelled McKinlay.

13. **Theodore Roosevelt**—Roosevelt's mother, Martha Bullock, came from a Scots-Irish and Huguenot family that had lived in County Antrim. His father's mother, Margaret Potts Burnhill, is said to have been born in County Meath.

14. **Woodrow Wilson**—Both of his paternal grandparents —James Wilson and Annie Mills (Wilson)—were from the Strabane area of County Antrim.

15. **John Fitzgerald Kennedy**—Kennedy's ancestors all came from Ireland. His paternal great-grandfather, Patrick Kennedy, had emigrated from Dunganstown, New Ross, County Wexford to Boston, and there married Bridget Murphy, another immigrant. The paternal grandparents of Kennedy's mother—Thomas Fitzgerald and Rose Mary Murray—had also immigrated from County Wexford.

16. **Richard M. Nixon**—Nixon numbered Irish Quakers among his forebears. His great-great-grandfather, Richard Milhous, was born at Timahoe, County Laois. While in the White House, the Nixons owned an Irish setter they named King Timahoe.

17. **Ronald W. Reagan**—Reagan's paternal great-grandfather, Michael Regan, emigrated from Ballyporeen, County Tipperary, in 1829.

Did You Know . . .

. . . That as many as one-third to one-half of American troops during the Revolutionary War were of Irish birth or descent. Among them were nearly 1,500 officers, including 26 generals (15 of them Irish-born).

100 Notable Irish-Americans,
Past and Present

▰▰▰▰▰▰▰▰▰

Americans of Irish descent have ranked among our country's leading achievers since long before there was a United States. In the political and military efforts that established American independence, in fact, individuals of Irish heritage—Catholic and Protestant alike—were unusually active as both leaders and rank-and-file. Since then—despite the once anti-Irish bias triggered by the mass influx of poor, mostly Catholic, famine victims in the 1830s and 1840s—Irish-Americans have earned fame and fortune in virtually every field.

As with some other sections of this book, we make no pretense that this is the final word on the subject. Our space is far too limited to do justice to the thousands of Irish-Americans who have a good claim to be represented here. Nor do we claim that the 100 individuals covered are *the* 100 most important Irish-Americans.

Such lists, of course, always reflect opinion and arbitrary judgment. Most of us would agree that the names John F. Kennedy, Charles Carroll of Carrollton, Eugene O'Neill, General Philip Sheridan, and a few others belong at or near the top in any selection of Irish-American "greats." However, after these, the going gets a lot tougher. What criteria do you use?

Is a famous Irish-American architect "more important" than a leading singer? How do you measure fame or importance, anyway? In a society that recalls too little of its past—and where opinion is often shaped by those with a flair for promoting themselves or others—how closely does someone's fame parallel his or her historical importance? Is popularity or name-recognition a measure, since quantifying a person's importance is otherwise nearly impossible?

The distinguished Irish-Americans covered are *among* the most important, living or dead. Collectively, their stories show the range and depth of the Irish contribution to America. *Note:* John F. Kennedy, Ronald Reagan and fifteen other U.S. presidents of Irish descent are covered in another chapter.

BUSINESS, INDUSTRY AND FINANCE

Alexander Brown (1764–1834)—A native of Ulster, who emigrated from Belfast to Baltimore in 1800. He soon became the city's largest importer of Irish linens. He was active in trading a variety of commodities, but came to specialize in cotton exports to Liverpool. Alexander Brown & Sons, the private mercantile and banking house Brown founded, is America's oldest investment banking firm. Brown entrusted each of his sons with a branch company, one of which survives as the prestigious New York-based firm, Brown Brothers Harriman. Alexander Brown was a major shareholder in the Bank of the United States and was instrumental in establishing the city waterworks of Baltimore. He and one of his sons were also key figures in founding the Baltimore & Ohio Railroad, a major step in bringing railroads to the United States. When he died, Brown was one of the nation's few millionaires.

Michael Cudahy (1841–1910)—One of the developers of the modern meatpacking industry, Cudahy was born in Callan, Ireland, and came to the United States with his family in 1849. He went to work as a meatpacker in Milwaukee at age fourteen, and gradually worked his way up to management, then establishing his own firm. Cudahy's firm pioneered the use of cold-storage facilities in packing plants. Because animals could now be slaughtered and frozen for later sale, his innovation revolutionized the industry by making possible for the first time the year-round marketing of livestock.

Henry Ford (1863–1947)—A household name if ever there was one, Henry Ford was the son of Irish immigrants. The pioneering American automobile manufacturer was perhaps most famous for introducing mass-production techniques with the famous Ford Model T. This innovation made the automobile affordable to the average American for the first time, and helped unleash a far-reaching social and economic revolution. Ford's creation, the Ford Motor Company, ranks among the world's largest industrial firms and has traditionally been second in the U.S. automotive market. Today it makes and markets not only cars but trucks, farm equipment, home appliances and aerospace vehicles and equipment.

William Russell Grace (1832–1904)—Grace, an Irish-American business leader, steamship line operator and public official, was born in County Cork. He emigrated first to Peru, where he founded William R. Grace & Co., a shipping line, before relocating in the United States. Thriving in his business pursuits, he ran successfully for mayor of New York in 1880. Grace was the first Roman Catholic to serve in that office, and a man known for his freedom from corruption.

William Randolph Hearst (1863–1951)—Legendary editor, publisher and political leader known for his grand style and autocratic manner. Hearst created the nation's largest newspaper chain, which has evolved into one of today's largest privately owned communications empires. He also served in Congress and found time to amass an impressive collection of art and antiquities, now housed at San Simeon, his palatial former estate in California. His life, achievements and methods inspired the classic film, *Citizen Kane*.

Howard R. Hughes (1905–1976)—U.S. aviation pioneer and industrialist who had built one of the world's largest fortunes at the time of his death. A colorful, flamboyant playboy during his early career, Hughes became a reclusive, eccentric Midas during the last two decades of his life, prompting endless curiosity and speculation. Hughes Aircraft and Hughes Tool Company brought him billionaire status.

Joseph Patrick Kennedy (1888–1969)—Boston-born businessman and politician-statesman who sired three U.S. senators (John F., Robert F., and Edward M. Kennedy), the first of whom became 35th President of the United States. After amassing a fortune in the pre-Depression stock market and in motion picture ventures, Kennedy was named chairman of the newly formed Securities and Exchange Commission (SEC) by President Franklin D. Roosevelt in 1934. He served as ambassador to Britain from 1937 to 1940.

Samuel S. McClure (1857–1949)—Emigrating from County Antrim as a child, McClure became an active journalist during his college days in Illinois. In 1884 he launched a literary syndicate— America's first—which within a few years was supplying newspapers with high-quality material by the leading U.S. and European writers of the day. *McClure's Magazine,* which was launched in 1893 and published for about three decades, featured exposés by leading social crusaders including Ida Tarbell and Lincoln Steffens. It became a leading force in reform journalism or—as some preferred to call it—muckraking.

Andrew W. Mellon (1855–1933)—After starting a successful lumber firm, Mellon joined the Pittsburgh bank his immigrant father had founded, rising to head it ten years later. He was an astute judge of business ventures, backing the start-up and growth of Aluminum Company of America, Gulf Oil, Union Steel and other firms that came to rank among the nation's largest. Though a major capitalist and one of the country's wealthiest men, Mellon was almost unknown to the public until he was named Treasury Secretary by President Harding in 1921. He guided the nation's financial affairs during the boom years of the twenties and into America's most severe depression, leaving office with the advent of FDR and the New Deal. Before his death Mellon donated his huge art collection to the government together with a major endowment, making possible the establishment of the National Gallery of Art, Washington, D.C.

Thomas F. Ryan (1851–1928)—Ryan, a financier and businessman of uncommon talent, began his career by establishing a brokerage firm in 1873. He went on to acquire the franchise for New York City's street railways, eventually consolidating the lines with August Belmont's subway interests. Later he organized the American Tobacco Company—dissolved in 1911 as an illegal monopoly —and held large interests in banks, railroads, insurance companies and natural-resource ventures. His middle name, aptly, was Fortune.

Alexander T. Stewart (1803–1876)—County Antrim-born Stewart pioneered the department-store concept in America. A. T. Stewart & Co., the great New York store he founded, was later acquired by the Wanamaker chain of Philadelphia and continued to operate until 1954. Stewart was reputedly the richest man in America at one time, and used part of his fortune to establish Garden City, New York, one of the nation's first planned communities.

EDUCATION

John R. Gregg (1867–1948)—Born in Rockcorry, County Monaghan, he emigrated to the U.S. in 1893. Here he eventually perfected the Gregg system of shorthand, the first practical, easily learned form of shorthand writing, which helped make office operations much more productive. Although its days seem numbered, Gregg shorthand is still taught and widely used in this age of dictating machines and automated word processors.

William H. McGuffey (1800–1873)—During an academic career in which he taught languages and moral philosophy at the college level, and served as president of Cincinnati College and Ohio University, McGuffey pursued a lifelong interest in public education. The result was his famous series of Eclectic Readers, used by generations of American elementary-school students. The six readers went through numerous revisions and expansions, ultimately selling more than 120 million copies. "McGuffey's Readers" had a major influence on how Americans thought during the nineteenth century.

ENTERTAINMENT: MUSIC, FILMS, THEATER AND BROADCAST

Walter Brennan (1894–1974)—Brennan is best remembered for the colorful old-timers he portrayed in scores of Westerns. He was named to the Cowboy Hall of Fame in 1970. He appeared in over 100 films, winning three Oscars as Best Supporting Actor. Brennan also did television work, most notably as the crochety but lovable Grandpa McCoy, the role he created in the television series, "The Real McCoys."

James Cagney (1904–1986)—From his first tough-guy role in *Public Enemy,* no gangster film in the 1930s seemed complete without him. When gangsters went out of vogue with the end of Prohibition, Cagney sweetened up his on-camera image. In 1942, he won an Oscar as Best Actor for *Yankee Doodle Dandy,* a movie in which he immortalized the life and career of the Irish-American composer and entertainer, George M. Cohan. His more recent film credits included *Ragtime* and *Terrible Joe Moran.* The American Film Institute bestowed its Life Achievement Award on Cagney in 1974.

Hoagy Carmichael (1899–1981)—"Hoagy," born Hoagland Howard Carmichael, was blessed with a multitude of talents. He is probably best remembered, however, as the songwriter who gave us such numbers as "Stardust," "Lazy River," "Georgia on My Mind," "Lazy Bones," and "Heart and Soul." At least 50 of his songs, in fact, made it to the hit lists. Carmichael also sang, acted and excelled on the piano; he wrote music for the theater, films, nightclub acts and his own television show.

George M. Cohan (1878–1942)—Generally considered the father of American musical comedy, Cohan was a man of legendary versatility: actor, songwriter, playwright, director and producer. His patriotic World War I composition, "Over There," earned him a Congressional Medal, and other songs, such as "You're a Grand Old Flag" and "Give My Regards to Broadway," also set Americans' toes a-tapping. Cohan's life and career were celebrated in the 1942 movie, *Yankee Doodle Dandy,* as well as the Broadway show, *George M.*

Harry L. ("Bing") Crosby (1904–1977)—One of America's best-loved entertainers, "Bing" was best known for his mellow, dreamy crooning. He gave us classic renditions of "Blue Skies," "Silent Night" and "White Christmas," with the last selling more copies than any other single ever released. Crosby made over 850 recordings and sold over 300 million records. He appeared in over 50 films—including the popular "Road" comedies with Bob Hope and Dorothy Lamour—and won an Oscar in 1944 for *Going My Way.* An avid golfer, Crosby established the Crosby National Pro-Am Golf Tournament.

The Dorsey Brothers: Jimmy (1904–1956) and *Tommy* (1905–1956)—As dance-band leaders, these brothers rode the crest of the swing craze during the big-band era of the 1930s and 1940s. With Jimmy playing saxophone and Tommy the trombone, they formed the first of their renowned jazz bands around 1920. Going their separate ways for 18 years, the Dorseys pursued successful careers as band leaders and in film and television appearances. Reunited in 1953, they put together one final, popular orchestra.

John Ford (1895–1973)—Ford, born Sean O'Feeney in Maine, directed over 130 films whose standards of excellence continue to inspire filmmakers today. Sweeping scenes of nature and an undercurrent of social concern characterize many of his works. Ford won Oscars for *The Informer, The Grapes of Wrath, How Green Was My Valley, The Battle of Midway* and *December Seventh*. He also received the American Film Institute's Life Achievement Award and the Presidential Medal of Freedom.

Jackie Gleason (1916–1987)—A rotund, irrepressible entertainer, Gleason became a cult figure for many Americans in his role as the bombastic but lovable Ralph Kramden in the television series, "The Honeymooners." He also starred in the "Cavalcade of Stars" series during the 1950s as well as winning the title Mr. Saturday Night as host of the popular, long-running "Jackie Gleason Show." Gleason brought his talents to Broadway and the screen as well, appearing in such films as *Requiem for a Heavyweight, Smokey and the Bandit* and *The Hustler*. As conductor of the Jackie Gleason Orchestra, he recorded some 40 albums.

Helen Hayes (1900–   )—Justly known as First Lady of the American Theater, Hayes's acting career spanned eight decades. Particularly notable among her stage credits were the title roles in *Mary of Scotland* and *Victoria Regina*. She also appeared in many films, earning Oscars for *Claudet* (1932) and *Airport* (1971). Hayes's other honors include an Emmy, the Medal of the City of New York and—perhaps the ultimate compliment for a living actress—having a Broadway theater named for her in 1955. Despite her active professional career, Hayes has also found time for major efforts on behalf of charitable causes. In private life, she is known as Mrs. Charles MacArthur.

Victor Herbert (1859–1924)—Dublin-born Herbert earned his most lasting fame as a composer of comic opera. He began his career as a cellist, playing with major orchestras in Europe and New York before accepting an offer to become conductor of the Pittsburgh Symphony in 1898. In 1904, Herbert turned to composing full time, and was soon delighting audiences with such operettas as *Babes in Toyland, Naughty Marietta,* and *Mlle. Modiste,* whose songs and music are still widely loved. The first American to compose an original score for a motion picture, Herbert also wrote two grand operas, *Natoma* and *Madeleine.*

Emmet Kelly (1898–1979)—America's most famous pantomime clown, Kelly was the son of a staunchly patriotic Irish immigrant who named him for the Irish patriot, Robert Emmet. Kelly's reputation was built on characterizations marked by pathos rather than slapstick comedy. He first created a tattered hobo, Weary Willie, as a cartoon character, then brought Willie to life in circus performances in the United States and Britain. Most closely associated with Ringling Brothers, Barnum & Bailey Circus, Kelly became a familiar face on television, in nightclub acts and in such movies as *The Greatest Show on Earth.*

Gene Kelly (1912–   )—One of the country's most popular dancers, Kelly pirouetted, flipped and tap-danced his way into American hearts in such musicals as *On the Town, An American in Paris* and *Singin' in the Rain.* His virile dance moves—combining ballet, gymnastics, tap and modern dance—revolutionized film choreography and helped create an American style of dance. In a career spanning more than four decades, Kelly not only danced but wore the hats of dramatic actor, singer, director, choreographer and producer.

Grace Kelly (1929–1982)—Rarely has life yielded to Hollywood fantasy as much as in Grace Kelly's career. Though the family she was born into was prosperous, even wealthy, it had come very far very quickly. Her immigrant grandfather had established a bricklaying firm in Philadelphia, and her father had worked at the craft as well as helping manage the business. Jack Kelly had gone on, however, to win laurels as an Olympic rower, and brothers George and Walter had gained reputations as a playwright and a vaudeville performer, respectively. After her stage debut in 1948, Grace

Kelly's career blossomed with a series of film roles. She starred in such movies as *Dial M for Murder, Rear Window, To Catch a Thief* and *High Noon,* and her performance in *The Country Girl* brought an Oscar in 1954. Not long afterward, having caught the eye and heart of Monaco's Prince Ranier, she was drawn into a whirlwind romance that ended in a fairytale marriage and her transformation into Her Serene Highness, Princess Grace of Monaco. As a real-life princess, Kelly never forgot her Irish roots, and devoted herself to family, charities and cultural projects until her tragic, untimely death in an auto accident in Monaco.

John McCormack (1884–1945)—Probably the most famous of Irish tenors, McCormack was born at Athlone, County Westmeath. After winning a gold medal at age 18 in Dublin's National Irish Festival, he studied in Italy and went on to a series of operatic successes in U.S. and European cities. By the time he became a U.S. citizen in 1917, McCormack had given up operatic performances in favor of concerts. He was equally at home with classical arias and traditional Irish songs, and is fondly remembered for his moving renditions of the latter.

Pat O'Brien (1899–1983)—All four of his grandparents were Irish immigrants, so it will come as little surprise that Pat O'Brien spent much of his career playing the stereotypical Irish-American—rugged, friendly and loquacious. He won roles in over 100 films, typically playing priests, policemen and soldiers. O'Brien is well-known for his screen portrayals of the legendary Notre Dame football coach in *Knute Rockne—All-American,* and of Father Duffy, famed chaplain of *The Fighting 69th.* In one of his last roles, he starred in the television series, "Harrigan and Son."

Carroll O'Connor (1924–   )—O'Connor made his reputation as Archie Bunker, the blue-collar bigot and bully known to millions from the controversial television comedy series "All in the Family." During the dozen years he ruled the airwaves as Archie, he won four Emmies and brought such explosive issues as integration into America's living rooms. O'Connor, a native New Yorker, returned to the land of his ancestors to study at the National University of Ireland, and traveled the country on an acting tour. At this writing, he holds a lead role in the television crime series, "In the Heat of the Night."

Maureen O'Hara (1921–   )—Born Maureen Fitzsimmons to a theatrical family in Dublin, O'Hara emigrated to the United States in 1939. The red-haired beauty, with her classic looks, was soon a sought-after actress, particularly as the heroine in swashbuckling adventure movies. Notable on her long list of credits are *How Green Was My Valley, The Quiet Man* and *Miracle on 34th Street.* In more recent years, she married an airline pilot who ran a Caribbean-based airline, then took over active management of the line following his death in a crash.

Gregory Peck (1916–   )—One of America's most distinguished film actors, Peck was born in San Diego, California, the son of Katerine Ashe, a native of Dingle, County Kerry. Between dozens of film credits—including *To Kill a Mockingbird,* which won him an Oscar, and *Keys of the Kingdom, The Yearling, Gentleman's Agreement* and *Twelve O'Clock High,* for which he received Oscar nominations —Peck has kept up his Irish connections, living in Galway for a time in 1970. One of his earlier films, *Moby Dick,* was filmed in Ireland.

Tyrone Power (1914–1958)—If acting can be said to be in someone's blood, it was in Tyrone Power's. The great-grandson of a noted Irish actor who had been a comedian at London's Drury Lane Theatre, Power also brought classic good looks and a swashbuckling flair to his roles. Beginning with a stage company in Shakespearean repertory, he went on to star in more than 40 movies. Power was particularly sought after for such historical romances as *The Black Rose* and *Blood and Sand.*

Anthony Rudolph Oaxaca Quinn (1915–   )—For many people, Anthony Quinn will always be Zorba the Greek, the role he made famous in the 1964 film and again, on Broadway, in 1983. Born in Mexico to a Mexican mother and an Irish father, his trademarks are his swarthy looks and the intensity he projects. Quinn has made over 175 films, winning Oscars for *Viva Zapata* and *Lust for Life.* *Requiem for a Heavyweight* and *The Shoes of the Fisherman* were other Quinn landmarks. He is less well-known, but nonetheless talented, as a writer and artist.

Mack Sennett (1884–1960)—Born Michael Sinnott, Sennett was a pioneering director and producer of American motion pictures. Although he made about 1,000 films during his career, he earned his reputation with *The Keystone Cops* and other slapstick comedy classics of the silent-film era. Custard-pie fights and automobile chases were typical Sennett touches. Among the renowned comic actors he directed were Charlie Chaplin, Buster Keaton and W. C. Fields.

Ed Sullivan (1902–1974)—Beginning his career in vaudeville and subsequently writing a syndicated Broadway gossip column, Ed Sullivan went on to become, in the opinion of many, the greatest impresario of the century. In 1948 he launched his television career with the show, "Toast of the Town." This program evolved into "The Ed Sullivan Show," which ran until 1970. Over the years he used his variety shows to introduce an enormous range of talent to American viewers—from the Beatles to Rudolf Nureyev. Sullivan's on-air style was marked by a deadpan expression and low-key presentation. Among many honors he received were four government citations for his extensive humanitarian work.

Spencer Tracy (1900–1967)—As an "actor's actor" whose hallmark was his quiet reserve, Spencer Tracy drew audiences to American cinemas for more than 30 years. He co-starred in nine films with longtime friend Katharine Hepburn and was often cast as a tough-minded man facing formidable odds, or as a strong father figure. Tracy won Oscars for his portrayal of a Portuguese-American fisherman in *Captains Courageous* (1937) and of Father Flanagan in *Boys Town* (1938). Notable among his other films are *The Old Man and the Sea, Inherit the Wind* and *Judgment at Nuremberg*.

FINE ARTS AND ARCHITECTURE

Mathew B. Brady (1822–1896)—An American-born photographer and historian, Brady documented the Civil War in a superb series of photographs that captured its sufferings and sacrifices for generations unborn. Taken by himself and the "photographic corps" he organized in 1861, the photography proved a personal financial disaster but left a priceless legacy for artists and historians. Brady died tragically, his last years marked by bankruptcy and alcoholism.

James E. Kelly (1855–1933)—A New York–born artist, Kelly earned the title, "the Sculptor of American History." Although few would recognize his name, Kelly's works are familiar to millions. They include *Sheridan's Ride* and *Paul Revere;* bronze busts of American military heroes, including Grant, Sherman, Sheridan and Admiral Dewey; and an equestrian statue of Theodore Roosevelt at San Juan Hill.

Georgia O'Keeffe (1887–1986)—O'Keeffe decided to become a painter at age twelve. It was, she recalled, ". . . the only thing I could do that was nobody else's business." She remained a staunch individualist throughout her long and distinguished artistic career. At a time when working outside the home was unusual for a woman—let alone blazing trails in a virtually all-male field— O'Keeffe soon became known for paintings that were strong, candid and colorful, offering fresh insights into their subjects. Her many paintings of desert scenes near her New Mexico home, and of natural objects such as flowers, shells and bones, have found their way into leading collections around the world and helped bring her prestigious awards as well as the admiration of her peers. O'Keeffe was married for many years to Alfred Stieglitz, the photographer.

Louis H. Sullivan (1856–1924)—Boston-born Sullivan, son of an immigrant from County Cork, is considered "the father of modernism in architecture." He revolutionized the face of America's cities with radical new building designs, including the Transportation Building for the World's Columbian Exposition of 1892–1893 and Chicago's Auditorium and Gage buildings. More than anyone, Sullivan created the modern skyscraper. He broke with classical traditions that had long governed architectural design and created buildings "whose form followed their function." Frank Lloyd Wright, a more recent architectural giant, cited Sullivan as his chief inspiration.

HUMAN SERVICE

Thomas Anthony Dooley (1927–1961)—Tom Dooley gave up the chance for a lucrative medical practice in the United States to serve suffering thousands in Southeast Asia. His first experience of the area came as a Navy doctor in 1954, helping refugees to flee Communist North Vietnam. Leaving the Navy in 1956, he began a medical mission in the jungle of neighboring Laos. His first book, *Deliver Us from Evil,* which recounts his naval service in Vietnam, was also published that year. With proceeds from its sale and 297 lectures, he and three colleagues established their first hospital, in Laos. The next year Dooley was instrumental in founding MEDICO (Medical International Cooperation Organization), which he used to channel money from further speaking engagements and from two additional books (*The Edge of Tomorrow,* 1958; *The Night They Burned the Mountain,* 1960) to help found more hospitals. He set up two in Laos and three more in other Southeast Asian countries. When cancer ended Dooley's life and career at age 34, he had accomplished more than most men do in a normal lifetime. Congress voted him a posthumous gold medal for his humanitarian service.

Father Edward J. Flanagan (1886–1948)—Born in County Roscommon, Flanagan came to the United States in 1904 and soon entered seminary. He continued his studies at the Gregorian University in Rome and the University of Innsbruck, Austria. Back in the United States, Flanagan was assigned a parish in Nebraska and soon took an interest in social service, founding a hostel for workingmen in Omaha. Soon his compassion turned him to helping disadvantaged boys who had broken the law or came from broken homes. He began appearing at juvenile court hearings, insisting that "there is no such thing as a bad boy" and usually persuading the judge to give boy offenders into his care for "another chance." These activities led him in 1917 to establish Boys Town, U.S.A., a haven for boys of all religions and races. His work there was immortalized in the 1938 movie, *Boys Town,* starring Spencer Tracy and Mickey Rooney.

INVENTORS AND PIONEERS OF TECHNOLOGY

Charles Edgar Duryea (1861–1938)—This American-born automobile pioneer, together with his younger brother, J. Frank Duryea (1869–1967), built the nation's first successful gasoline-powered automobile. The Duryea brothers, natives of Illinois, ushered the United States into the automotive age on September 21, 1893, with a one-cylinder, two-cycle vehicle first shown at Springfield, Massachusetts. In 1895 they founded the Duryea Motor Wagon Company, and that same year one of their automobiles won the nation's first gasoline-automobile race, from Chicago to Evanston, Illinois.

Robert Fulton (1765–1815)—A Pennsylvania-born artist, civil engineer and inventor, Fulton began his career painting portraits, miniatures and landscapes. From this he turned to designing canals, bridges and aqueducts, then to building a semi-successful submarine mine and torpedo. Although he did not, in fact, invent the steamboat, his fame rests on his success in designing and building the *Clermont,* which in 1807 demonstrated that steam-powered navigation was commercially as well as technically feasible.

John P. Holland (1840?–1914)—Holland, a native of County Clare, began his career as a schoolteacher. He went on to invent the first practicable submarine, demonstrating its potential as a major naval weapon. Holland had begun drawing plans for a submarine while in Ireland, but it was only after he came to the United States that he was able to build his first successful boat, the *Fenian Ram* (1881), with funds from the Irish republican group. Despite some support from U.S. naval officers, most of Holland's early offers to design submarine craft were rebuffed by the American naval establishment. He financed the *Holland,* launched in 1898, with his own money, and finally convinced the skeptics. The U.S. Navy ordered six of his prototype, and others were built for Britain, Russia and Japan in the run-up to World War I. Holland also invented an escape device for use by craft that were disabled underwater.

Stephen H. Horgan (1854–1941)—Horgan, who was born near Norfolk, Virginia, developed the process that newspapers still use to reproduce photographs on their pages. Fascinated by photography from childhood, Horgan joined the New York *Daily Graphic* as a staff photographer. There he discovered how to use a line screen to convert black-and-white photographs—so-called continuous-tone art—into "halftones" suitable for printing. The *Graphic* published the first newspaper halftones in 1880. In 1893, Horgan became art director at the *New York Herald,* where he improved the halftone process so that newspapers could print photos using high-speed presses. He later worked on a process for transmitting color photographs by wire.

Thomas E. Murray (1860–1929)—Trained as an engineer, Murray in the late 1880s became a technical adviser to Anthony Brady, who operated a number of utility companies. As general director of the New York and Brooklyn Edison companies, he consolidated and managed much of the system and also oversaw the design and construction of New York City's main power plants as well as similar facilities throughout the nation. Murray's greatest legacy, however, was his inventive genius. He conceived useful devices for a wide range of industries and received patents on over 1,100—second only to Thomas Edison himself among American inventors.

JOURNALISM AND LITERATURE

Jimmy Breslin (1929–   )—Known for his outspoken, colorful style, street-smart Breslin ranks among America's best-known and most widely read journalists and novelists. Readers first took notice of the Queens native while he was a sports writer for New York's now-defunct *Herald Tribune;* he has since come to be regarded as a key developer of "the new journalism." During the early 1960s, Breslin also began writing novels on the side, initially to help support his growing family. *The Gang That Couldn't Shoot Straight, Forsaking All Others, World Without End, Amen,* and other Breslin books have been widely acclaimed. Breslin's award-winning syndicated column has a large, enthusiastic following; its subjects are far-ranging, from humorous profiles of his low-life cronies to impressionistic pieces on the events of the day. Much of his non-fiction writing shows a strong concern for those he sees as disadvantaged or oppressed. Breslin has also brought a convincing command of "the Queens [New York] English" to television as a network commentator. In a digression from his usual pursuits, he campaigned unsuccessfully in 1969 for president of the City Council of New York, together with novelist Norman Mailer, who lost his bid for the mayoralty. One critic has observed that, though the "bulky, rumpled" Breslin may have the appearance of a "slob" and the vocabulary of a "hood," he "writes like a man of wit, intelligence and sensitivity."

William F. Buckley (1925–   )—American editor, writer, novelist and champion of conservative causes—a prolific and versatile talent, whether you love or hate his views and manner. Buckley first came to national attention with *God and Man at Yale* (1951), a book criticizing the alleged liberal tendencies of his alma mater. In 1955 he co-founded the conservative journal, *National Review,* where he continues as editor-in-chief. Branching out into the electronic media, Buckley in 1966 launched his own television program, *Firing Line,* a showcase for his often acerbic wit and criticism. In recent years, he has shown a penchant for fiction with such novels as *Who's on First, Airborne* and *Saving the Queen,* among many.

Francis Scott Key Fitzgerald (1896–1940)—"F. Scott," the "spokesman of the roaring twenties," ranks among the most gifted writers America has produced. Born in St. Paul, Minnesota, and educated a Catholic in New Jersey, his life followed a course stamped by extremes—from the heights of glamor, fame and success, to the depths of desperation and despair, a pattern mirrored in many of his characters. Fitzgerald attended Princeton starting in 1913, but left before graduation to enlist in the army. Much of his writing chronicled the carefree, decadent younger generation of the Jazz Age. His first novel, *This Side of Paradise* (1920), painted a picture of life among the typically privileged students at his beloved alma mater. *Paradise* propelled him to financial success and paved the way for his marriage to Zelda Sayre. Their life together began in gaiety and desperate fun-seeking, but gradually deteriorated, with a retreat to Europe for several years. She suffered two breakdowns, never recovering; he took to heavy drinking. Along the way, however, Fitzgerald managed to produce *The Beautiful and Damned* (1922); regular short stories for leading magazines; *The Great Gatsby* (1925), his masterpiece, which was highly acclaimed but a financial bust; and *Tender Is the Night,* a critical failure. He spent his last years in the seclusion of a small Southern town and in Hollywood, writing movie scripts.

Walt Kelly (1913–1973)—Comic-strip cartoonist and political-social critic who created the famous newspaper feature, *Pogo.* On the surface, *Pogo* was about a self-effacing 'possum who lived in Georgia's Okeefenokee Swamp with an assortment of other animals. Much of their conversation, however, contained veiled commentary on the events of the day, and millions considered *Pogo* an essential part of their daily reading.

Margaret Mitchell (1900–1949)—For several years after college, Mitchell worked as a feature writer for the *Atlanta Journal*. Turning to fiction, she wrote *Gone With the Wind,* a romantic novel set in her native Atlanta during and after the Civil War. The book was an immediate success. It is thought, in fact, to be the best-selling work of fiction ever produced in America, having supplanted *Uncle Tom's Cabin,* the previous record-holder. *Gone With the Wind* received a Pulitzer Prize and also was made into perhaps the most popular motion picture of all time.

Edward R. Murrow (1908–1965)—Murrow, one of the most influential personalities in twentieth-century broadcast journalism, joined CBS as a radio reporter in 1935. Sent to Britain as a war correspondent with the coming of World War II, he became familiar to millions from his radio reports to America during the German "Blitz" bombing of the British capital. During the 1950s and 1960s, the chain-smoking Murrow became a familiar face on television in the "See It Now" and "Person to Person" series. Before his death from lung cancer, he served for a time as Director of the United States Information Agency (USIA).

Flannery O'Connor (1925–1964)—A novelist and short-story writer, O'Connor is remembered for unconventional works that are typically set in the rural South and deal with alienation and the relationship of individuals to God. *A Good Man Is Hard to Find, and Other Stories,* published in 1955, established her as a master of the short story. O'Connor's other works include a novel, *The Violent Bear It Away* (1960) and a collection of stories, *Everything That Rises Must Converge* (1965).

John O'Hara (1905–1970)—Born into a wealthy Irish-American family in Pottsville, Pennsylvania, O'Hara gave up plans to attend Yale after the death of his father. Traveling widely, he settled in New York, working as a critic and reporter. This journalistic experience would show in his subsequent writing style. In the late 1920s, O'Hara began the writing for which he is most remembered: a series of novels and short stories that mirror the social history of upwardly mobile Americans between the 1920s and 1940s. In such novels as *Butterfield 8* (1935) and *From the Terrace* (1958), O'Hara showed his fascination with how class, money and sexuality affect

Americans. The dialogue and detail that mark his writing form a valuable record of the decades he wrote about. O'Hara's novel, *Ten North Frederick,* won a National Book Award in 1955.

Eugene G. O'Neill (1888–1953)—Son of a touring actor known for his portrayal of Dumas' Count of Monte Cristo, Eugene O'Neill remains perhaps the finest playwright America has produced. His plays typically explore the tormented dimensions of human relationships, especially man's struggle with God and religion. Many scholars have linked these themes to his insecure childhood, which was marked by constant moving around required by his father's theatrical engagements—and influenced by the "peasant Irish Catholicism" of his father and the more refined, mystical religiosity of his mother, who succumbed to drug addiction. Young O'Neill attended Princeton briefly (1906–1907), a prelude to six years marked by work as a merchant seaman, a derelict's life on the waterfronts of three continents, alcoholic nightmares and three suicide attempts. He would later see this period of adventure, danger and low life as an invaluable education for his career as a dramatist. O'Neill's first play, *Bound East for Cardiff,* opened in Provincetown, Massachusetts, in 1916, and was restaged later that year as his New York debut. Four years later he brought his first full-length effort, *Beyond the Horizon,* to Broadway. Twenty long plays and several shorter ones followed between 1920 and 1943. Among his more powerful and enduring works are *Anna Christie, The Emperor Jones, Mourning Becomes Electra, The Iceman Cometh, Long Day's Journey into Night,* and *A Moon for the Misbegotten.* O'Neill won four Pulitzer Prizes for drama; and was the first and, to date, the only American playwright to win the Nobel Prize for Literature (1936). He spent his last years in a Boston hotel, withdrawn, unproductive and waiting for death—as tragic a figure as he had ever created for the stage.

LABOR LEADERS

Elizabeth Gurley Flynn (1890–1964)—The first woman to head the U.S. Communist Party, Flynn was born in New Hampshire into a socialist family that moved to New York in 1900. At age 15, Flynn began giving street-corner speeches for workers' rights. In

1906 she joined the radical labor group, the International Workers of the World (IWW), where she led several bloody strikes. She was a cofounder of the American Civil Liberties Union in 1920, and in 1937 she joined the U.S. Communist Party. Over the next two decades Flynn rose to head that organization and in 1955 went to prison for violating the Smith Act. This law, which jailed many communist leaders during the strongly anticommunist fifties, forbade preaching the violent overthrow of the U.S. government. The Supreme Court ruled in 1957 that teaching communism was not in itself illegal—and Flynn was released from jail, but went into self-imposed exile in Moscow, dying there in 1964.

George Meany (1894–1980)—A gruff, formidable individual, Meany was the American labor movement's undisputed "power" for nearly three decades. Born in New York, he began his career at 16 as an apprentice plumber. Meany soon became active in union management, and by 1952, had been elected president of the American Federation of Labor (AFL). Three years later, in 1955, he was instrumental in merging the group with the Congress of Industrial Organizations (CIO), forming a national labor organization of unprecedented size and strength. Meany presided over the united organization until his retirement in 1979. As head of the AFL-CIO, he worked vigorously to reduce corruption in the labor movement, and was a key mover in expelling the powerful Teamsters Union from the organization in 1957, after serious charges of unethical conduct were brought against its leaders. Meany also tried to strengthen U.S. labor's stand against communism, both at home and abroad, and he strongly backed the Vietnam War from start to finish.

Peter James McGuire (1852–1906)—Peter McGuire is best remembered today as the Father of Labor Day, but his contributions to the welfare of American workers were much broader. Born in New York City, McGuire left school at age 11 to help support his family, while continuing his education at night. During the late 1870s he worked as an organizer for the Social Democratic Party, also sponsoring legislation in Missouri that established one of the country's first bureaus of labor statistics. After a time as deputy commissioner of the Missouri bureau, he returned to his trade, furniture making. McGuire organized the St. Louis carpenters and then became the driving force behind a national convention of carpenters' unions that resulted in the formation of the United Brotherhood of Carpenters and Joiners (UBC). As chief administrator of the UBC and editor of its newspaper, *The Carpenter,* McGuire issued the call for a conference of national labor union leaders in Chicago, which led to the creation in 1881 of the Federation of Organized Trades and Labor Unions of the United States and Canada. Moving the UBC's headquarters to New York City, McGuire became an active champion of the eight-hour day; was a leader of the May Day demonstrations of 1886 and 1890; and led the movement that ultimately resulted in enactment of the national Labor Day holiday in 1894. McGuire was one of the founders of the American Federation of Labor (AFL) in 1886, which he served as first secretary and vice president.

Terence Vincent Powderly (1849–1924)—A pioneering labor leader, Powderly joined the Knights of Labor in 1874, rising to head the organization five years later. During the 1880s, with K of L membership over 700,000, Powderly was the nation's most powerful union leader. He served for a time as mayor of Scranton, Pennsylvania, and in 1897 was appointed Commissioner General of Immigration by President McKinley.

Michael Joseph Quill (1905–1966)—Born in Kilgarvan, County Kerry, Mike Quill became a volunteer in the Irish Republican Army and served in the Rebellion of 1919–1923. He came to New York in 1926 and, after several jobs, became a gateman with the Interborough Rapid Transit Company. In 1934 Quill was one of the founders of the Transport Workers Union of America (TWUA), which elected him its full-time president and organizer the following year. In the decades that followed, he was active in local and national union affairs, becoming president of the new International Transport Workers Union after it affiliated with the Congress of Industrial Organizations (CIO) in 1937. Quill also served, off and on, as a member of the New York City Council. In 1965 he led a strike against New York's bus and subway lines that paralyzed the city for 12 days. Refusing a court order to end the strike, he was sent to prison. There he suffered a heart attack that probably hastened his death the following January. Quill had generally followed the communist line early in his career, but he ultimately became strongly anticommunist and worked to eliminate communist influence in the U.S. labor movement.

MILITARY SERVICE

John Barry (1745–1803)—Barry, one of the most prominent American naval officers during the American Revolution, is considered by many to be the Father of the U.S. Navy. Born in Tacumshane, County Wexford, Barry emigrated to Philadelphia and became a shipmaster. When the Revolution erupted, the Continental Congress commissioned him and gave him command of several ships which became the nucleus of the American fleet. At his death, Commodore Barry was the Navy's senior officer.

Patrick R. Cleburne (1828–1864)—A native of Cork, Cleburne was one of several Irish-born soldiers who held high rank in the South during the Civil War. His skill and courage earned him the rank of major general, and his military exploits along the Mississippi won him the sobriquet, Stonewall Jackson of the West. Cleburne was killed in action after winning commendations for valor at Shiloh, Chickamauga and Missionary Ridge.

William J. Donovan (1883–1959)—Soldier, politician and statesman, Donovan is best remembered as founder of the OSS (Office of Strategic Services), World War II predecessor of the CIA. He first came to national attention during World War I, when his heroic exploits as colonel of the Fighting 69th, the famous New York Irish-American regiment, earned him the Medal of Honor and the nickname, Wild Bill. After World War II, Donovan became active in New York politics and served briefly as ambassador to Thailand.

Colin P. Kelly (1915–1941)—Captain Kelly, a U.S. Army Air Force officer, became one of America's first World War II heroes when he crash-dived his crippled bomber into a Japanese battleship off the Philippines three days after Pearl Harbor. The battleship was sunk, and for his courageous self-sacrifice, Kelly was posthumously awarded the Distinguished Service Cross.

William D. Leahy (1875–1959)—Born in Hampton, Iowa, Leahy attended the U.S. Naval Academy, followed by active service in the Philippines during the Spanish-American War, with U.S. occupation forces in Nicaragua, and during World War I. Between the wars he headed the Navy Bureau of Ordnance and served as Chief of Naval Operations, retiring as an admiral in 1939. When the Germans overran France in 1940 and established a puppet government at Vichy, Leahy was appointed ambassador to this sensitive capital. Recalled to active duty in 1942 as a fleet admiral, Leahy served as Chief of Staff to Franklin D. Roosevelt until the president's death, and continued to hold the post under Harry Truman, retiring in 1949.

Alfred Thayer Mahan (1840–1914)—A U.S. naval officer and historian, Mahan was the son of a professor at West Point, the U.S. Military Academy. He attended Annapolis and served with the U.S. Navy during the Civil War. By 1884, he had compiled a sufficiently impressive reputation to be invited to lecture on naval history and tactics at the Naval War College. He taught there for several years, basing his lectures on his extensive study of naval history from ancient times to the nineteenth century. Far more influential were Mahan's three books: *The Influence of Sea Power upon History, 1660–1783* (1890), *The Influence of Sea Power upon the French Revolution and Empire, 1793–1812* (1892), and *The Interest of America in Sea Power, Present and Future* (1897). The first two books showed convincingly how British political and economic supremacy from the seventeenth through the early nineteenth centuries had resulted largely from her commercial and naval sea power. The last book helped shape America's development as a major naval power after the Spanish-American War, and influenced naval thinking around the world.

Anthony McAuliffe (1893–1975) McAuliffe is perhaps best remembered for his timely use of a four-letter word. As an American general commanding airborne troops who were desperately defending the key Belgian town of Bastogne during the Battle of the Bulge, the last great German counteroffensive of World War II, McAuliffe found himself faced with a German ultimatum demanding his surrender. He sent a reply to his German counterpart consisting of a single word: "Nuts!" His terse, no-nonsense response made McAuliffe an instant legend, symbolizing dogged defiance and courage in the face of overwhelming odds.

Audie Murphy (1924–1971)—A U.S. war hero and movie actor, Murphy won the Medal of Honor in 1945 for single-handedly killing some 240 German soldiers. This and other brave feats helped make the modest young man the most decorated U.S. soldier of World War II. After the war, he played himself in *To Hell and Back,* a film about his life and war exploits, launching a film career that included starring roles in *The Red Badge of Courage* and a series of low-budget Westerns. Murphy died in an airplane crash.

Philip H. Sheridan (1831–1888)—Born into a Catholic family in County Sligo (some sources say County Cavan), Sheridan ranked among the foremost Union generals during the Civil War. His brilliant leadership won several battles for the North, and he played a key role in forcing Robert E. Lee's surrender at Appomatox. After notable service on the Western frontier, Sheridan was named commander-in-chief of the U.S. Army in 1884 and became a full general shortly before his death.

John Sullivan (1740–1795)—The son of immigrant parents, Sullivan was born at Somersworth, New Hampshire. He began his career as a successful lawyer. In 1774, as a major in the New Hampshire militia, he was sent as a delegate to the Continental Congress. Sullivan became a brigadier general in 1775 and for a time commanded Continental forces in the Northern colonies. Promoted to major general in 1776, he was captured at the Battle of Long Island but was soon released in a prisoner exchange. He served with distinction at the critical battles of Trenton and Princeton, then resigned in 1779 because of ill health. Recovering, Sullivan served again as a New Hampshire delegate to the Continental Congress and, during the Confederation period, was governor of his state for three years.

POLITICS AND PUBLIC SERVICE

William G. Brennan (1906–   )—Born in Newark, New Jersey, Brennan became a judge in the state's Superior Court in 1949. His distinguished record there earned him national attention, and in 1956 he was named an associate justice of the U.S. Supreme Court. On the nation's highest court, Brennan has been a consistent champion of individual liberties and civil rights, often leading the Court's now-dwindling liberal faction.

James F. Byrnes (1879–1972)—South Carolina–born Byrnes was one of few individuals who have served at high levels in all three branches of the Federal government as well as in state posts. The Charleston native had little formal schooling as a boy but, like Lincoln and others, entered the legal profession after reading law on his own. In 1911 Byrnes was elected a Democratic member of the U.S. House of Representatives for South Carolina. He served there until 1925 followed, beginning in 1931, by a decade in the Senate. In 1941, Franklin Roosevelt named Byrnes to the Supreme Court, persuading him the next year to transfer to the executive branch. Byrnes held major agency posts during World War II, heading the Office of Economic Stabilization and the Office of War Mobilization. He was named Secretary of State in 1945, showing increasing firmness in the face of Soviet violations of the Yalta agreements and Allied-Soviet friction in Germany. Leaving Washington, Byrnes returned to his native state to serve as governor from 1951 to 1955.

Charles Carroll (1737–1832)—Considering what he achieved and how widely he was respected while he lived, Charles Carroll's name is surprisingly unfamiliar to the vast majority of Americans. Born into a distinguished Irish-Catholic family in Maryland—it might justly be called America's first Irish-Catholic dynasty— Charles Carroll of Carrollton was given an "underground" Catholic education. Maryland's laws at the time prohibited Catholics from voting, from holding office, from worshipping openly and from having their children educated as Catholics. Yet, through his own brilliance, Carroll overcame anti-Catholic prejudice and won the respect of many citizens of Maryland in opposing the Stamp Act and other British laws that affected the American colonies. First in Maryland, and then on behalf of all the colonies, he took a leading role in public affairs, and signed the Declaration of Independence as a representative from Maryland. His business and legal skills were instrumental in helping the colonies acquire the money and materials they needed to resist Britain's military power. After the Congress was established in 1789, Carroll served for a time as a U.S. senator. He then turned his attentions to business affairs, managing vast personal landholdings and helping to found and direct companies engaged in building canals and railroads for the infant United States. When he died, he was the last surviving signer of the Declaration and was also reputedly the wealthiest man in America. According to one account, he was selected by the Federalist party to be its presidential candidate if George Washington had declined to serve a second term in 1792. Under slightly different circumstances, then, the United States would have had a Roman Catholic chief executive of Irish descent a full 169 years before John F. Kennedy was inaugurated.

Richard Joseph Daley (1902–1976)—Though he never held public office beyond the local level, Richard Daley became one of the nation's most powerful Democratic leaders. The future Chicago mayor was born on that city's West Side and received his law degree from De Paul University. Daley was elected to the Illinois legislature in 1936 and became a close associate of Governor Adlai Stevenson, serving the future Democratic presidential candidate as a legislative adviser. After serving as clerk of Cook County and county Democratic chairman during the early 1950s, he was elected mayor of Chicago in 1955, winning reelection by decisive margins every four years through 1975. As mayor, Daley reduced traditional political graft, made reforms in the police and fire departments and helped rejuvenate the city's economy. At the same time, he built a masterful political machine that could "deliver votes to order": Last of the Bosses, some called him. He was Democratic leader of Illinois as well as of Chicago, and provided support that proved critical to the presidential nominations of Adlai Stevenson, John F. Kennedy, Hubert Humphrey and Jimmy Carter. Daley attracted widespread attention after the Democratic party held its 1968 national convention in Chicago. Chicago police clashed with demonstrators who opposed the Vietnam War, and hundreds of demonstrators, journalists and police were hurt. Four years later, the convention refused to recognize Daley and his delegates, opting for delegates it contended were more representative of Illinois Democrats.

Sir Thomas Dongan (1634–1715)—A colonial governor of New York, Dongan was the first Catholic governor in the American colonies. He was born in Castletown Kildrought (Celbridge), County Kildare, son of a member of the Irish parliament, Sir John

Dongan. When Charles I was executed in 1649, Dongan went into exile in France, subsequently becoming colonel of an Irish regiment there. He returned to England in 1678 and went to Tangier as lieutenant governor. In 1682, Dongan was appointed governor of the bankrupt colony of New York. Though he served for only six years, he achieved much. Dongan set what are essentially the current boundaries of New York State, after conferring with officials from Connecticut, Pennsylvania and Canada; developed a sensible Indian policy that kept the powerful Iroquois on England's side; set up a post office; and granted charters to the cities of New York and Albany. Most notable, however, was his Charter of Liberties, an abortive attempt to establish parity between the New York provincial legislature and Parliament, to guarantee religious freedom, and to uphold the principle of no taxation without representation as well as a number of other principles that were ahead of their time. Dongan was replaced in 1688, and returned to England in 1691, later succeeding his brother as Earl of Limerick.

The Kennedy Brothers—Of the four sons born to Joseph Patrick Kennedy (see Business, Industry and Finance) and Rose Fitzgerald Kennedy, three were destined for prominent careers in national Democratic politics. The Kennedys trained their children to compete and achieve from childhood, beginning with ***Joseph P. Kennedy, Jr.*** (1915–1944), their eldest son. Joe Jr.'s death on a secret World War II air mission quashed the plans his wealthy and influential father had made to launch him on what many expected would have been a brilliant political career. The details of the Kennedy family's subsequent fortunes are familiar enough to require no detailed recounting. Briefly, however, Joe's death thrust the family mantle onto ***John Fitzgerald Kennedy*** (1917–1963), who, after heroic Navy service in the South Pacific, won election to Congress from Massachusetts in 1946. He subsequently served as U.S. senator and, in 1961, was sworn in as the first Roman Catholic president of the United States. Following his assassination in 1963, JFK's younger brother, ***Robert Francis Kennedy*** (1925–1968), came to the fore. RFK, or Bobby, as he was known, had been his brother's closest political adviser and attorney general in his cabinet. He left the Johnson administration in 1964, ran successfully for the Senate representing New York, and was himself assassinated in

1968 during his campaign for the Democratic presidential nomination. ***Edward Moore Kennedy*** (1932–   ), the last representative of his generation among the Kennedy males, has represented Massachusetts in the Senate since 1962. Perhaps the Senate's most prominent liberal, "Teddy" has served as Democratic whip (assistant leader) and as chairman of the Senate Judiciary Committee. After a 1969 incident in which the car he was driving plunged off a bridge on Chappaquiddick Island, Massachusetts, drowning the young woman with him, serious questions were raised about Kennedy's role in the event and his subsequent handling of it. Charges of a cover-up, which have continued to this day, have reportedly been a major factor in persuading Kennedy to defer his presumed plans to seek the presidential nomination; he failed in a 1980 bid. One is hard-pressed to name an American family that has been so widely loved and admired—or so distrusted.

Mike Mansfield (1903–   )—As Majority Leader in the U.S. Senate, this Montana Democrat served in that post longer than any other person (1961–1977). Michael Joseph Mansfield, born in New York City and reared in Montana, left school at age 14 to join the Navy during World War I. Then, enlisting in the Army, he served there and in the Marine Corps until 1922. He worked as a miner and mining engineer for the rest of the 1920s, then earned bachelor's and master's degrees from Montana State University, despite the fact that he had never attended high school. After teaching Hispanic and Far Eastern history there, he entered Congress in 1943, moving up to the Senate ten years later. He left his Senate post in 1977 to become U.S. Ambassador to Japan, and proved so effective and well-liked by the Japanese that he continued to serve under Ronald Reagan.

Eugene McCarthy (1916–   )—McCarthy, a Minnesota native who began his career teaching high school and college students, left the classroom in the late 1940s to enter Democratic politics. He was elected to Congress from Minnesota in 1949, moving up to the Senate a decade later. McCarthy's opposition to the Vietnam conflict won him strong backing, particularly among college students, and led him to seek the Democratic presidential nomination in 1968. Although he ultimately lost the nomination, his primary successes helped persuade Robert Kennedy to enter the race and also put pressure on Lyndon Johnson to abandon a bid for a second presidential term. McCarthy ran as an independent presidential candidate in 1976, and afterward returned to his first loves: teaching, lecturing and writing poetry.

Joseph Raymond McCarthy (1908–1957)—A Senator from Wisconsin (1947–1957) whose political career was marked by extreme controversy, McCarthy is best remembered for the campaign he launched in 1950 to expose alleged communist penetration of the U.S. State Department and other government agencies. His anticommunist crusade, which many came to see as a self-serving political gambit, was centered on the hearings he conducted as chairman of the Senate's Permanent Subcommittee on Investigations. The so-called McCarthy Hearings, televised in 1954, tainted the reputations of many public officials, some justly, but most unfairly. In the end, however, they also showed the senator up as a demagogue in the eyes of most Americans.

Daniel P. Moynihan (1927–)—Born in Tulsa, Oklahoma, Moynihan grew up in the tough Hell's Kitchen section of Manhattan, graduating from Tufts University with both bachelor's and doctoral degrees. He quickly gained a reputation for expertise on urban problems and minority groups, and wrote influential books on immigration, the antipoverty program and black family life. After teaching at Harvard and M.I.T., Moynihan was lured to Washington as an adviser to President Nixon, then returned to Cambridge until his appointment as U.S. Ambassador to India from 1973 to 1975. Over the next year, he served as U.S. Ambassador to the United Nations, winning high visibility for his outspoken attacks on those who criticized the administration's policies. Democrat Moynihan has represented New York in the U.S. Senate since 1977.

Sandra Day O'Connor (1930–)—The first woman ever appointed to the United States Supreme Court (1981), Mrs. O'Connor is descended on her father's side from the O'Deas (Day is a corruption). Born in El Paso, Texas, she graduated third in her class at Stanford University Law School, where a classmate was now-Chief Justice William Rehnquist. O'Connor practiced law in California and Arizona until 1965, when she became assistant attorney general of the state. She then served, in succession, in the Arizona Senate, as Superior Court Judge, Maricopa County, and as a member of the Arizona State Court of Appeals. Since her appointment to the highest U.S. court by Ronald Reagan, O'Connor has written moderate to conservative opinions on most cases, on many issues disregarding political ideology.

Thomas P. ("Tip") O'Neill (1912–   )—Speaker of the U.S. House of Representatives from 1977 to 1986, this Massachusetts Democrat was first elected to his state's house of representatives in 1936, the same year he graduated from Boston College. O'Neill became leader of the Democratic minority in 1947, rising the next year to become House Speaker. Winning election to the U.S. House of Representatives in 1952, he began a course that paralleled his state political career. He was named Majority Whip (assistant leader) in 1971, Majority Leader in 1973 and Speaker in 1977. Among O'Neill's major accomplishments were his successful leadership of a fight to have all votes in the House publicly recorded, and his early opposition to the Vietnam conflict.

Alfred Emanuel Smith (1873–1944)—A child of New York's Lower East Side, where he attended the school of St. James Church, Smith became active in city politics at age 22. Starting within the Tammany Hall organization, he won election to the state legislature in 1903. The governorship of New York followed in 1919, and in 1924 Smith was an unsuccessful candidate for the Democratic presidential nomination. With the backing of Governor Franklin Delano Roosevelt, Smith tried again in 1928. This time the so-called "Happy Warrior" won nomination but was defeated at the polls by Herbert Hoover, who benefited from continuing anti-Catholic prejudice and Smith's desire to repeal Prohibition.

RELIGION

John Carroll (1735–1815)—Maryland-born Carroll, member of one of the leading Catholic families that had settled the colony under Lord Baltimore, studied for the priesthood in France. After his order, the Jesuits, was suppressed in 1773, he returned to America. Carroll was consecrated America's first Catholic bishop in 1790, and became Archbishop of Baltimore in 1808. He was instrumental in organizing the American Catholic community during its infancy, and was a leading founder of Georgetown University, the nation's oldest Catholic institution of higher learning. (He was a first cousin of Charles Carroll of Carrollton.)

James Gibbons (1834–1921)—As an American cardinal, Gibbons took the lead in guiding the Roman Catholic Church through a troubled period of adjustment to its new status as a leading church in the United States. He was born in Baltimore, Maryland, but was taken to Ireland by his parents at age three. Gibbons returned to this country in 1853, settling in New Orleans. Following his ordination in 1861, he served as pastor of St. Bridget's Church in Baltimore. He moved on to serve as secretary to the archbishop of Baltimore in 1865 and, three years later, was named titular bishop of Adramyttium and first vicar apostolic of North Carolina. He was consecrated bishop of Richmond in 1872, during which service he wrote *The Faith of Our Fathers* (1876), a book that clearly explained Catholic doctrine for both Catholics and non-Catholics. After succeeding to the archbishopric of Baltimore in 1877, Gibbons led the delegation of American bishops that convened at Rome in late 1883 to make plans for the Third Plenary Council of Baltimore. As apostolic delegate he served as president of the council in 1884. Called to Rome the following year to receive his cardinal's hat, Gibbons, a frequent activist for just causes, interceded to prevent the Holy See from condemning the Knights of Labor, the leading American labor organization of the day. He was also instrumental in helping the Roman curia better understand the United States and the Church's role there at a time when the American church was being criticized for ultraliberal tendencies—the so-called heresy of Americanism. Gibbons died in Baltimore in 1921.

John Joseph Hughes (1797–1864)—Hughes, a native of County Tyrone, served as first archbishop of New York. There he began construction of the present St. Patrick's Cathedral, though he did not live to see it completed. Emigrating to America at age 21, Hughes worked as a laborer and seminary gardener in Chambersburg, Pennsylvania, beginning study for the priesthood there in 1820. He was ordained in 1826 for the Philadelphia diocese, and was consecrated coadjutor bishop of New York in 1838. He succeeded to the bishopric in 1842 and became archbishop in 1842 with the creation of the Archdiocese of New York. Hughes set in motion the building of a new cathedral for the archdiocese in 1858. As leader of New York's Catholic community, Hughes opposed abolition while criticizing slavery; encouraged Irish immigrants to remain in the cities, under Church guidance, instead of moving West; promoted the growth of parochial schools; and checked the growing control of local church affairs by laymen.

Francis Makemie (1658?–1708)—The founder of American Presbyterianism was born in Rathmelton, County Donegal, and pursued a business career before emigrating to the colonies. Here he was ordained into the Presbyterian ministry, afterward traveling widely in the mainland colonies and the West Indies, preaching and founding many new churches. In 1706, Makemie founded the Presbytery of Philadelphia, the first in America, which united scattered churches in Maryland, Pennsylvania, New York and Virginia. The following year, not long before his death, he was arrested in New York and prosecuted for preaching without a license. His subsequent acquittal was considered a major victory for religious toleration in America.

John McCloskey (1810–1885)—The first American cardinal of the Roman Catholic Church, McCloskey was born in Brooklyn, New York, the son of immigrants from County Derry. He received a private school education in New York and, after studies at Mount St. Mary's College, Emmitsburg, Maryland, followed by seminary, was ordained in 1834. McCloskey studied in Rome for two years, returning to New York in 1837, where he was assigned to St. Joseph's Church. In 1841 he was appointed first president of St. John's College (now Fordham University), but returned to parish duties after a year. Soon afterward, on the recommendation of New York Bishop John Joseph Hughes, McCloskey was appointed titular bishop of Axiere and coadjutor of New York. In 1847, he was transferred to Albany, where he remained for 17 years and built many churches and related institutions, including the Cathedral of the Immaculate Conception. McCloskey succeeded Hughes as archbishop of New York on the latter's death in 1864, and in 1875 became the first American cardinal. He completed the construction of St. Patrick's Cathedral, begun by Hughes, and officiated at its dedication in 1879.

John Joseph O'Connor (1920–   ) has established a reputation for plain speaking on issues of the day since his installation as archbishop of New York in 1984. O'Connor, a Philadelphia native, was ordained in 1945 and then taught high school for seven years, followed by service as a chaplain in the United States Navy and Marine Corps. He was appointed to head the Navy's chaplain corps in 1975, and four years later became an auxiliary bishop of the Military Ordinariate, a diocese that serves the nation's armed forces. After less than a year as bishop of Scranton, Pennsylvania, O'Connor was appointed archbishop of New York in 1984, receiving his cardinal's hat the following year. O'Connor has been active in condemning the nuclear arms race, and has also made plain his views on such controversial issues as homosexuality and artificial birth control.

Fulton J. Sheen (1895–1979)—One of the best-known, eloquent spokespersons for Catholic theology in modern times, Sheen was born Peter Sheen in El Paso, Texas. He was ordained in 1919, then studied philosophy at the Catholic University of Louvain, Belgium. Returning to the United States in 1926, he began a quarter-century teaching career at Catholic University of America. He also published the first of 50 books, *God and Intelligence in Modern Philosophy*. The Church had long recognized Sheen's persuasive powers —he had given talks on radio's "Catholic Hour" since 1930. In 1950 he was named director of the Society for the Propagation of the Faith in the United States, where he used his talents in raising funds for mission work abroad. During the 1950s, he also became a familiar television personality with his program, "Life is Worth Living." Sheen was not only effective with mass audiences; he acquired a reputation as a personal proselytizer, converting a number of well-known Americans including Claire Booth Luce. Sheen was named bishop of Rochester, New York, in 1966 and titular archbishop of Newport in 1969 but, to many's surprise, never received a cardinal's hat.

Francis Spellman (1889–1967)—Spellman, a native of Whitman, Massachusetts, earned his B.A. at Fordham and took holy orders in 1916. After service in Boston, he was assigned to the Papal Secretariat at Rome from 1925 to 1932. Returning to the United States, Spellman served as auxiliary bishop of Boston before being named archbishop of New York in 1939 and elevated to cardinal in 1946. Spellman served as apostolic vicar to the U.S. armed forces, making several wartime visits to battle zones. Thanks to his acquaintance with church leaders throughout the world, he also took on several missions as an envoy for presidents Roosevelt and Truman.

SPORTS

Charles Albert Comiskey (1858–1931)—An American baseball player and manager, Comiskey founded the Chicago White Sox in 1900. The Baseball Hall of Fame recognized his outstanding achievements by inducting him into its membership in 1939. The White Sox' home stadium, Comiskey Park, also honors him.

James ("Jimmy") Connors (1952–   )—The American tennis star first gained wide notice by winning the men's singles title at Wimbledon in 1974. Ranked number one internationally in 1974 and 1976, Connors remains, at age 38, among the top echelon of contenders in an increasingly competitive field.

James John ("Gentleman Jim") Corbett (1866–1933)—An American boxer, Corbett was born in San Francisco. In 1892 he won the first heavyweight title to be fought with gloves by defeating fellow Irish-American John L. Sullivan. Corbett lost the title to Bob Fitzsimmons in 1897.

William H. ("Jack") Dempsey (1895–1983)—One of the United States' greatest boxers, Dempsey became known as the Manassa Mauler after his Colorado birthplace. He defeated Jess Willard for the world heavyweight title in 1919, finally losing it to Gene Tunney in 1926. Dempsey was inducted into the Boxing Hall of Fame in 1926.

William Benjamin ("Ben") Hogan (1912–   )—Hogan, one of the immortals of U.S. golf, won four U.S. Open competitions (1948, 1950, 1951 and 1953), two PGA titles (1946, 1948), two Masters tournaments (1951, 1953), and the British Open (1953).

Connie Mack (1862–1956)—Among American baseball's greatest managers of all time, Mack was born Cornelius McGillicuddy in Brookfield, Massachusetts. As manager of the Philadelphia A's

(Athletics) from 1901 to 1950, he achieved the highest win record in baseball history—3,776 games. Mack entered the Baseball Hall of Fame in 1937.

John McEnroe (1959–)—Known as much for his on-court temper tantrums as for his skill with a racket, the Queens, New York–born tennis player rose to prominence with first-place finishes in the U.S. Open singles championships in 1979, 1980 and 1981. He also took top honors at Wimbledon in 1981.

Samuel Jackson ("Sam") Snead (1912–)—An American golf star, Snead won a record 84 professional tournaments. He is also the only pro to have won competitions over a span of six decades. "Slammin' Sammy" Snead was elected to the PGA Hall of Fame in 1953.

John L. Sullivan (1858–1918)—Perhaps the first American boxer to achieve wide recognition, Sullivan fought bare-knuckled from 1878 until his 1892 match with James J. Corbett, when he adopted gloves. Corbett knocked out the long-time champion in the 21st round of their heavyweight match.

Did You Know . . .

. . . That you don't have to pay taxes in Ireland *if* you're a writer, painter, composer or other artist *and* your creative work is "generally recognized as having cultural or artistic merit," in the opinion of the Revenue Commissioners. This policy has helped stop the export of creative talent—long one of Ireland's most important national resources—and has even attracted well-known actors and authors from Britain and other countries.

Irish-American Landmarks

▬▬▬▬▬▬▬

T o do justice to the subject of Irish-American landmarks would easily require a book in itself. We attempt here to cover a number of the more important, though "more important" is always, naturally, a matter of judgment. Collectively, the landmarks described illustrate some essential aspects of the Irish-American experience, including immigration, building the nation, military service and sacrifice, political life, the Irish-American religious heritage, and achieving the American Dream.

California

MILL VALLEY: THE REED SAWMILL RESTORATION

This Marin County landmark, across the Golden Gate from San Francisco, played a key role in the birth of the Empire City of the Pacific. Built in the 1840s by John Reed, a Dublin native and first non-Spanish settler of the Marin area, the sawmill was working when the forty-niners descended on California after James Marshall discovered gold at Sutter's Mill. Tens of thousands—a large percentage of Irish birth or parentage—arrived at San Francisco and, almost overnight, erected a city of tents and shacks. It was Reed's mill that supplied the lumber to build the first permanent structures. Meanwhile, another Dubliner, Jasper O'Farrell, had planned and laid out the city that has long been called one of the most beautiful on the continent. He named his vast estate outside San Francisco, Annaly, after a territory once ruled by the O'Farrells in County Longford. Reed's sawmill has been preserved as a landmark, and is open to the public. O'Farrell is commemorated in the name of one of San Francisco's major streets.

SAN FRANCISCO: ROBERT EMMET STATUE, GOLDEN GATE PARK

Erected to commemorate the great Irish patriot who was executed in 1803 for leading an unsuccessful uprising, the statue has long been a popular site for Irish-American speeches and events. Each year Emmet's eloquent and prophetic Speech from the Dock is read here as a memorial.

SAN FRANCISCO: ST. PATRICK'S CHURCH, 756 MISSION STREET

This has been called "the most Irish church on the continent." The present structure, built of brick with a slender tower and steeple, is the fourth erected by the parish since it was established in 1851 by Father Maginnis, then the only English-speaking priest in San Francisco. The church interior is faced with translucent green Connemara marble, brought from Ireland, and Caen stone. The crucifix and vestments were inspired by Irish designs of the sixth and eighth centuries. A series of stained-glass windows tells the stories of various Irish saints, each a patron of, or closely associated with, one of the 32 counties.

SAN FRANCISCO: THE FORMER JAMES FLOOD MANSION, CORNER OF CALIFORNIA AND MASON STREETS, NOB HILL

Nob Hill looks down, figuratively and literally, on most of San Francisco. It was here that much of the city's elite chose to build imposing mansions in the late 1800s. Irish-Americans formed a disproportionate share of these self-made men. While their experience was scarcely typical of their fellow immigrants from Ireland, scores of shrewd, able and lucky men with names such as O'Brien, Fair, Brown and Downey found in the West a chance to build fortunes in mining, building and contracting, transportation and other fields. James C. Flood was one of the Irish-American Big Four—four immigrants who bought out Henry Comstock's interest in a Nevada silver strike for $11,000 before he realized that the Comstock Lode held hundreds of millions in silver and gold. Flood spent $1.5 million in the 1860s to build a massive mansion atop Nob Hill. The brass railing in front of the house ran for two blocks and reportedly required a full-time worker to keep it polished and bright. Flood's was the only house on the hill to survive the San Francisco Fire of 1906. You can still see it today—if you settle for an outside view. It is now occupied by the exclusive Pacific Union Club.

District of Columbia

WASHINGTON: GEORGETOWN UNIVERSITY, GEORGETOWN

This world-famous Jesuit institution, founded in 1789 by soon-to-be-bishop John Carroll and other leading Irish-American Catholics, was the country's first Catholic institution of higher learning. Other well-known institutions with Irish-Catholic roots include Boston and Holy Cross colleges, Boston, Mass.; Seton Hall University, South Orange, N.J.; Fordham University and Iona College, The Bronx, N.Y.; and Villanova University, Villanova, Pa. Despite the fact that its teams are called the Fighting Irish, however, Notre Dame University, at South Bend, Ind., owes its founding as much to Franco-Americans as to Irish-Americans. Princeton University, Princeton, N.J., grew largely out of efforts by Irish-Americans of Ulster Presbyterian origins, who helped found it in 1746 to serve the Middle colonies and also to counter the theological liberalism of Harvard and Yale.

Illinois

CHICAGO: OLD ST. PATRICK'S CHURCH, 718 WEST ADAMS

If you believe in miracles, there may be one in the fact that this church still stands. During the Great Fire of 1871, most of the city's center—and its churches—was destroyed. The flames devastated everything around St. Patrick's as well, even the adjoining buildings, but stopped abruptly at the church steps. Dedicated on Christmas Day, 1856, and built in Romanesque style, St. Patrick's is Chicago's oldest standing church—and perhaps its oldest public building. Two towers, one Gothic, the other Byzantine, were added later to symbolize the meeting of East and West in the ethnically mixed area surrounding the church. St. Patrick's is especially known for its stained-glass windows. Designed by Chicago artist Thomas O'Shaughnessy in 1911, the nave windows depict the major saints of Ireland, including Patrick, Brigid, Finbarr, Colman, Brendan, Columbanus, and Columcille (Columba). Most celebrated, however, is O'Shaughnessy's McSwiney Memorial Window, honoring the revolutionary Lord Mayor of Cork who died after a hunger strike in 1920. It is a triptych representing Faith, Hope and Charity, containing 150,000 pieces of glass in a seemingly unlimited palette of pastels. Throughout the church, decorative touches taken from the *Book of Kells* and ancient Celtic design motifs abound.

Louisiana

LAKEVIEW: NEW BASIN CANAL PARK

During the 1830s, the city of New Orleans built the New Basin Canal, which was designed to connect Lake Pontchartrain with what is now the Howard Avenue section of the city. Thousands of recent Irish immigrants were employed to dig the waterway along a route that ran mostly through fever-infested cypress swamp. Eight thousand workers died before the project was completed— and some estimate the death toll as high as 20,000. Their sacrifice, embodied in the new canal, brought increased trade and prosperity to New Orleans and made it a major regional city for the first time. The Irish Cultural Center of New Orleans recently erected a monument to their sacrifice in the form of a Celtic cross suitably inscribed.

Maryland

BALTIMORE: BASILICA OF THE ASSUMPTION, CATHEDRAL AND MULBERRY STREETS

Designed by Benjamin Latrobe, this was the first Catholic cathedral built in the United States. In 1806, the year the cornerstone was laid by John Carroll, more than half the nation's Catholics lived in Maryland. Carroll, the nation's first Catholic bishop (and archbishop) and a member of one of the oldest and most distinguished Irish-American families, did not live to see the project completed. The War of 1812 and other problems delayed construction, and it was 1821 before the Classical Revival–style structure was opened to worshippers. Because of its seniority among U.S. cathedrals, the Basilica is sometimes called the Holy See of the United States. Pope Pius XI designated it a minor basilica in 1936, recognizing its special historical importance. The basilica is laid out in a cruciform with a vaulted, domed interior. Among the prelates buried in the crypt beneath the altar are Archbishop John Carroll and James Cardinal Gibbons. The basilica is open to visitors between 6:30 a.m. and 3:30 p.m. daily.

WARWICK: ST. FRANCIS XAVIER/ OLD BOHEMIA MISSION

Established in 1704, this church on Maryland's Eastern Shore was one of the earliest permanent Catholic foundations in the colonies. Jesuits also operated an academy here starting in 1745. Among its pupils were both John Carroll, the nation's first bishop, and his cousin, Charles Carroll of Carrollton, a signer of the Declaration of Independence. Although the school was illegal, and closed after a few years, the gracious Georgian-style building that housed it still stands at the site. The former rectory now contains a museum, and in the adjoining cemetery can be seen the gravestones of many early parishioners. Mass is celebrated at the church at 4 p.m. on the third Sunday of April, May, September and October. The rectory and museum are open, 12:00 to 3:00 p.m., on Sundays during the summer.

Massachusetts

BOSTON: ST. STEPHEN'S CHURCH, 401 HANOVER STREET

Located in what is now the largely Italian North End, St. Stephen's was originally built for a Protestant congregation and known as New North Church. It was designed in 1804 by Charles Bulfinch, the great Boston architect. (Five years earlier, Bulfinch had donated the design for Boston's first Catholic church, the original Church of the Holy Cross, on a site nearby.) In 1862 New North Church was sold to St. Stephen's Parish and soon became the parish church for many of Boston's leading Irish families. The Fitzgeralds—who gave the city a mayor and, through marriage with the Kennedys, three U.S. senators and a president—worshipped here; and here they baptized the infant Rose Fitzgerald (Kennedy). Of several Boston churches designed by Bulfinch, only St. Stephen's still stands. The rest have gone the way of the original Church of the Holy Cross—a close architectural cousin of St. Stephen's—which was demolished in 1875 when its parish moved into the present Cathedral of the Holy Cross. In 1965, then-Cardinal Cushing had St. Stephen's restored to its original condition. In the course of the project, workers uncovered copper nails and sheathing that had been fabricated over 160 years earlier in Paul Revere's forge. Revere also cast the church's large tower bell.

BOSTON: JOHN BOYLE O'REILLY MEMORIAL, THE FENWAY

Boston abounds with mementos of this nineteenth-century Irish-born journalist and poet, who became owner and editor of *The Boston Pilot* in 1876. O'Reilly not only made *The Pilot* the most influential and respected Irish-American journal of its day, but also won many admirers through his public speaking, his poetry and his outspoken championing of oppressed groups, including blacks and Jews as well as his fellow Irish and Irish-Americans. In addition to the Fenway memorial, Boston has a John Boyle O'Reilly Plaza; and Brookline's Holy Rood Cemetery contains his funeral monument. O'Reilly's home, now a private residence, still stands in Charlestown, and his summer home, at Hull, is now the public library.

BROOKLINE: KENNEDY NATIONAL HISTORIC SITE, 83 BEALS STREET

Birthplace of the 35th U.S. president, the first Irish-American Catholic to attain that office. Joseph and Rose Kennedy lived here from 1915 until 1921, when the needs of their growing family forced them to move to a larger house nearby. JFK's birthplace is furnished as it was during those years and contains a collection of Kennedy family memorabilia. Maps are available showing other local sites associated with the family. Open daily, 10 a.m. to 4:30 p.m. (President Kennedy is buried in Arlington National Cemetery, Arlington, Va. Most of his official papers as well as exhibits relating to his life and career are housed in the Kennedy Memorial Library, University of Massachusetts Campus, Boston.)

COHASSET: THE ST. JOHN MEMORIAL, COHASSET CENTRAL CEMETERY

In 1849, the *St. John,* a two-masted ship bringing Famine immigrants from Galway and County Clare, foundered in a storm on the Grampuses, hidden rocks about a mile off the port town of Cohasset. Only 20-odd souls survived and, of the 99 who drowned, 45 were never identified. Henry David Thoreau visited Cohasset several days after the wreck and wrote movingly of what he saw in the first chapter of his book *Cape Cod.* In 1914, the Ladies Ancient Order of Hibernians erected a 20-foot Celtic cross to the memory of the nameless victims of the *St. John* disaster. The cemetery is private; you might need permission to enter.

Michigan

DEARBORN: HENRY FORD BIRTHPLACE, GREENFIELD VILLAGE, 20900 OAKWOOD BOULEVARD

Ford, the son of Famine immigrants from County Cork, pioneered standardization and mass-production techniques in the infant U.S. automobile industry, enabling the average American to afford a car for the first time. Relocated here by Ford, who brought together at Greenfield Village homes and buildings linked with many famous Americans, the Ford Birthplace is open seven days a week.

New York

GREENE COUNTY: CAIRO AND EAST DURHAM

Set amid the northern Catskill Mountains of New York State, these Greene County resort communities have been a summer and holiday retreat for Irish-Americans for half a century. Hotels and guest houses bearing names from every corner of Ireland stand along the wooded roads, and at least three Irish-American festivals are held in the area each summer. The local chamber of commerce bills Greene County as "Ireland's 33rd county." East Durham has recently consolidated its role as a retreat for Irish-Americans by beginning construction of an Irish Sports and Cultural Center, which will have complete facilities for Gaelic sports such as hurling, handball and Gaelic football as well as ample indoor facilities for lectures, classes and step-dancing lessons. The 58-acre site will also boast a new Irish Heritage Museum, including a large library.

NEW YORK: THE NEW YORK PORT OF ENTRY

The experience of millions of immigrants from Ireland and elsewhere can be relived, to some degree, by visiting the former immigration facilities and associated museums in Lower Manhattan and New York Harbor: (a) South Street Seaport, South Street, Manhattan, which provides a restored and sanitized picture of the scene awaiting Irish immigrants who landed from the Liverpool packets that docked along South Street until 1856; (b) Castle Clinton

National Monument, Battery Park, Manhattan, where immigrants were processed between 1855 and 1889; and (c) Ellis Island National Monument (formerly the United States Immigration Station), where most immigrants were processed between the early 1890s and 1954. (Immigrants from Ireland formed the second-largest group to come through the station; in fact, a 15-year-old colleen from County Cork was the first person officially processed after Ellis Island opened on January 2, 1894.) Ellis Island is open in season and can be reached via the Liberty Island ferry from Battery Park. The museums of immigration on Liberty and Ellis islands are being greatly expanded, and the American Museum of Immigration, 15 Pine Street, New York, is also worth a visit.

NEW YORK: OLD ST. PATRICK'S CATHEDRAL, CORNER OF MOTT AND PRINCE STREETS

New York's second-oldest Catholic church, Old St. Patrick's was begun in 1809—a year after the Diocese of New York was established—and completed in 1815. Its architect was Joseph Mangin, who codesigned New York's City Hall during the same period. Although little survives of the original church after an 1868 fire, experts consider St. Patrick's the second-oldest example of Gothic Revival architecture in the United States. Old St. Patrick's became a cathedral in 1850 and remained the seat of the Archdiocese of New York until 1879, when the more familiar structure uptown was dedicated. It was here, in 1875, that John McCloskey was installed as the first American cardinal. An adjoining cemetery contains the graves of many well-known parishioners. Others are buried in catacombs below the church.

NEW YORK: ST. PATRICK'S CATHEDRAL, FIFTH AVENUE AT 50TH STREET

Built over a 21-year period, 1858 to 1879, "St. Pat's" was begun by the Right Reverend John Joseph Hughes, New York's first Catholic archbishop, and dedicated by John Cardinal McCloskey, America's first cardinal. A truly magnificent symbol of the country's wealthiest archdiocese, the cathedral is a fine example of the Gothic Revival style and was largely modeled after the Cathedral of Cologne, West Germany. The cathedral interior is 306 feet long and 108 feet high; its twin spires soar 330 feet above the street. From its very name, to its central role in New York's annual St. Patrick's Day Parade, to the heritage of its resident archbishops and much of its congregation, St. Patrick's has always been closely associated with New York's Irish community.

NEW YORK: ST. JAMES CHURCH, 23 OLIVER STREET

St. James Parish was first organized in the mid-1820s by Felix Varela, a refugee Cuban priest, who arranged to purchase nearby Christ Church from its Episcopalian congregation. When fire destroyed this structure several years later, the parish bought a new site adjacent to James Street, and renamed itself in honor of St. James. The present building was completed between 1836 and 1837, and with its colonnaded front reflects the Greek Revival style so popular during the early 1800s. From the beginning, the parish was largely Irish-born, drawing many members from Five Points, a crowded slum on the other side of Chatham Square where newly arrived immigrants often settled. In 1836, the same year it opened its new building, the parish also witnessed a landmark event in Irish-American history, the founding of the Ancient Order of Hibernians in America (AOH). During the late 1870s, Al Smith—later governor of New York and the first Catholic nominated for president by a major party—attended the parish elementary school.

ROME: OLD ERIE CANAL STATE PARK, STATE ROUTES 5 AND 46

Here, as at some other points between Albany and Buffalo, surviving sections of the original Erie Canal can be seen. Built largely by immigrant Irish muscle working for Irish-born contractors, the historic waterway was completed in 1825. It helped open America's interior to large-scale settlement and trade for the first time. And this, in turn, helped make New York City the nation's leading port. New York Governor DeWitt Clinton, whose brainchild the canal was, had an Irish-born grandfather himself. From the early years of the nineteenth century and into the twentieth, not only canals but countless other public works were, more often than not, the fruit of Irish-American efforts: railroads, such as the Baltimore

& Ohio and the Union Pacific; bridges, including that engineering marvel of its day, the Brooklyn Bridge; and the subway systems of New York, Boston and other great cities, to give just some examples.

Pennsylvania

GETTYSBURG: GETTYSBURG NATIONAL MILITARY PARK

Here in the summer of 1863 a Confederate army under General Robert E. Lee sought a dramatic breakthrough victory on Northern soil. Instead, in three days of savage fighting, Northern forces commanded by Irish-American George G. Meade turned back the attempt, helping hasten the Union's final victory at Appomattox. For both sides, however, Gettysburg was a costly battle, paid for in 7,000 lives and 45,000 wounded and missing. Irish-Americans fought courageously on both sides, but the largest and most famous unit in which they fought as a group was the Union's Irish Brigade, organized by Colonel Michael Corcoran, a County Sligo native. The brigade had already suffered heavy losses at Bull Run, Fredericksburg, Antietam and Chancellorsville as well as lesser-known clashes, but so many were killed or wounded at Gettysburg that the brigade ceased to exist thereafter. The courage and sacrifice of those who served in the brigade is commemorated at Gettysburg in a poignant monument: a mourning wolfhound at the base of a Celtic cross. Park rangers will direct you to the monument.

READING: DANIEL BOONE HOMESTEAD, NORTH OF BAUMSTOWN, SEVEN MILES EAST OF READING

A descendant, like Davy Crockett, of eighteenth-century immigrants from Donegal via Derry, Daniel Boone became a symbol of the first large-scale Irish settlements in America. Most of those who formed the so-called Ulster migration were Protestants driven from Ireland by economic hardship. Once in America, many drifted to the western frontier, where land was abundant and government minimal. The early phase of America's push westward is in large measure a story of hardy pioneers of Irish and Scots-Irish stock.

(*Note:* The latter term only emerged in the early 1800s, when many whose forebears had arrived earlier from Ireland found it useful to distinguish themselves from the impoverished Catholic masses whose arrival was triggering prejudice against anything Irish.) Daniel Boone was born in this house in 1734, when Reading was on the edge of the frontier. He was given his first rifle at age 10, and had become an expert at living in the wilds by the time the Boones moved to North Carolina in 1750. The stone homestead has been restored to reflect life in the early nineteenth century; there are also a blacksmith shop, a smokehouse and other buildings. Open daily, 9:30 a.m. to 4:30 p.m. Monday through Saturday, and Sunday, 1:00 to 4:30 p.m.

Rhode Island

PROVIDENCE: GEORGE M. COHAN BIRTHPLACE, 536 WICKENDEN STREET

Famous for such patriotic songs as "Yankee Doodle Dandy" and "Grand Old Flag," George Michael Cohan (1878–1942) was a giant of the American musical theater. He was not only a composer and dramatist, but was widely praised for his acting and song-and-dance routines. During a theatrical career that spanned over half a century, Cohan had a hand (or voice) in scores of popular productions. Cohan's success inspired many younger Irish-Americans to enter the world of entertainment.

South Carolina

CHARLESTON: HIBERNIAN HALL NATIONAL LANDMARK

The Hibernian Society of Charleston was originally founded, in part, to raise money for the relief of needy Irish immigrants who had emigrated to Charleston following the unsuccessful Irish uprising of 1798. Its membership has always been nonsectarian, with the presidency alternating each year between a Protestant and a Catholic. Between 1839 and 1841, the Society erected a headquarters in the form of a classical temple in the Greek Revival style. The designer, Thomas U. Walter, later designed the Capitol Building in Washington, D.C. During the late 1840s, the Society led efforts throughout the Southeast to aid victims of the Great Famine in Ireland. Essentially a social and charitable organization, the Society is a closed group of about 400 members, mostly drawn from the business and professional communities.

Texas

HOUSTON: THE DICK DOWLING MEMORIAL, HERMANN PARK

This memorial commemorates the courage and fighting skill of a handful of Irish-born Houstonians who fought and won the Battle of Sabine Pass, a dramatic Confederate Civil War victory. On September 8, 1863, 42 members of the Jefferson Davis Guards manned six cannon behind a simple earthwork at Sabine Pass, where the Sabine and Neches rivers empty into the Gulf of Mexico near Port Arthur. Nearly all of the men were County Galway natives, like their commander, 25-year-old Lieutenant Richard W. "Dick" Dowling. Offshore, a Union expedition of 20 ships prepared to disembark an invasion force of 5,000 troops. When the three Union gunboats moved inshore to "soften up" the defenses, however, the Davis Guards turned the tables. With just three or four shots, they put the first Federal gunboat out of action and then quickly disabled the second. The surrender of the second gunboat ended the battle, which had lasted only 45 minutes. The remaining Union ships sailed back to New Orleans, giving the expedition's commander, General Franklin, the honor of being the first American general to lose a fleet to shore batteries alone.

SAN ANTONIO: THE ALAMO—SHRINE OF TEXAS LIBERTY

Originally founded as a Franciscan mission station in the early 1700s, this famous landmark had become a presidio—a Spanish military post—by the end of the century. Its fame rests on the pivotal role it played in the War for Texas Independence, when 186 Texas volunteers under Colonel William Barrett Travis fought to the last man against forces vastly superior in number under Mexican General Santa Ana. At least 12 of the Texan defenders were Irish-born, and another 32 were of Irish descent, including Travis and several other prominent leaders. The self-sacrifice of these men at the Alamo bought just enough time for General Sam Houston, who was also of Ulster stock, to regroup his forces at San Jacinto. There he shortly afterward inflicted on the Mexicans the decisive defeat that secured Texas independence. The Alamo remained the property of the Roman Catholic Church until early in this century, when Clara Driscoll, an Irish-American philanthropist, bought the property on behalf of the Daughters of the Republic of Texas, who operate the shrine today.

SAN PATRICIO COUNTY: SAN PATRICIO

Located some dozen miles northeast of Corpus Christi, San Patricio de Hibernia was one of the first two Irish colonies established in Texas. In the late 1820s, James McGloin and John McMullen secured a land grant for this area from the Mexican government, which looked favorably upon settlement in Texas by Irish people who shared their Roman Catholic faith. The men recruited about 250 Catholic settlers, mainly in Donegal, Leinster and Connaught. In 1829, with a roster including names such as Brennan, Carroll, Conway, Dwyer, Fadden, Haughey and O'Docharty, they established the new town. San Patricio (the "de Hibernia" was soon dropped) became chiefly a farming and ranching community. On the orders of General Sam Houston, San Patricio County had the honor of being the first county organized in the newly independent Texas Republic, on March 17th, St. Patrick's Day, 1836. Most of the settlers had moved on by the end of the nineteenth century, and the town effectively ceased to exist. Since then, however, it has been reincorporated (1971), and visitors can tour the restored old courthouse and several of the original houses each St. Patrick's Day.

Wyoming

CODY: CODY BIRTHPLACE/BUFFALO BILL HISTORICAL CENTER, 720 SHERIDAN AVENUE

Son of an Irish immigrant, "Buffalo Bill" Cody came to symbolize the exploits of Americans in taming the western frontier. He excelled as a scout and a hunter, and later became a world-famous showman, entertaining hordes with his Wild West troupe. The Cody Birthplace contains a fascinating collection of memorabilia. Within blocks, you may also visit the Whitney Gallery of Western Art, the Plains Indian Museum, and Buffalo Bill Village & Western Exhibits, a recreated town of the early West. All facilities are open daily, 7 a.m. to 10 p.m., June through August.

Did You Know . . .

. . . That Ireland has more golf courses per square mile than any other country. Among these are several world-class links: for example, Ballybunion, County Kerry; Royal Dublin and Portmarnock, both in County Dublin; and Lahinch Golf Club, County Clare—Ireland's oldest course.

Irish-American Festivals:
A Directory

~~~~~~~~~~

Arizona

PHOENIX IRISH FEIS
St. Gregory Parish Grounds
3434 North 18th Avenue
Phoenix, AZ

Late October, Saturday and Sunday. Competition in traditional music and dancing events. Heritage Room with Irish-American historical exhibits and video presentations. Slide presentations on Ireland. Irish crafts and other imports on sale. Irish food and drink. CONTACT: Chris Dobyns, Treasurer, 3249 East Windrose, Phoenix, AZ 85032; or phone John Corcoran, (602) 939-1183.

California

GRAND NATIONAL IRISH FAIR & MUSIC FESTIVAL
Los Angeles Equestrian Center
480 Riverside Drive
Burbank, CA

Mid-June, Saturday and Sunday. Features continuous entertainment on several stages, with show bands, traditional music groups

and musicians from Ireland and the United States. Also: pipe
bands, parades, Gaelic sports, traditional food; Irish merchandise
vendors; genealogical information; children's entertainment. Sunday morning: liturgy in Irish. CONTACT: Irish Fair Foundation, P.O. Box 341, Pasadena, CA 91102. (818) 843-3644 or
(714) 523-5784.

Connecticut

GREATER HARTFORD IRISH FESTIVAL
The Irish American Home
132 Commerce Street
Glastonbury, CT

Late July, Friday through Sunday. Irish entertainers and show
bands; "Miss Irish Festival" competition; children's games and
rides; craft demonstrations and exhibits; Irish imports on sale; food
and drink. CONTACT: Mike Connolly, Festival Chairman, (203)
666-0022.

CONNECTICUT IRISH FESTIVAL & FEIS
Yale Field
Central Avenue and Route 34 (near Yale Bowl)
New Haven, CT

Early July, Saturday and Sunday. Musical entertainment, featuring
leading show bands and traditional groups as well as individual performers. Pipe bands. Competitions in dancing, singing, music,
Irish language and other feis events. Irish cultural and historical
exhibits. Gaelic football, hurling and camogie games. Irish imports
and food and drink on sale. Mass celebrated at 9 a.m. Sunday.
Most events are under cover. CONTACT: Connecticut Irish Festival, P.O. Box 1184, New Haven, CT 06505. (203) 281-3563.

Delaware

ANNUAL FEIS
University of Delaware
Newark, DE

Mid-August, Sunday. Competition in Irish dance, music, arts, crafts, poetry, essays and other feis events for all age levels. Irish soda bread. Food and drink. Celebration of Mass. CONTACT: Bob McHugh, Irish Culture Club of Delaware, P.O. Box 9326, Wilmington, DE 19809. (302) 478-2819.

Florida

SAINT PATRICK'S IRISH FESTIVAL
Pompano Beach Municipal Stadium
1601 N.E. 8th Street
Pompano Beach, FL

Weekend preceding St. Patrick's Day, March 17th. Friday through Sunday. Continuous musical entertainment, including top name folk groups, show bands. Traditional dancers. Bagpipers. Gaelic football game. Irish fashion show. Traditional storytellers. Contests and drawings for prizes. Special entertainment for children. Sponsored by the Irish Cultural Institute of Florida, P.O. Box 541, Deerfield Beach, FL 33441. (305) 429-1542 or (407) 395-3725.

Georgia

ANNUAL CELTIC FESTIVAL
Oglethorpe University Campus
4484 Peachtree Road
Atlanta, GA

Late April. Saturday and Sunday. Instrumentalists, singers, dancers, pipe bands and other performers representing the three major Celtic traditions—Irish, Scottish and Welsh. Exhibits of handmade traditional crafts. Traditional Celtic food on sale. Special entertainment for children, including theatrical presentations of traditional

Celtic folk tales. Celtic Gala featuring folk music and dance held Saturday at 8:00 p.m. CONTACT: A. J. Murray at (404) 429-0107 or Kathy Lane at (404) 873-5621.

Illinois

GAELIC PARK IRISH FESTIVAL
Chicago Gaelic Park
6119 West 147th Street
Tinley Park, IL

Memorial Day weekend, Thursday through Monday. Opening ceremonies are scheduled for 5:00 p.m. Thursday. The festival features big-name Irish popular musicians, singers and groups; step dancers; set (county) dancing and waltz competitions; red-hair and freckled-face contests; ceili performance; pipe bands; seanachies (Irish storytellers). Also: craft demonstrations; crafts and imports on sale; carnival rides, puppet shows and musicians for children; Irish and American food and drink. CONTACT: Frank Bradley, 11516 Burr Oak Lane, Burr Ridge, IL 60525. (312) 246-9596.

IRISH FEST CHICAGO
Downtown on the Lakefront
Chicago, IL

Normally between middle and end of July. Friday afternoon through Sunday. Continuous entertainment by Irish and Irish-American performers, including well-known show bands, traditional groups, etc. Pipe band. Culture booths and heritage center. "Most Freckles" and "Reddest Hair" contests for children. Art exhibit and sale. Irish shopping mall featuring over one dozen Irish import stores. Food and refreshments. Indoor Mass at noon Sunday. Sponsored by Irish Fest Chicago in cooperation with the Office of Tourism, Illinois Department of Commerce and Community Affairs. CONTACT: Mary Cannon at (708) 424-2974.

IRISH FEST ON THE MISSISSIPPI
18th Street and Second Avenue
Rock Island, IL

Late August. Saturday and Sunday. Popular and traditional Irish musical entertainment. Ceili and step dancing. Bagpipers. Riverboat cruise on the Mississippi featuring Irish entertainment and food. 10:30 a.m. Mass on Sunday. Co-sponsored by the St. Patrick's Society of the Quad Cities and Roche's of Ireland. CONTACT: Debra Roche Wehrheim at (319) 359-1750.

TASTE OF IRELAND
Irish American Heritage Center
Chicago, IL

Mid-September, Saturday and Sunday. Big-name popular Irish musicians and singers. Traditional music groups. Irish drama. Continuous ceili dancing and instruction. Step and set (county) dancing. Seanachie (Irish storyteller). Pipe bands. Special entertainment for children. Irish and American food and drink. Irish imports on sale. Fine dining and beverages in the Club Room. CONTACT: Mike Shevlin, 207 Cedar Street, Arlington Heights, IL 60005. (312) 439-9439, or phone the Irish American Heritage Center at (312) 282-7035.

Maryland

BALTIMORE IRISH FESTIVAL
Harborplace Festival Hall
Sharp & Pratt Streets
Baltimore, MD

Mid-September. Friday evening through Sunday. Traditional ceili music and ballad groups. Mid-Atlantic Stepdancing Competition. Irish craftmaking demonstrations. Currach races (traditional boats from the West of Ireland). Irish storyteller. Crafts and imports on sale. Irish food and drink. CONTACT: Phone The Irish Hotline at (301) 747-6868; or Bill McCloskey at home (301) 747-3575, or at work (301) 799-6233.

ANNUAL IRISH DANCE COMPETITION
Glen Echo Park
McArthur Boulevard
Glen Echo, MD

Saturday of Memorial Day weekend. The program for this feis includes competition in traditional dancing and music events as well as selected arts and crafts. CONTACT: Irish Dance Festival of Northern Virginia, c/o Mr. Ben Malcom, P.O. Box 71, Merrifield, VA 22116. (703) 591-5191.

Massachusetts

BILLERICA IRISH AMERICAN FESTIVAL
616 Middlesex Turnpike
Billerica, MA

Third weekend in July. Friday evening through Sunday night. Vocal and instrumental music provided by a full line-up of popular individual performers and groups. Step dancers. Imported Irish merchandise. Irish-style food. Mass at 11 a.m. Sunday. Sponsored by Billerica Irish American Social Club. CONTACT: Phone (508) 663-8230.

Michigan

IRISH FESTIVAL OF DETROIT
Waterfront Plaza (Downtown)
Detroit, MI

Early June, Friday through Sunday. One of a series of ethnic heritage weekends in downtown Detroit. Features celebrity entertainers and groups from Ireland, traditional Irish musicians and step dancers, ceili dancing, movies about Ireland, cultural exhibits, demonstrations of traditional crafts, Irish drama, and a seanachie (Irish storyteller). Irish imports on sale. Irish and American food and drink. CONTACT: Irish Festival of Detroit, Inc., c/o Chris Murray, Chairman. (313) 584-3888.

DETROIT INTERNATIONAL FEIS
Ford Field
Livonia, MI

Early June. A day of competition in traditional Irish music, dancing, oratory, poetry and other events. 1990 marks this festival's

28th year. CONTACT: John Fallon, Feis Chairman, (313) 420-0962.

Minnesota

MINNESOTA IRISH HERITAGE FAIR
St. Paul Civic Center Complex
St. Paul, MN

September or October, Saturday and Sunday. Traditional music, dancing and singing. Dramatic performances. Irish craft demonstrations. Pipe band. Irish imports and gifts on sale. CONTACT: Hibernian Life Insurance, 790 South Cleveland Avenue, Suite 221, St. Paul, MN 55116. (612) 690-3888 or (800) 677-ERIN.

New Jersey

IRISH FESTIVAL
Garden State Arts Center
Holmdel, NJ

Last Sunday in June. One of a series of ethnic festivals held at the Arts Center each year. Opens with a pipe band competition at 9:00 a.m., followed by Mass at 11:00 a.m. The afternoon lineup includes Irish popular music groups, singers, traditional musicians, folk dancers, harpists, step dancers and celebrities. CONTACT: Irish Festival, Garden State Cultural Center Fund, Garden State Parkway, Holmdel, NJ 07733. (201) 888-5000.

IRISH FESTIVAL
Action Park
Vernon, NJ

Late July or early August, Saturday and Sunday. Held under a tent that can accommodate 5,000 people, this festival features Irish show bands and folk singers, Irish dancing, pipe bands, and Irish craftspeople. Irish and American food and drink on sale. CONTACT: Irish Festival, P.O. Box 848, McAfee, NJ 07428. (201) 827-2000.

New York

BUFFALO IRISH FESTIVAL
Weimar's Grove
Broadway and Bowen Roads
Lancaster, NY

Late August, Friday through Sunday. Started in 1983, this festival features traditional Irish entertainment by leading U.S. and Canadian musical groups, ceili and step dancing, singers, free consultation with a specialist in Irish genealogy, a children's entertainment area, food and drink, and booths selling Irish imports. CONTACT: Kevin Townsell, Coordinator, Buffalo Irish Festival, 6861 Main Street, Williamsville, NY 14221. (716) 632-0552.

EAST DURHAM IRISH FESTIVAL
East Durham Irish Cultural Centre
Route 145
East Durham, NY

Memorial Day Weekend. Saturday through Monday. Leading Irish show bands, traditional music groups. Bagpipers. Step dancers. Working craftsmen and artists. Games. Children's entertainment. Imported Irish gifts. Irish food and drink. Mass celebrated at 11 a.m. Sunday. CONTACT: East Durham Irish Festival, c/o Irish Cultural and Sports Centre, P.O. Box 320, East Durham, NY 12423. (518) 634-2286 or (800) LIL-ERIN; or East Durham Vacationland Association, P.O. Box 67, East Durham, NY 12423. (800) 542-2414 ext. 206.

THE GREAT IRISH FAIR
Coney Island (Steeplechase Park)
Brooklyn, NY

First weekend after Labor Day, Saturday and Sunday. A well-attended event cosponsored since 1981 by the Ancient Order of Hibernians and the Brooklyn Borough President's Office. This festival features music, dancing and sports competitions, including show band and traditional Irish music performed by well-known entertainers; step dancing and ceili performances; races in currachs, traditional boats from the West of Ireland; and a Gaelic sports com-

petition matching an Irish championship team with an all-star team
from the New York Gaelic Athletic Association. Also: demonstrations of traditional arts and crafts, sale of Irish imports, games and
rides for children, and Irish-style food and drink. CONTACT:
Mary Henry, 37 Joval Court, Brooklyn, NY 11229. (718) 648-
3931.

INTERNATIONAL CELTIC FESTIVAL
Hunter Mountain
Hunter, NY

Mid-August, Friday through Sunday. A celebration of Irish, Scottish, Welsh and Breton cultures and their common Celtic origins.
Events include pipe band competitions, Highland games, Highland
dancers or step dancers, dancing competitions, singing groups, and
workshops on the Celtic harp and the bagpipe. Irish, Scottish and
Welsh food specialties as well as more standard refreshments. The
festival ends with a parade down the mountain by 400 pipers
a-playing—guaranteed to send chills down your spine. CON-
TACT: Exposition Planners, Bridge Street, Hunter, NY 12442.
(518) 263-3800.

IRISH TRADITIONAL MUSIC FESTIVAL
Snug Harbor Cultural Center
Staten Island, NY

Late June/early July, Saturday or Sunday. A festival highlighting
traditional music, song and dance. Includes performances by big-
name Irish traditional entertainers and others from Ireland and the
United States. Ceili instruction is held throughout the day, both for
beginners and for experienced dancers. Also: workshops in various
instruments (harp, flute, fiddle, tin whistle, and the like) and singing techniques. A children's area offers song, dance and games.
Irish food and drink are on sale, as is Irish-related merchandise. A
ceili follows in the evening. CONTACT: Irish Arts Center, 553
West 51st Street, New York, NY 10019. (212) 757-3318.

LEEDS IRISH FESTIVAL
Leeds, NY

Labor Day weekend, Saturday through Monday. Program highlights include show bands, bagpiping, traditional music and danc-

ing, and children's games. Irish food, drink and imports on sale. CONTACT: Leeds Irish Festival, P.O. Box 6, Leeds, NY 12451. (518) 943-9820 or (518) 943-3736 (after 6 p.m.).

ROCKAWAY IRISH FESTIVAL
Beach 108th and 109th Streets
Rockaway Beach, NY

Late July. Saturday and Sunday. Music by a full array of singers, groups and other entertainers, including prominent Irish and Irish-American performers. Step dancers. New York City Emerald Society pipe bands. Irish arts and crafts. Imports on sale. Food and refreshments on sale. Events held rain or shine. CONTACT: Phone Sheila Hynes at (718) 474-1226 or Adrian Flannelly at (718) 634-4242.

UNITED IRISH COUNTIES ASSOCIATION FEIS
St. Joseph's Seminary
Yonkers, NY

Second Sunday of June. This is one of the nation's largest Irish festivals and—after nearly 60 years—almost certainly its oldest. Some 250 competitions cover such categories as Irish music, harp playing, pipe bands; the Irish language, poetry, oratory; art, Celtic design, and needlecrafts. CONTACT: United Irish Counties Association of New York, 599 Van Cortlandt Park Avenue, Bronx, NY 10705. (914) 476-8569.

Ohio

CLEVELAND'S IRISH CULTURAL FESTIVAL
7863 York Road
Parma, OH

First weekend in August, Friday through Sunday. Features singers, show bands and traditional Irish musical groups; ceili and step dancing exhibitions; Irish drama; Gaelic football and camogie (hurling for women); a seanachie (Irish storyteller); and folklore demonstrations. Also: ceili workshops, demonstrations of traditional arts and crafts, and booths selling Irish imports. Noon Mass on Sun-

day. CONTACT: John O'Brien, Irish Festival Chairman, 14708
Westland Avenue, Cleveland OH 44111. (216) 251-0711.

Pennsylvania

IRISH DAYS
Coal Street Park
Wilkes-Barre, PA

First *full* three-day weekend following July 4th, Friday through
Monday. Entertainment lineup for this weather-sheltered festival
includes show bands and traditional Irish music groups, step and
ceili dancing, pipe bands, a seanachie (Irish storyteller), cultural
exhibits and a children's playland. Also: Irish imports on sale, and
Irish-style food and drink. Mass in Gaelic on Sunday. CONTACT:
George Horn, The Donegal Society of Greater Wilkes-Barre, P.O.
Box 184, Wilkes-Barre, PA 18701. (717) 822-7376.

IRISH FESTIVAL AT MONTAGE MOUNTAIN
Exit 51—Interstate 81
Scranton, PA

Memorial Day weekend, Saturday through Monday. Leading Irish
entertainers: singers, instrumentalists and groups. Step dancers.
Irish imports on sale. Irish food and drink. Gaelic Mass at noon on
Sunday. CONTACT: Irish Cultural Society, P.O. Box 573, Scran-
ton, PA 18501. (717) 961-0143 or (717) 347-4609; or, Montage Ski
Resort, (717) 969-7669.

IRISH JUBILEE AND CELTIC FESTIVAL
Rocky Park Glen
Avoca, PA

Late August, Friday through Sunday. A full schedule of traditional
and popular Irish music, dancing and entertainment. Sunday Mass
in Gaelic. CONTACT: Rocky Park Glen, P.O. Box 37, Avoca,
PA 18641-0037 (717) 457-7401 or (717) 655-5500.

TRADITIONAL IRISH MUSIC AND DANCE FESTIVAL
Fischer's Pool
Lansdale, PA

Mid-September, one day. CONTACT: The Philadelphia Ceili Group, Attn. Robin Cook, Room 2, The Irish Center/Commodore Barry Club, 6815 Emlen Street, Philadelphia, PA 19119. (215) 849-8899.

Rhode Island

IRISH HERITAGE MONTH
Newport, RI

March. A month-long lineup of Irish-related festivities sponsored by the Newport Irish Heritage Committee. Features performances by musicians, dancers and singers; an Irish marketplace, offering imported craft and gift items; special dinner and pub nights; the John J. Jameson's road race; talks by experts on Irish history and culture; and an annual St. Patrick's Day parade on March 17th. CONTACT: For a free Irish Heritage Month calendar and other information, phone the Newport County Convention & Visitors Bureau at (800) 458-4843, toll-free, or (401) 849-8048.

RHODE ISLAND IRISH FESTIVAL
Providence, RI

First weekend in June: Saturday and Sunday. A festival emphasizing traditional Irish music and dance. Features leading traditional instrumentalists and groups playing fiddle, flute, accordion, and uillean pipes. Step dancers. Children's entertainment area. Workshops in traditional dance and instruments. Evening concerts and ceili dance. Irish imports on sale. Craft booths. Food and drink. Co-sponsored by the Providence Ceili Club and the Irish Subcommittee of the Rhode Island Heritage Commission. CONTACT: (401) 274-9804.

Texas

HOUSTON IRISH FOLK FEST
(Location varies)
Houston, TX

Late October, Saturday. Big-name Irish show bands and traditional music groups. Competition in Irish dancing and harp playing. Pipe band. Gaelic sports exhibitions. Cultural exhibits. Children's fair. Irish gifts and crafts on sale. Irish food and drink. Midnight seisun. Co-sponsored by Harris County A.O.H. and the Houston Irish Folk Fest Committee. CONTACT: Patrick Patton, 11422 Cold Spring, Houston, TX 77043. (713) 496-7897.

NORTH TEXAS IRISH FESTIVAL
The Embarcadero and Adjacent Buildings
Fair Park
Dallas, TX

Early March, Saturday and Sunday. An indoor festival featuring "name" Irish entertainers, traditional Irish music groups, step dancing exhibitions, a Texas "Rose of Tralee" competition, Irish stew cook-off, Irish food and drink, and arts and crafts booths. CONTACT: North Texas Irish Festival, P.O. Box 4474, Dallas, TX 75208.

SOUTH TEXAS IRISH FESTIVAL
La Villita Plaza
San Antonio, TX

March, Friday through Sunday, the weekend before St. Patrick's Day. Live Irish music. Step dancing exhibitions. Irish food and drink. CONTACT: Rev. Bill Davis, St. Mary's Church, 202 North St. Mary's Street, San Antonio, TX 78025. (512) 226-8381.

TEXAS FOLKLIFE FESTIVAL
Festival Grounds
Institute of Texan Cultures
San Antonio, TX

First weekend in August, Thursday through Sunday. This festival celebrates many of Texas' ethnic groups, each in a separate area.

The Irish section features a traditional thatched cottage with an exhibit on the Irish cultural heritage of Texas. Also: ceili bands, step dancing performances, a seanachie (Irish storyteller), and bagpipers. Food and refreshments. CONTACT: Patrick Dowd, Harp & Shamrock Society, 19843 Encino Brook, San Antonio, TX 78259. (512) 497-8435.

Wisconsin

IRISH FEST
Henry W. Maier Lakefront Festival Grounds
Milwaukee, WI

Mid–August, Thursday through Sunday. One of the country's biggest Irish events, with an exceptional lineup of Irish bands and entertainers, plus step dancers, Irish drama, children's theater, cultural exhibits, an Irish marketplace, wandering performers, Gaelic football and rugby, parades, and contests, including a bake-off. CONTACT: Irish Fest, Box 599, Milwaukee, WI 53201. (414) 466-6640.

Did You Know . . .

. . . That blue has a better claim to be called Ireland's traditional national color than green! The official color for several centuries was St. Patrick's blue, and one of Ireland's historic flags shows the harp on a blue ground, later changed to green. Green was commonly considered the nation's official color by the 1800s, when it became associated with the nationalist movement in general, and the Catholic majority in particular.

The Green Pages

The Green Pages

AIRLINES—SCHEDULED
SERVICE BETWEEN THE
UNITED STATES AND
IRELAND

**AER LINGUS: IRISH
INTERNATIONAL
AIRLINES
(800) 223-6537; in New York
State, (800) 631-7917**

Regularly scheduled 747 service
connecting New York/Shan-
non/Dublin and Boston/Shan-
non/Dublin. Operates five days
a week from April through
October. In addition, once-
weekly service (Fridays)
connects Chicago (O'Hare
International Airport) and Shan-
non/Dublin from April through
October. Aer Lingus offers special through fares between Ireland and at least 80 U.S. cities
by arrangement with leading
U.S. airlines. It is also seeking
to increase service on at least
some of the routes it now flies,
as well as applying for landing
rights at additional U.S. air-
ports. Phone toll-free for fares,
flight schedules, terms/condi-
tions and other information.

**DELTA AIR LINES
(800) 241-4141**

Delta inaugurated direct flights
between Atlanta International
and Shannon in May 1986.
From two to four wide-body
flights are offered weekly. These
provide direct service between
Atlanta and Shannon, connect-

ing with Dublin without a change of aircraft. Phone toll-free for further information and reservations.

PAN AMERICAN WORLD AIRWAYS
(800) 221-1111

Daily wide-body flights connect New York's JFK International Airport and Shannon. Phone for further information.

ALCOHOLIC BEVERAGES— BEER IMPORTERS

Finding the following Irish brands at a store in your community should be no problem. If you're unable to locate one, however, contact the appropriate importer for the location of your nearest retail dealer.

GUINNESS IMPORT COMPANY
**Six Landmark Plaza
Stamford, CT 06901
(203) 323-3311**

Guinness Stout, Harp Irish Lager, Kaliber Non-Alcoholic Brew, Bass Ale, Guinness Gold (available only in the Northeast United States at present).

CENTURY IMPORTERS
**210 Allegheny Avenue
Baltimore, MD
(301) 296-0010**

Beamish Stout.

ALCOHOLIC BEVERAGES— IRISH WHISKEY AND VODKA IMPORTERS

Note: Several Irish whiskey labels are no longer available: Powers, Murphy's, Dunphy's, Paddy and Tullamore Dew.

BLACK BUSH IMPORT COMPANY
**600 West Main Street
Louisville, KY 40202
(502) 589-5559**

Black Bush Irish Whiskey.

BROWN-FOREMAN COMPANY
**P.O. Box 1080
Louisville, KY 40201
(502) 585-1100**

Old Bushmill's Irish Whiskey.

FEDERAL DISTILLERS
**15 Monsignor O'Brien Highway
Cambridge, MA 02141
(617) 742-9700**

Celtic Vodka.

PARK BENZINGER AND
    COMPANY
70 Grand Avenue
River Edge, NJ 07661
(201) 489-9393

Midleton Very Rare Irish
Whiskey.

JOSEPH SEAGRAM
375 Park Avenue
New York, NY 10152
(212) 572-7000

Jameson Irish Whiskey. Jameson
1780.

ALCOHOLIC BEVERAGES—
LIQUEUR IMPORTERS

PADDINGTON
    CORPORATION
Parker Plaza
Fort Lee, NJ 07024
(201) 592-5700

Bailey's Irish Cream Liqueur.

AGE INTERNATIONAL,
    INC.
36 Main Street
Roslyn, NY 11576
(516) 621-2656

Emmets Cream. Emmets
Bananas 'N Cream.

CAROLANS
50 Charles Lindbergh
    Boulevard
Suite 400
Uniondale, NY 11553
(516) 227-2320

Carolans Cream Liqueur.

HIRAM WALKER
85 North Stemmons
Suite 739
Dallas, TX 75247
(214) 630-3070

Irish Mist liqueur, a blend of
Irish whiskey and honey.

SCHENLEY INDUSTRIES
12770 Merit Drive
Dallas, TX 75247
(214) 233-6165

O'Darby's Irish Cream Liqueur.

ANTIQUITIES, CELTIC—
GENUINE

ERIN RARE COIN
    COMPANY
P.O. Box 170
Merrick, NY 11566
(516) 868-8828

Sells a selection of ancient and
medieval Celtic items excavated
in Ireland and Britain. These
have included flint arrowheads

(pre-Celtic); earthenware urns (circa 300 B.C.–300 A.D.); and medieval jewelry, including bracelets, rings and other silver items. Erin acquires additional items as they become available. Request descriptive literature.

ANTIQUITIES, CELTIC— REPRODUCTIONS

ALL THINGS IRISH, INC.
P.O. Box 94
Glenview, IL 60025
(312) 998-4510

As agent for the Wild Goose Studio, Kinsale, County Cork, this firm sells small sculptures, bas-reliefs, statues and pendants hand-cast from models of medieval Celtic art or interpretations by contemporary artists. Each piece consists of a thick shell cast in bronze, iron or nickel silver and backed by ceramic resin compound. Among the pieces are a 7-inch statue of St. Patrick modeled after a carving on a twelfth-century cross at Kilfenora; a replica of a sixteenth-century lion from Lynch's Castle, Galway; and several Celtic crosses. Request free catalog.

ARTISTS—LANDSCAPES AND OTHER IRISH SUBJECTS

IRISH ARTS
7364 El Dorado Drive
Buena Park, CA 90620
(714) 739-4195

Peter Walsh, the owner, paints in oils, specializing in Irish landscapes. He also represents Edmund Sullivan, the New York–based landscape painter, and Jim Fitzpatrick, who has made his reputation painting Irish historical scenes. Write for descriptive literature, or phone evenings or weekends.

TEERNAHILAN IRISH ARTS
26 Francis Street
Norwalk, CT 06851
(203) 846-1881; (800) 548-8619

Offers limited-edition prints from original paintings of Irish country scenes by Kevin Callahan. Request free color brochure.

THE IRISH SCENE
49 Lantern Circle
Stamford, CT 06905
(203) 322-8211

Offers a set of six prints by Dublin-born Hugh O'Neill. Each depicts in realistic style one of the various types of dwellings found in rural Ireland, but now disappearing as more modern homes are built. These include, for example, the farmer's cottage, the fisherman's cottage, and the "egg house." Prints are 8¼ inches by 11¾ inches, ready to frame, and cost $49.95 per set. Individual oak-framed prints are also available. Request free brochure.

MARY McSWEENEY
P.O. Box 971
Libertyville, IL 60048
(312) 816-7168

A graduate of Cork College of Art, Mary McSweeney draws her subjects from the land and people of Ireland. Her work is available in original oil paintings as well as prints of them. Two of her works have been unveiled at public ceremonies by Irish Prime Minister Charles Haughey. McSweeney accepts commissions to do original paintings. Request free color brochure.

VAL McGANN
Val McGann Studio &
** Gallery**
Route 1, Box 395
Ogunquit, ME 03907
(207) 646-3167

Request free brochure with representative Irish scenes by McGann.

EDMUND SULLIVAN
166 Brookdale Drive
Yonkers, NY 10710
(914) 337-1585

Artist Sullivan offers realistic paintings of Irish landscapes, equestrian scenes and other subjects by Irish and Irish-American artists. For a viewing, phone between 11:00 A.M. and 6:00 P.M. Sullivan also sells his own paintings—both as originals and as numbered prints in limited editions, suitable for framing. Request free color catalog.

FITZPATRICK IRISH BOOK
** & ART GALLERY**
1576 Oakmount Road
South Euclid, OH 44121
(216) 291-2373

Offers a wide selection of fine and graphic art, including oil paintings, watercolors, silkscreen prints, facsimiles, photographs and wall hangings. Request free catalog, which describes some items available.

BAKERIES—SPECIALIZING IN IRISH BREADS AND CAKES
(See also "Food Specialties.")

STAR BAKERY
1701 Church Street
San Francisco, CA 94131
(415) 648-0785

Irish soda bread and other specialties. Open seven days.

KELTIC KRUST
1915 Dorchester Avenue
Dorchester, MA 02122
(617) 265-6488

Bakes a wide variety of Irish breads and cakes. These include soda bread, wheaten bread, fruit soda, crusty loaf, potato loaf, griddle bread, barm bracks, plain scones, fruit scones and apple tarts.

O'BRIEN'S BAKERY
9 Beale Street
Wollaston, MA 02170
(617) 472-4025/4027

Features Irish breads, cakes, cookies and rolls.

THE TRADITIONAL IRISH BAKERY
4268 Katonah Avenue
Bronx, NY 10470
(212) 994-0846

Second location:
4947 Broadway
New York, NY 10034
(212) 567-9415

Sells soda bread, scones, apple tarts, barm brack, Irish sausages, Irish bacon and black pudding. Also: Irish grocery items.

GAELIC IMPORTS
4882 Pearl Road
Cleveland, OH 44109
(216) 398-1548

Sells fresh soda bread, potato bread and scones. Also makes black pudding, white pudding and Irish sausages, and stocks a variety of biscuits, sauces and other imported grocery items.

BANKS, IRISH—OFFICES IN THE UNITED STATES

ALLIED IRISH BANKS, LTD.
U.S. branch offices at:

3 First National Plaza
Suite 4412
Chicago, IL 60602
(312) 630-0044

405 Park Avenue
New York, NY 10022
(212) 223-1230

A full-service commercial bank serving both individuals and businesses. Consumer banking services include checking accounts, money market funds, traveler's checks, international money orders, and changing of money into Irish currency. The New York office also represents the Cayman Islands branch.

BANK OF IRELAND
Branch office at:
640 Fifth Avenue
New York, NY 10019
(212) 397-1700

A full-service commercial bank
catering to both individuals and
corporate customers. Among its
services are traveler's checks,
savings and checking accounts,
international money orders, and
currency exchange.

IBI INTERNATIONAL
  INVESTMENT SERVICES
  LTD.
3 First National Plaza
Suite 1400
Chicago, IL 60602
(312) 419-8224

Investment banking subsidiary
of the Bank of Ireland.

BOOKS—IRISH-LANGUAGE

ALICORN/IRISH BOOKS &
  THINGS
3428 Balboa Street
San Francisco, CA 94118
(415) 751-9129

Books in Irish, both current and
out of print. Also, Irish dictio-
naries, grammars and other
language-learning materials.

IRISH BOOKS AND MEDIA
1433 Franklin Avenue East
Minneapolis, MN 55404-2135
(612) 871-3505

A mail-order service. Stocks a
wide selection of Irish-language
titles, including children's
books, literary classics, dictio-
naries and grammars, and
contemporary fiction. Write
for a free list, enclosing a self-
addressed, stamped envelope.
Sells at wholesale as well as
retail.

IRISH BOOKS AND
  GRAPHICS
90 West Broadway
New York, NY 10007
(212) 962-4237

In addition to its impressive
selection of new and used
English-language books, IB&G
has stocked its smallish shop
with what may be the largest
selection of Irish-language
books on this side of the Atlantic, including adult and children's titles. Request free Irish
title list.

BOOKS—PUBLISHERS &
DISTRIBUTORS
(See also "Genealogical
Resources" and "Directories—
Irish-American.")

**THE DEVIN-ADAIR
  COMPANY, PUBLISHERS**
6 North Water Street
Greenwich, CT 06830
(203) 531-7755

Publishes "Books of Irish Interest," including reprints of out-of-print titles as well as newer works. Among subjects covered are poetry, history, politics, fiction, travel, culture, customs and folklore. Request free copy of their descriptive price list.

GREENWOOD PRESS
88 Post Road West
P.O. Box 5007
Westport, CT 06881
(203) 226-3571

Among the 600 books GP issues each year is a small but growing number of Irish-related reference works. These include *Irish-American Voluntary Organizations* (1983), edited by Michael Funchion; *Irish Research: A Guide to Collections in North America, Ireland and Great Britain,* edited by DeeGee Lester; *A Companion to Joyce Studies* (1984), edited by Zack R. Bowen and James F. Carens; *Dictionary of Irish Literature* (1979), Robert Hogan, Editor-in-Chief; *Hibernia America: The Irish and Regional Cultures,* by Dennis Clark; and *Sean O'Casey's Autobiographies: An Annotated Index* (1983), by Rob-

ert G. Lowery. Request free catalog or descriptive literature.

PROSCENIUM PRESS
P.O. Box 361
Newark, DE 19715
(302) 255-4083

In addition to *The Journal of Irish Literature,* Proscenium publishes books of Irish fiction, poetry collections and full-length plays by Irish and Irish-American writers. Request publication price list.

**QUINLIN, CAMPBELL
  PUBLISHERS**
P.O. Box 651
Boston, MA 02134
(617) 296-4306

Publishes or distributes about 40 titles on Irish history, politics and nationalism, and women's studies—as well as such topical works as *Guide to the New England Irish,* which is updated about every two years. Also sells Irish records. Request free descriptive brochures.

**CATHOLIC UNIVERSITY
  OF AMERICA PRESS**
P.O. Box 4852
Hampden Station
Baltimore, MD 21211
(301) 338-6953

Publishes "Reprints in Irish History"—important works previously out of print. Request free catalog.

LONGWOOD PUBLISHING GROUP, INC.
27 South Main Street
Wolfeboro, NH 03894-2069
(603) 569-4576/4577

Distributes a variety of books on Irish subjects from Irish and British publishers, including The Educational Company of Ireland and Caliban Books. Some titles are scholarly, others are aimed at general readers.

HUMANITIES PRESS INTERNATIONAL
171 First Avenue
Atlantic Highlands, NJ 07716-1289
(201) 872-1441; (800) 221-3845

HPI's Irish Studies series includes titles in history, poetry, drama, literature, literary criticism and other categories. Request free catalog(s) covering history and/or literature.

CAMBRIDGE UNIVERSITY PRESS
32 East 57th Street
New York, NY 10022
(212) 688-8885

Publishes a growing list of books on Irish subjects, particularly history, biography, litera-

ture and criticism. Request free catalog(s).

SYRACUSE UNIVERSITY PRESS
1600 Jamesville Avenue
Syracuse, NY 13210
(315) 423-2596

SUP's Irish Studies series includes books on literary history and criticism, politics, history, and biography. Request brochure.

WAKE FOREST UNIVERSITY PRESS
Box 7333
Winston-Salem, NC 27109
(919) 724-3750

Irish-related books are chiefly poetry and literary criticism. Request free catalog.

BOOKS—RETAIL STORES AND MAIL-ORDER SERVICES

IRISH BOOKS
P.O. Box 2388
Dublin, CA 94568-9991

Write for catalog.

THE IRISH IMPORT SHOP
738 North Vine Street
Hollywood, CA 90004
(213) 467-6714

Contact for information about books in stock.

ALICORN/IRISH BOOKS & THINGS
3428 Balboa Street
San Francisco, CA 94121
(415) 221-5522

Books of Irish interest: new, used and out of print. Includes texts and tapes for language instruction, cookbooks, and genealogical material, as well as books on various cultural and historical topics. Also: Irish records and books about other Celtic nations. Request free catalog.

IRISH CASTLE GIFT SHOP
2123 Market Street
San Francisco, CA 94114
(415) IRISH 32

Carries a large selection of books on Irish and Irish-American subjects. Contact for details.

GUILD BOOKS
2456 North Lincoln Avenue
Chicago, IL 60614
(312) 525-3667

Perhaps the largest, most diverse selection of Irish literature, history and music in Chicago, including many imported items.

CONNOLLY BOOKS
Books of Irish Interest
P.O. Box 24744

Detroit, MI 48224
(313) 885-5618

Offers a mail-order selection of books on Ireland and Irish-related subjects. Most titles are politically oriented. Request catalog.

IRISH BOOKS AND MEDIA
1433 Franklin Avenue East
Minneapolis, MN 55404-2135
(612) 871-3505

This mail-order book service is "the largest supplier of books on Ireland in the United States, and a distributor for all major Irish publishing houses." Request catalog(s).

RUANE'S IRISH BOOK SHOP
239 South First Street
Hammonton, NJ 08037
(609) 561-7733

Current books from U.S. and Irish publishers on "nearly any subject dealing with Ireland, the Irish and Irish America." Also offers free book search service. Request free catalog.

BOOKS BRITAIN
2170 Broadway
New York, NY 10024
(212) 749-4713

Sells a wide selection of books of Irish interest, both at retail and wholesale. Request free catalog. Write or phone only.

IRISH BOOKS AND GRAPHICS
90 West Broadway
New York, NY 10007
(212) 962-4237

Stocks new and backlist works as well as out-of-print titles. In addition to English-language materials, IB&G carries a large number of Irish-language books for adults and children.

CELTIC HERITAGE BOOKS
59-10 Queens Boulevard, #9B
Woodside, NY 11377
(718) 478-8162

Books from Irish, British and U.S. publishers on various Celtic nations and their cultures: Irish, Scottish, Welsh, Manx and Breton. Categories covered include archaeology, art, history, literature, music and children's literature. Also: maps and cut-out models. Request free catalog.

FITZPATRICK'S IRISH BOOK & ART GALLERY
1576 Oakmount Avenue
South Euclid, OH 44121
(216) 291-2373

Stocks books from U.S. and foreign publishers on nearly

all aspects of Irish and Irish-American history and culture. Request free catalog, which includes video titles as well.

DUFOUR EDITIONS, INC.
Box 449
Chester Springs, PA 19425
(215) 458-5005

Sells by mail only the large list of Irish-related books it distributes or publishes. Its selection includes history, literature, criticism, philosophy, music, art, social sciences, politics, biography, folklore, and more. Sells both at retail and wholesale. Request free catalog.

BOOKS—SPECIALISTS IN OUT-OF-PRINT, USED, RARE AND ANTIQUARIAN TITLES

ALICORN/IRISH BOOKS & THINGS
3428 Balboa Street
San Francisco, CA 94121
(415) 221-5522

Books of Irish interest: new, used and out of print.

MURPHY BROOKFIELD BOOKS
219 North Gilbert
Iowa City, IA 52245
(319) 338-3077

History and literature. Write or phone for information.

STEPHEN GRIFFIN
9 Irvington Road
Medford, MA 02155
(617) 396-8440

Irish books bought and sold: new, used and out of print; English- and Irish-language items. Request free catalog.

IRISH BOOKS AND
**   GRAPHICS**
90 West Broadway
New York NY 10007
(212) 962-4237

HELEN HARTE,
**   BOOKSELLER**
6525 51st Avenue, N.E.
Seattle, WA 98115
(206) 526-5284

Books from, and about, Ireland and Irish America, including history, literature, biography and travel. Request free catalog. Vistors welcome by appointment.

CALENDARS AND
APPOINTMENT BOOKS

Most of the bookshops and mail-order sources previously listed also offer a selection of calendars and appointment books produced in Ireland or by Irish-American organizations. Also check, in particular:

IRISH CASTLE GIFT SHOP
2123 Market Street
San Francisco, CA 94114
(415) IRISH 32

GATEWAY
Box 403
Greenwich, CT 06830-0403
(203) 531-7400

Offers a variety of Irish calendars, including *Beautiful Ireland*. Request free color catalog, *Best of Ireland*.

IRISH BOOKS AND MEDIA
1433 Franklin Avenue East
Minneapolis, MN 55404-2135
(612) 871-3505

Write for information in the fall, when Irish Books and Media begins stocking several Irish- and American-produced calendars for the coming year.

CELTIC LEAGUE
**   AMERICAN BRANCH**
2973 Valentine Avenue
Bronx, NY 10458

A calendar based on the traditional Celtic year that celebrates not only the holidays and heritage of the Irish, but those of their sister Celtic nations, the Scots, Manx, Cornish, Welsh and Bretons. Illustrated with drawings in the traditional Celtic style. Send $6 per calendar.

IRISH BOOKS AND
    GRAPHICS
90 West Broadway
New York, NY 10007
(212) 962-4237

As the old year wanes and the
new one begins, you'll find several calendars of Irish and Celtic
interest in this singular book-
store. Request a copy of IB&G's
Book News.

CALLIGRAPHY AND GRAPHIC DESIGN—CELTIC STYLE

Celtic-style hand lettering and
decoration by a professional can
add special touches to invitations, announcements, posters
and other printed material. The
following is a selection of
sources who can provide one or
both services. We suggest you
request samples of their work:

CALLIGRAPHIC DESIGN
    STUDIO
10141 South Kedvale
Oak Lawn, IL 60453
(312) 425-9348

Celtic-style hand-lettering for
your posters, invitations,
announcements and other
graphic decoration needs.

GALLOWGLASS
    COMMERCIAL ART

4 Greenlay
Nashua, NH 03063
(603) 880-3706

Celtic-style calligraphy and
graphic design for invitations,
posters, album covers, publication mastheads and organiza-
tional logos. Arthur Ketchen,
the owner, also teaches at
nearby schools, and privately by
appointment. Request free brochure and samples.

CELTIC FOLKWORKS
RD #4, Box 210
Willow Grove Road
Newfield, NJ 08344
(609) 691-5968

Custom design of various items
using traditional Celtic motifs:
wall hangings, stationery, note
cards. Also stocks a variety of
ready-made items as well as
books on Celtic subjects. Send
$1 for catalog.

LISTOWEL CELTIC ART
3217 Beacon Hill Avenue
Pittsburgh, PA 15216

Sells full-color hand renderings
of individual letters of the alpha-
bet, each ornamented with
zoomorphic and other traditional Celtic designs. Renderings
come on quality stock, 8 inches
by 10 inches, suitable for framing. Send $50 check or money

order plus $3 postage and handling.

CEMETERY MONUMENTS—IMPORTED—TRADITIONAL

IRISH ART INDUSTRIES OF AMERICA
1921 Bellaire Avenue
Royal Oak, MI 48067
(313) 399-8804

Irish stonemasons began carving the famous high crosses of Ireland over 1,000 years ago. Today IAI carries on this tradition, employing master stone-carvers at Durrow, County Laois, to produce cemetery monuments reminiscent of the great Celtic high crosses.

Three standard crosses are available—each in three sizes, mounted on a pedestal that can be suitably inscribed. The face of the cross may be ordered with ivy leaf, shamrock or interlace pattern. IAI also offers a contemporary memorial that combines a rectangular stone with a Celtic cross carved adjacent, and a flat marker stone inspired by the Celtic grave slabs at the monastery of Clonmacnois. Monuments may also be custom-carved to your order. Request free color brochure.

CHARITABLE ORGANIZATIONS—GRANT-MAKING

FOUNDATIONS (See also "Industrial Development in Ireland—Programs to Assist.")

FUND FOR RECONCILIATION IN NORTHERN IRELAND
c/o National Conference of Catholic Bishops
3211 4th Street, N.E.
Washington, DC 20017-1194
(202) 541-3000

This fund, established by the NCCB in cooperation with the Irish Episcopal Conference, provides money to existing organizations working to help improve the human climate in Northern Ireland. The emphasis is on programs that promote inter-religious human relations and reconciliation of traditionally hostile groups. Contributions are tax-deductible, and checks or money orders should be made payable to "NCCB Fund for Reconciliation."

THE AMERICAN IRELAND FUND
Attn.: William J. McNally
Executive Director
150 Federal Street
25th Floor
Boston, MA 02110
(617) 951-8547

The AIF, the nation's largest Irish-related charitable organization, has supported over 1,000 charities and cultural projects of all types throughout Ireland, North and South. At the present time, however, it is concentrating its efforts on helping "find an alternative to the painful struggle going on in Ireland."

As a nonpolitical, nonsectarian foundation, the AIF seeks to help children and others affected by the agony of Ireland's unrest. It supports projects that work on a small, local level, and encourages self-help and community involvement. One organization it has aided is the Northern Ireland Children's Holiday program, which provides opportunities for Catholic and Protestant young people from strife-torn areas to interact in a safe and nonthreatening environment. The children's holidays are designed to emphasize reconciliation. When they are over, they are followed up with a series of weekend youth leadership workshops. The Fund also provides assistance to groups that serve children, the elderly, the injured and the unemployed, among others.

With a membership that encompasses all parts of the United States and Ireland, the AIF holds fund-raising events throughout the country. All contributions are tax-deductible,

and, depending on their level, entitle the donor to a variety of membership benefits. You can join the Ambassador's Circle with an annual contribution of $5,000, the National Committee for $1,000, and the Regular membership for $200. In fact, a contribution in any amount up to $200 entitles you to receive regular mailings about the work of the Fund, and invitations to regional events. Write for further details, or send your check made out to "The American-Ireland Fund."

CHARITABLE ORGANIZATIONS— MISCELLANEOUS

Among the charities, those involved in aiding victims of "The Troubles" in Northern Ireland do so without taking sides in the conflict. Contributions are tax-deductible under U.S. law.

IRISH CHILDREN'S FUND
c/o Joe and Pat Fortune
784 Spring Road
Elmhurst, IL 60126
(312) 833-1910

Since the early 1980s, ICF has been bringing 11- and 12-year-old boys and girls—Catholic and Protestant—from Northern

Ireland to the Chicago area for six-week stays with local families. After the children return home, the program works to follow up with them in an effort to reinforce healthy values and attitudes that will work against the prevailing cycle of bitterness and hatred. Please make checks, which are tax-deductible, payable to "Irish Children's Fund."

THE IRISH WAY
Irish American Cultural
  Institute
Mail 5026
2115 Summit Avenue
College of St. Thomas
St. Paul, MN 55105
(612) 647-5678

IACI welcomes contributions to help it finance The Irish Way program, which sends American high-school students to Ireland each summer to experience Irish life and culture first-hand. Information on the program will be sent to you on request, or see description under "Travel to Ireland—Student Travel and Travel/Study Programs."

TREES FOR IRELAND
Irish American Cultural
  Institute

Mail 5026
2115 Summit Avenue
College of St. Thomas
St. Paul, MN 55105
(612) 647-5678

For a $10 donation—tax deductible—you can aid the Irish government's reforestation program and have a tree planted in any county of the republic. For $50, six trees will be planted in the name(s) of any one person, or couple, in the county you specify. The name(s) in which each donation is made—whether your own, a friend's or a relative's—will be recorded in the local register of the Forestry and Wildlife Service, and a certificate will be issued and sent to you by the IACI's Trees for Ireland program. Contact IACI for details.

PROJECT CHILDREN
c/o Gaelic Cultural Society
P.O. Box 933-L
Greenwood Lake, NY 10925
(914) 477-3472

This organization brings Protestant and Catholic children from Northern Ireland to the United States each summer for a six-week vacation. Since 1975, nearly 3,000 Irish children have been guests of American families under this program. Donations are tax deductible; checks should be payable to "Project Children."

THE UNITED IRISH FOUNDATION, INC.
319 West 48th Street
New York, NY 10036
(212) 581-1619

A nonmember agency under The United Way. Aids elderly and needy residents of New York City—of Irish and other heritages—through counseling services and referrals to appropriate government agencies and nonprofit organizations.

CHINA—IMPORTED

Most Irish import shops stock some Irish chinaware. The following sources specialize in these products or represent the Irish manufacturers:

ROYAL TARA CHINA
P.O. Box 341
Kearny, NJ 07032
(201) 997-1059

Royal Tara fine bone china, handmade in county Galway, is available at selected Irish import stores and gift shops in the United States. Write for a free catalog sheet and addresses of local dealers.

THE BELLEEK COLLECTORS' SOCIETY
2 Cranberry Road
Parsippany, NJ 07054
(201) 316-0299

For generations, Belleek china has been not only a popular, prestigious giftware, but has attracted avid collectors. The Collectors' Society serves a growing number of enthusiasts —now 3,500 in the United States—by informing them of newly issued Belleek items, product revivals, and retirements in the current product line. Other benefits include (1) a special new-member presentation package, (2) a four-color periodical, (3) chances to acquire special limited editions, (4) local chapter events, and (5) Belleek's annual Collectors' Tour of Ireland and the Belleek Pottery. Request further information.

BELLEEK IRELAND, INC.
2 Cranberry Road
P.O. Box 6112
Parsippany, NJ 07054
(201) 316-0299

Belleek, the classic Irish porcelain chinaware, has 2,000 dealers throughout the United States. Its U.S. headquarters will be pleased to refer you to dealers in your area, and will also send you literature about Belleek products.

IRISH DRESDEN, LTD.
c/o Ebeling and Reuss
 Company
P.O. Box 189
477 North Lewis Road
Royersford, PA 19468
(215) 948-4255

This is the U.S. distributor for Irish Dresden, Ltd., makers of porcelain figurines. They don't sell directly to individuals, but will refer you to local dealers.

COINS, IRISH—DEALERS

ERIN RARE COIN
 COMPANY
P.O. Box 170
Merrick, NY 11566
(516) 868-8828

Deals in Irish coins minted from 995 A.D. to the present. Normally stocks proof sets of all coins issued since the Irish Free State started minting coins in 1928. Also carries commemorative medals, trade tokens and paper money issued during the last two to three centuries. Will send items to you on approval. That is, you examine them, decide which you wish to buy—

if any—and return the remainder undamaged along with payment for those you keep. Request free descriptive price list.

CORPORATIONS (U.S.)
OPERATING IN IRELAND

UNIWORLD BUSINESS
 PUBLICATIONS, INC.
50 East 42nd Street
New York, NY 10017
(212) 697-4999

Publishes *The Directory of American Firms Operating in Foreign Countries,* which includes a listing of U.S. businesses with offices, factories or other operations in Ireland. Updated regularly, the directory may be ordered from Uniworld or used without charge at many public, corporate and college libraries.

CRAFTS AND CRAFTSPEOPLE
—TRADITIONAL (See also "Needlecrafts—Traditional" and "Musical Instruments, Traditional—Sources.")

LONG SHOTS
809 North Lafayette Park
 Place
Los Angeles, CA 90026
(213) 413-1374

Traditional Irish fabrics, designed and woven by Eileen

O'Dwyer using centuries-old techniques. To assure authenticity, Ms. O'Dwyer—a UCLA graduate in Ethnic Arts specializing in folklife studies—researches each new project. In addition to looming tweeds and other fabrics, she makes crios (belts) and spins some of her own thread and yarn, dyeing them with either vegetable or synthetic dyes. Ms. O'Dwyer also fills orders for customized items, exhibits her work, and gives public demonstrations of her crafts.

LENORE KEANE
8420 South Kenneth Avenue
Chicago, IL 60652
(312) 582-3097

Trained in Ireland, Ms. Keane is a skilled maker of Carrickmacross lace, Limerick lace, traditional Irish crochet items and Mount Mellick embroidery. Though she does not make items for sale, she does teach, demonstrate and exhibit throughout the United States.

CELTIC FOLKWORKS
RD #4, Box 210
Willow Grove Road
Newfield, NJ 08344
(609) 691-5968

Hand-etched silver earrings, brooches and bracelets incorporating serpentine, interlace, zoomorphic and other traditional Celtic motifs. (Some items are also available in gold.) Also, sterling silver pendant necklaces and brooches made in Dublin, in interlace patterns and other designs taken from the *Book of Kells;* torcs and penannular brooches combining silver and bronze; and silk scarves featuring Celtic designs. Send $1 for catalog.

SIMON PEARCE GLASS
Quechee, VT 05059
(802) 295-2711

County Cork–born Simon Pearce was surprised to find several years ago that no one was still making Irish glassware using traditional styles, materials and techniques. So he came to the United States and set up an authentic traditional glass mill in Vermont. Here you can watch lead-glass items being hand-blown and -worked: everything from pitchers, wine glasses and tumblers to bowls, vases and candlesticks. The designs are simple yet elegant, and authentic. You can also enjoy a traditional Irish meal in the mill's own restaurant. Send $2 for catalog, which also includes traditional clay dinnerware handmade in Ireland by the potteries of Simon's father and brother.

CELTIC SWAN FORGE
P.O. Box 123
Freeland, WA 98249
(206) 221-8734

The ancient Celts were known for their jewelry and metal-work. Splendidly worked items of precious metal or bronze sometimes served practical purposes as well, such as fastening clothing. Celtic Swan Forge recreates these items today, hand-forging and -working each so that no two are exactly alike. Among the items they make are Celtic-inspired torcs, or neck rings; lyre-shaped penannular brooches, which are attractive fasteners for scarves, shawls and sweaters; shawl straight pins; bracelets; sleying hooks for weavers; crochet hooks; and threading hooks for spinners. Some items can be ordered in bronze, some in .999 pure silver, and some in either metal. Write or call for free descriptive literature and price list.

CRYSTAL AND GLASS—IMPORTED (See also "Crafts and Craftspeople—Traditional.")

Most Irish import shops carry at least some of the famous crystal ware of Ireland. The following specialize in these products:

IRISH CRYSTAL COMPANY
1815 East Thousand Oaks Boulevard
Thousand Oaks, CA 91360
(805) 496-8363

Sells Tyrone Crystal exclusively, at discounted prices.

IRISH TREASURE TROVE LTD.
17W424 22nd Street
Oakbrook Terrace, IL 60181
(312) 530-2522

Stocks Waterford's entire line of crystal items. Request free catalog.

IRISH CRYSTAL OF CHICAGO
815 East Nerge Road
Roselle, IL 60172
(312) 351-3722

A shop dealing exclusively in Tyrone Crystal. Claims to be "the only factory-direct warehouse in the U.S.A.," offering "50-percent savings and more." Stocks over 300 items. Specializes in custom pieces and hand-engraving of trophies, business gifts and presentation awards.

WARD'S
24-26 High Street
Medford, MA 02155
(617) 395-4099/2420

Stocks Waterford and Galway Crystal.

GALWAY CRYSTAL
83 Flagship Drive
North Andover, MA 01845
(508) 688-3376

U.S. headquarters for Galway
Crystal. Request location of
dealer(s) near you.

WATERFORD CRYSTAL,
   INC.
1330 Campus Parkway
Wall, NJ 07719
(201) 938-5800

Waterford's U.S. headquarters
will send you information on
their famous crystal products
and provide the names of
dealers in your area.

IRISH CRYSTAL
   COMPANY, INC.
7 Main Street (Route 25A)
Cold Spring Harbor, NY
   11724
(516) 367-6394

Stocks Tyrone Crystal exclusively. Fully leaded superior
crystal in stemware, decanters,
bowls, vases, accessory pieces,
and more. Request free catalog,
which shows full line.

CLARINBRIDGE CRYSTAL
c/o Paul Secon
301 East 53rd Street
New York, NY 10022
(212) 505-1363

Clarinbridge Crystal is a fully
leaded, hand-blown, hand-cut
product available in stemware,
giftware and accessory items.
Request their free catalog and
the location of dealer(s) near
you.

ST. BRENDAN'S CROSSING
Station Square Shops, #7
Pittsburgh, PA 15219
(402) 471-0700

Carries full line of Cavan Crystal. Ask to be put on their mailing list.

CAVAN CRYSTAL
c/o Ebeling and Reuss
   Company
P.O. Box 189
477 North Lewis Road
Royersford, PA 19469
(215) 948-4255

U.S. distributor for Cavan
Crystal, a line of hand-blown,
hand-cut and fully leaded items,
including giftware, stemware
and accessories. Ask for location
of retailer(s) near you.

IRISH CRYSTAL COMPANY
4046 Westheimer
Highland Village
Houston, TX 77027
(713) 963-0550

Offers Tyrone Crystal's full
line. Request free catalog.

DANCING, TRADITIONAL—INSTRUCTION

Irish dancing schools aren't usually located in a fixed place. Instead, instructors—often national or world champions in one or more events—typically rent rooms at schools or commercial dance studios. Many teach in different locations, even different states, on different days or evenings, permitting them to "bring the school to their students." Look for notices or advertisements in Irish-American newspapers that cover your area, or check with local Irish-American organizations to find out about local dancing schools.

DANCING, TRADITIONAL—SUPPLIES

IRISH TREASURES
P.O. Box 5449
Mill Valley, CA 94942
(415) 388-5024

Imports shoes for ceili and step dancing, poodle socks, Tara brooches, lace collars, and headbands. Contact for prices and other details.

DIRECTORIES (See also "Irish Studies—Resources.")

GREENWOOD PRESS
88 Post Road West

P.O. Box 5007
Westport, CT 06881
(203) 226-3571

Irish American Voluntary Organizations (1983), edited by Professor Michael Funchion, is the single best source on Irish-American (including Scots-Irish) organizations of every type. Groups covered—active and defunct, national as well as notable local organizations—include charitable, fraternal, social, nationalist, cultural, religious and educational groups. The history, objectives and activities of each are covered in detail. Cost: $45. Request brochure.

DOLLS AND TOYS—IMPORTED

IRISH IMPORTS, LTD.
1735 Massachusetts Avenue
Cambridge, MA 02138
(617) 354-2511

Miniature (7-inch) lambs and rams handmade with real wool in Mayo. Contact for prices and details.

THE IRISH TINKER SHOP
Seaport Mall
59 West Front Street
Keyport, NJ 07735
(201) 888-8399

Sells handmade, thatched-roof dollhouses, with two rooms,

modeled on an Irish country cottage. Cost: $125. Request details.

TULLYCROSS
602 South Hancock Street
Philadelphia, PA 19147
(215) 925-1995

Offers several handmade Irish-character dolls as well as hand-made dolls with porcelain faces. Request free catalog.

NUN-STALGIA
P.O. Box 1167
Midlothian, VA 23113
(804) 379-4050

Offers "the genuine Nun Doll," an 18-inch heirloom-quality doll crafted in meticulous detail. Available in the traditional habits of 33 different orders (Dominican, Franciscan, Sisters of Mercy, etc.), including all of those active in Ireland. Can also be customized for any order that may not now be in the collection. Price: $139.99. Request free color brochure depicting all standard dolls.

DRAMA GROUPS—IRISH THEATER

Many of the great plays of Irish masters such as Shaw, Synge, Yeats and Wilde—and more recent playwrights—are performed throughout the country by amateur companies that devote themselves to keeping alive the Irish repertory. With very few exceptions, they do not have their own permanent theaters. To keep up with the schedule of performances in your city or region, we suggest you follow the advertisements and announcements in one or more appropriate Irish-American newspapers. (See "Newspapers—Irish-American.")

ENTERTAINMENT— BOOKINGS

The Irish-American newspapers listed elsewhere in these pages run many advertisements by singers, instrumentalists and groups specializing in Irish entertainment. You may also wish to contact one of the booking agencies that follow and discuss the type of entertainment you're interested in.

IRISH PROMOTIONS, INC.
P.O. Box 1308
Dedham, MA 02026
(617) 484-2275 or 326-5017

Specializes in booking traditional Irish dancers, singers and instrumentalists for functions in the New England states.

GALLOWGLASS MUSIC AGENCY
4 Greenlay
Nashua, NH 03063
(603) 800-3706

Represents traditional musicians, including *sean nos* (old style) singers, step dancers and instrumental groups as well as pipers, harpists, fiddlers and other soloists. Request free brochure and/or demonstration tape(s).

ACE ENTERTAINMENT
600 Palisades Avenue
Englewood Cliffs, NJ 07632
(201) 871-4776; (212) 586-7880

Books a variety of Irish talent for functions nationwide, including bands, step dancers, instrumentalists, comedians and singers.

BLARNEY PROMOTIONS
c/o Tom O'Donoghue
30 Grant Avenue
Pittsburgh, PA 15223
(412) 781-1666

Handles bookings throughout the United States for leading entertainers from Ireland, including comedians, singing and instrumental groups, and individual performers.

EVENTS, CALENDARS OF— IRISH-AMERICAN

Several Irish-American newspapers (See "Newspapers— Irish-American") regularly publish schedules of forthcoming events, including meetings of Irish-American organizations, entertainment events and other happenings of special interest to Irish-Americans in the states these newspapers serve:

THE IRISH AMERICAN PRESS
Marina del Rey, CA

THE IRISHMAN
San Francisco, CA

IRISH AMERICAN NEWS
Chicago, IL

THE IRISH STAR
Boston, MA

THE IRISH ECHO
New York, NY

THE IRISH EDITION
Philadelphia, PA

Depending on where you live, the following publications and services may be helpful:

**SOUTHERN CALIFORNIA
 IRISH CALENDAR**
c/o Dennis Doyle
1135 Norton Avenue
Glendale, CA 91202
(818) 956-1311

Monthly. Subscriptions: $12/yr.

**THE IRISH INFORMATION
 SERVICE**
Baltimore, MD/Washington,
 DC Metro Area
(301) 747-6868

This telephone recording lists
upcoming Irish events in the
Greater Baltimore and Washington areas. A new tape is produced each week.

**IRISH EVENTS
 NEWSLETTER**
c/o EIRE (Emerald Isle
 Renaissant Enthusiasts)
5420 Acorn
Houston, TX 77092

This newsletter, covering events
in the Houston area, is available
free with membership in EIRE.
Membership dues are $5/yr. for
individuals, $10 for families.

THE CEILI
c/o Southwest Celtic Music
 Association
P.O. Box 4474
Dallas, TX 75208

Bimonthly. Devoted to music
of Ireland and the other Celtic

nations, particularly to performances and festivals in Texas
and adjacent states. Includes features, news stories and details of
forthcoming events, including
listings of Celtic music programs on radio. Subscription
comes with SCMA membership, at $25/yr.

THE GUARDIAN
5747 Spring Moon
San Antonio, TX 78247
(512) 656-2666

Bimonthly. Covers Irish events
throughout Texas as well as
major events in such neighboring states as Louisiana, Oklahoma, New Mexico, Arizona
and Nevada. Subscription: $12/
yr.

**AN NUAIDEACT (THE
 NEWS)**
c/o Mr. Coilin Owens, Editor
6008 Waynesboro Circle
Springfield, VA 22150
(703) 971-4265

Published four to six times a
year, this newsletter covers Irish
activities, events and organizations in Washington, DC, and
suburban Maryland/Virginia.
Subscription is included with
Gaelic League of Washington
(GLW) membership, at $10/yr.

EXPORTS, IRISH— INFORMATION

The Irish Export Board is the Irish government's agency for export promotion. From its principal North American office in New York, an office in Chicago, and associate firms in Atlanta, Boston and San Francisco, the board provides a comprehensive range of marketing services to Ireland's exporters as well as to potential U.S. importers of their products.

Staff marketing executives provide specialist consulting in consumer and industrial products and internationally traded services. They work with exporters to insure product development and merchandising that reflects the tastes and needs of the American buying public.

The board's communications and promotions executives work closely with U.S. retailers on special events and merchandising support for Irish products. A network of nearly 400 retail stores in every region of the United States specialize in the selling of fine products from Ireland. The Irish Export Board maintains a close association with these retailers, and advises interested merchants on the setting up of such specialty ventures. Trade inquiries may be directed to the following offices:

IRISH EXPORT BOARD
North American
Headquarters
320 Park Avenue
New York, NY 10022
(212) 371-3600

IRISH EXPORT BOARD
75 East Wacker Drive
Suite 600
Chicago, IL 60601
(312) 236-0001

FAMILY-NAME ITEMS

PATRICK MANGAN
37 Westbrook Road
West Hartford, CT
(203) 561-1862

Mangan will hand-paint the coat of arms associated with your Irish family name, mounting a painted copper shield on a mahogany base. You may order your wall shield in any of several styles and sizes. Allow four to six weeks for delivery. A $10 deposit, payable when you order, will be refunded if no arms can be found for your name. Request descriptive literature.

ANNIE'S ATTIC
P.O. Box 755
Freeland, MI 48623
(517) 695-2733

Sells kits for making counted-cross-stitch coats of arms "for most Irish names." Delivery in six to eight weeks. Price: $20.45, including shipping.

B/C CRESTS
100 West Emerson Street
West St. Paul, MN 55118
(612) 457-9224

Offers buttons ($2), key chains ($4) and "parchment" scrolls ($6) bearing the coats of arms associated with some 500 Irish family names. Prices include mailing. Send family name and any necessary explanation.

ANN CESTREE
INNOVATIONS
210 Tavistock
Condominiums
Cherry Hill, NJ 08034
(609) 428-0556

Offers a variety of items bearing coats of arms of Irish families, including stationery, scrolls, bookplates, jewelry, plaques, ashtrays and mugs. Specimen set of stationery with arms: $2 postpaid.

PLANXTY PRODUCTIONS
376 North Fullerton
Avenue
Montclair, NJ 07043
(201) 783-5870 after 6:00 p.m.
for information and credit-card orders.

Centuries ago, wandering Irish musicians composed special tunes as gifts for their patrons and friends. The recipient's family name was included in the title, and henceforth the tune was associated with that surname. Many a *planxty,* as the melodies were called, has been preserved—and many Irish surnames have their very own.

Planxty Productions offers a three-in-one package for each family name it has a planxty for: a transcription of the music on "parchment" decorated with Celtic-style art, and framed in a deep-green and gold mat; an audiocassette recording of the melody by an outstanding traditional musician; and the story behind your family's planxty. The items come in an attractive presentation folder. Each planxty package costs $42.40 postpaid, plus $2.42 tax for New Jersey residents. Write or phone to find out if a planxty is available for the name of your choice.

FARNAN JEWELERS
105 North Wayne Avenue
Wayne, PA 19087
(215) 687-1232

Offers 14-carat gold family crest rings engraved to order with the arms associated with your family name. You may bring or mail a picture of the arms you wish engraved, or have Farnan see if there is one for your name in its reference books.

FASHIONS, IRISH—IMPORTED (See also "Lace—Irish" and "Woolens—Imported.")

THE IRISH SHOP
334 2nd Street
Eureka, CA 95501
(707) 443-8343

Imported clothing for men, women and children: hand-knit sweaters (Aran, mohair, lambswool and linen), capes, shawls, skirts, caps, hats, ties, plaid kilts, and men's Donegal tweed jackets. Also: bedspreads, blankets, throws, and table linen.

THE IRISH SHOP OF MENDOCINO

45090 Main Street
P.O. Box 1636
Mendocino, CA 95460
(707) 937-3133

See preceding entry.

TIPPERARY FINE IRISH IMPORTS
5510 College Avenue
Oakland, CA 94618
(415) 428-9222

Emphasizes traditional items, including Aran sweaters, capes, shawls, scarves, caps, ties, Donegal tweed hats, and mohair and wool blankets.

MY IRISH COTTAGE
3302 N.E. 33rd Street
Fort Lauderdale, FL 33308
(305) 564-5542

Designer fashions for men and women, tweeds, Aran knits.

ROCHE'S OF IRELAND
Duck Creek Plaza
Bettendorf, IA 52722
(319) 359-1750

Traditional and designer fashions, including coats, capes, jackets, shawls and throws. Also: Aran sweaters, linen dresses, hats and scarves for men and women.

IRISH IMPORTS
1735 Massachusetts Avenue
Cambridge, MA 02138
(617) 354-2511

Sells Donegal tweed jackets and overcoats; dresses, skirts, coats and sweaters in mohair and wool, from Mary Hackett; capes, coats and jackets by Jimmy Hourihan; blankets, throws and capes from Avoca Weavers; hand-knit sweaters in traditional designs; jumpers and other linen items; Irish-style work shirts; and mohair capes, throws and blankets.

THE IRISH SECRET
155 Spring Street
New York, NY 10012
(212) 334-6711

Imported designer fashions for men and women, including items by such Irish designers as Jimmy Hourihan, Brian Tucker, Michael Mortell, Paul Costello and Mickey Wallace. Categories include linen suits, jackets and dresses; mohair throws and blankets; men's caps and hats; ties and scarves; traditional Aran knit sweaters; and Fermoy waxed cotton raincoats.

ST. BRENDAN'S CROSSING
Station Square, #7
Pittsburgh, PA 15219
(402) 471-0700

Offers designer fashions from Henry White, Jimmy Hourihan, Shandon Wools, Studio Mayo and Blarney Castle. Many items have a distinctively Irish look, and most are made of natural materials—linen, cotton or wool. Stocks men's and women's wear, including business and formal items; handmade wool and linen sweaters; hats, caps and scarves; capes and winter coats.

AVINGTON OF SLIGO &
**   KILDARE**
8 East Gay Street
West Chester, Pa 19380
(215) 692-2871

This shop specializes in couture and ready-to-wear collections by Ireland's leading designers; among them, Vonnie Reynolds, Ruari OSiochain, Evelyn Cahill and Henry White. Includes coats, capes, skirts, dresses, blouses, sweaters and caps. Many items have a traditional Irish look, though with a high-fashion cut.

IRISH IMPORTS
Bowen's Wharf
Newport, RI 02840
(401) 847-3331

See entry for Irish Imports, Cambridge, MA, above.

FESTIVALS AND FEISANNA
(See Table of Contents in *The Irish-American Almanac* section of this book.)

FILMS—DOCUMENTARY

**MODERN TALKING
  PICTURE SERVICE, INC.
General Offices
5000 Park Street North
St. Petersburg, FL 33709
(813) 541-7571**

Among hundreds of films available through this distribution service is a 16mm title sponsored by Budweiser: *Irish-Americans: Heart of a New Land.* The film traces the Irish contribution to America. Your school, college, church, club or other organization may borrow the film without charge for a limited time, paying return postage and insurance charges. Contact MTPS for details, referring to Film #16818.

**UNIVERSITY OF
  MINNESOTA
University Film and Video
1313 S.E. 5th Street
Suite 108
Minneapolis, MN 55414
(612) 627-4270**

Rents the "Ireland Rediscovered" series—12 half-hour 16mm films on Irish history and literature, which were produced by KTCA-TV in cooperation with the Irish American Cultural Institute. Request film catalog.

**TRIBUNE FILMS
303 Fifth Avenue, #1908
New York, NY 10016
(212) 689-3181**

Rents out about 15 films, all in 16mm with color and sound and from 10 to 30 minutes long. Included are travelogues and special-interest films about such subjects as ancient Celtic gold ornaments and jewelry; the Burren, a natural wonder in the West of Ireland; golfing in Ireland; and racing, hunting, horse shows, trekking and other horse-related activities in Ireland. Request descriptive brochure and reservation application.

FILMS—FEATURE

Hundreds of feature films with Irish or Irish-American themes have been produced since the 1910s. Many of the more familiar, such as *The Quiet Man, Going My Way* and *The Fighting 69th,* are described in *The Irish-American Almanac* section of this book. If you'd like to rent a 16mm print of one of these movies, consult the classified phone directory in your area under "Motion Picture Film Libraries" or similar headings.

Many feature films of Irish interest are also available on videocassette. Ask your local dealer to order titles that are available if he or she doesn't have them in stock.

FLAGS AND BANNERS

GEORGE LAUTERER CORP.
310 West Washington Street
Chicago, IL 60606
(312) 332-5584

Request free catalog describing flags in stock. They'll make anything else you want to order.

NEW ENGLAND FLAG AND BANNER, INC.
125 North Beacon Street
Boston, MA 02135
(617) 782-1892; (800) 922-1892 outside Massachusetts

Stocks the flags of Ireland in standard sizes—in nylon and cotton. Also makes flags and banners to order. Request price list.

THE FLAG CENTER
2267 Massachusetts Avenue
Cambridge, MA 02140
(617) 868-2026

Stocks the flag of Ireland in several standard sizes, and will also make flags to order.

GRAVESEND FLAG COMPANY
236 Avenue U
Brooklyn, NY 11223
(718) 449-9027

Stocks the flag of Ireland in various sizes. Also custom-makes flags and banners to your specifications. Request free catalog.

THE FLAG GUYS
RD 2, Bethlehem Road, #345
Newburgh, NY 12550
(914) 562-0088; (800) 232-3524

Irish tricolor in various sizes, most of them in stock. Nylon and other materials available. Also makes customized flags and banners to your specifications. Request free mail-order catalog.

AMERICAN FLAG CENTER
135 Lanark Plaza
San Antonio, TX 78218
(512) 655-2898

Ready-made flags of Ireland. Custom-made flags in any size or design.

CHRIS REID COMPANY
P.O. Box 1827
Midlothian, VA 23113
(804) 744-5862

Stocks Irish flag in four sizes—2 feet by 3 feet up to 5 feet by 8 feet—in nylon fabric. Makes other sizes to order. Request free catalog.

FOOD SPECIALTIES—IRISH
(See also "Bakeries.")

IRISH IMPORT SHOP
738 North Vine Street
Hollywood, CA 90004
(213) 467-6714

Imported sausages and rashers, soda bread, black pudding, and white pudding. Also: a large selection of Irish grocery items.

JOSEPH TIERNEY FINE
MEATS
2051 Balboa
San Francisco, CA 94121
(415) 751-8810

Homestyle Irish sausages, black pudding, and rashers.

WINSTON'S IRISH BAKERY
AND SAUSAGE SHOP
4701 West 53rd Street
Chicago, IL 60620
(312) 767-4353

Irish sausages, soda bread, corned beef, bacon, and black pudding.

SHANNON TRADITIONAL
FOOD IMPORT
P.O. Box 364E
Belmont, MA 02178
(617) 484-4545

Exclusive importer for the United States (except the New York metro area) of Shannon bangers (sausages) and Shannon bacon (rashers), made by Limerick Bacon Company. Write or phone for location of nearest retailer of these products. Dealer inquiries also welcome.

KELTIC KRUST
1915 Dorchester Avenue
Dorchester, MA 02122
(617) 265-6488

In addition to its freshly baked Irish cakes and breads, Keltic Krust stocks a good selection of Irish teas, soups, jams, biscuits and other grocery items. Also: beverages and sweets.

IRISH CROCHET
TREASURES, LTD.
P.O. Box 1625
562 Milk Street
Fitchburg, MA 01420
(617) 342-1152

This firm also sells imported Irish teas, oatmeal, jams and jellies, steak sauces and tea biscuits. Request price list.

IRISH IMPORTS, INC.
13251 Michigan Avenue
Dearborn, MI 48126
(313) 548-1404

Makes and sells Irish pork sausage; pasties filled with beef, chicken or corned beef/cabbage/potatoes; homemade fruit cakes; and soda bread. Will ship orders.

IRISH BAY
50 Avenue L
Newark, NJ 07105
(201) 465-4337; (800) 222-0645
  outside New Jersey

Sells "prime Irish smoked salmon . . . imported weekly." Pre-sliced and interleaved portions, available in 16-oz. pack or 2 to 2¼-lb. fillets. Phone for prices and/or to place an order using VISA or MasterCard. Delivery by air freight. Bulk inquiries also welcome from local distributors and others.

O'SULLIVAN'S IRISH
  IMPORTS
82-15 Northern Boulevard
Jackson Heights, NY 11372
(718) 478-2430

Stocks a wide selection of meats and grocery items. Irish-style meats include pork and beef sausages; black and white puddings; rashers; corned spareribs; boiling bacon; pigs' knuckles, toes and heads; and fresh pork steaks. Groceries include soups, sauces, trifle mix, plum puddings and fruitcakes, teas, canned vegetables, and beverages.

CHEESES OF ALL
  NATIONS
153 Chambers Street
New York, NY 10007
(212) 732-0752

Stocks several Irish-made cheeses, including Shannondale, Irish Blarney, Erin Gold and Irish cheddar. Will ship anywhere in the United States. Phone orders accepted. Send $1 for catalog.

MATTIE HASKINS
  SHAMROCK IMPORTS
205 East 75th Street
New York, NY 10021
(212) 288-3918

Sells bangers, black pudding, Irish soda bread (raisin and plain), raisin scones, hot cross buns, and grocery items.

SHANNON ENTERPRISES
New York Metro Area
(718) 780-0692

Importer for the New York metro area of Shannon bangers

(sausages) and Shannon bacon (rashers) from the Limerick Bacon Company. Ask for these products in your local delicatessen, or phone for the location of your nearest retailer.

IRISH TEA SALES CORPORATION
92-16 95th Avenue
Ozone Park, NY 11417
(718) 845-4402

This firm sells a lot more than Irish tea (and teapots). Its stock of imported Irish food includes jams and marmalades, sauces, canned goods, biscuits, black pudding and plum pudding. To order by mail, contact for information and prices.

STANTON ENTERPRISES
31-21 68th Street
Woodside, NY 11377
(718) 424-0421

Sells Irish smoked salmon, available in amounts from two pounds (a full side) up. Comes vacuum-packed in a gift box. Phone for current prices, which include postage and handling, or to place a C.O.D. order.

GAELIC IMPORTS
4882 Pearl Road
Cleveland, OH 44109
(216) 398-1548

Specialists in food items: Irish soda bread, potato bread, scones; black pudding, white pudding and Irish sausage; biscuits, sauces and other imported grocery items.

INTERNATIONAL GOURMET LTD.
Division of Howarth Imports
3216 North Front Street
Philadelphia, PA 19140
(215) 739-1264

Second location:
8117 Old York Road
Yorktown Courtyard of Shops
Elkins Park, PA 19117
(215) 576-1274

Specialties include Irish bacon, blood pudding, Irish sausage, meat pies, steak and kidney pies, potato scones, sausage rolls and Irish steak sauce.

BEWLEY IRISH IMPORTS
606 Howard Road
West Chester, PA 19380
(215) 696-2682

Established by the immigrant great-grandson of the founder of Bewley's Cafes Ltd., a chain of coffee-and-tea houses known to generations of Dubliners. BII imports Bewley's tea and coffee products as well as breads, cakes and other Irish food products. In addition to selling through over 400 retail stores across the United States, the firm offers mail-order service. Its catalog is free on request.

FRAGRANCES—IMPORTED

FRAGRANCES OF IRELAND
c/o Heather Smith
Accent on Irish Wares
600 East Street
New Britain, CT 06051
(203) 827-8270

Imports Innisfree and Patrick fragrances in colognes, after-shaves and soaps. Call for trade terms, if a retailer, or for the location of stores nearest you that stock these items.

FURNITURE—ANTIQUE

ISLAND HOUSE ANTIQUES
Route 7
Wilton, CT 06897
(203) 544-9151

Offers an impressive selection of eighteenth- and nineteenth-century Irish country furniture, crafted from pine. Includes armoires, tables, chests of drawers, cupboards, chairs, washstands and trunks.

PADDY'S ON THE SQUARE
Long Grove Road
Long Grove, IL 60047
(312) 634-0339

Offers a selection of antique pine furniture typical of what was used by rural Irish families during the nineteenth century: dressers, cupboards, settle beds, tables and chairs.

ESSEX FELLS TRADING
** CO., LTD.**
Lyons Mall
Basking Ridge, NJ 07920
(201) 766-2211

Second location:
Panther Valley Village
Route 517
Allamuchy, NJ 07820
(201) 850-4070

Imports and sells Irish pine antiques as well as a varied selection of other Irish wares. Call for details.

PITCH PINE IRISH
** COUNTRY ANTIQUES**
547 6th Avenue
Brooklyn, NY 11215
(718) 469-0919

Stocks antique country pine furniture from eighteenth- and nineteenth-century Ireland. Will also build reproductions of antique furniture. Write or call for details on items currently in stock. Open for limited hours, Wednesday through Saturday, or by appointment.

BYERLY'S ANTIQUES, INC.
4311 Wiley Davis Road
Greensboro, NC 27407
(919) 299-6510

Stocks a wide selection of
Irish country pine furniture, including corner cupboards,
armoires, linen presses, tables,
cottage chests and dressers.
All items have been stripped
and waxed. For a $1 fee per
item (refundable if you buy something), Byerly's will send you
photos and descriptions
of items you may wish to
purchase.

FURNITURE, ANTIQUE— REPRODUCTIONS

Admittedly inspired by English
models, Irish craftsmen in
recent centuries turned out classic pieces of furniture to grace
the homes of the aristocracy.
Generally, however, they
endowed their creations with a
distinctively Irish flavor, incorporating such traditional Irish
motifs as acanthus leaves, shells,
masks, trifid feet and animal-
like forms. Two U.S. furniture companies, Baker and
Kindel, have marketed collections that consist of authentic
replicas of fine furniture
found in some of Ireland's
great houses:

**BAKER FURNITURE
   COMPANY**
917 Merchandise Mart
Chicago, IL 60654

Many pieces in Baker's Stately
Homes of Ireland Collection
reflect the lavish decorative
carving that is common in fine
traditional Irish furniture.
Included are chairs, mirrors,
cabinets, tables and other items
suited for bedroom, living room
or dining room. The Collection
may be seen at selected U.S.
stores. For the names of local
dealers, or for further information on the Collection, write the
company.

**KINDEL FURNITURE
   COMPANY**
100 Garden Street, S.E.
Box 2047
Grand Rapids, MI 49501
(616) 243-3676

As official licensee of the Irish
Georgian Society, Kindel Furniture has brought to market its
Irish Georgian Collection. This
collection of mahogany reproductions includes 19 chairs,
tables, sofas and desks, based on
originals at Castletown, the
Guinness estate; Leixlip Castle,
Kildare; and Glin Castle, Limerick. Contact Kindel for free literature or the names of dealers
near you.

*GENEALOGICAL RESOURCES
—ORGANIZATIONS AND
RESEARCH COLLECTIONS*
(See also "Libraries and
Research Facilities.")

**BRANCH GENEALOGICAL
LIBRARY SYSTEM
Church of Jesus Christ of
Latter-Day Saints (The
Mormons)**

Genealogy is more than a hobby
for Mormons—their faith
requires them to identify as
many ancestors as possible so
that they can be baptized by
proxy as Mormons. Thus, the
LDS Church has systematically
collected vital records extending
centuries into the past from
many countries, including Ireland. The Mormons' library in
Salt Lake City is the largest
depository of genealogical records in the world. Non-Mor-
mons may use most of these
materials without charge, and
other materials for a small fee,
through any of the 460 local
branch libraries the Church
maintains in towns and cities
throughout the United States.

Without ever setting foot in
Ireland, you may learn much
about the family lines you're
tracing by using, for example,
microfilmed birth, marriage and
death records the Church has
acquired from Catholic, Church

of Ireland and other parishes
throughout the 32 counties. At
the very least, this could save
you costly and time-consuming
searching once you get to Ireland.

For the location of local LDS
libraries, consult phone directories for nearby cities under
"Church of Jesus Christ of Latter-Day Saints." Or you may
request a list of these libraries
and information on the services
available by writing to:

Genealogical Society
Church of Jesus Christ of
    Latter-Day Saints
50 East North Temple Street
Salt Lake City, UT 84150

**THE NATIONAL ARCHIVES
Pennsylvania Avenue
    between 7th and 9th
    Streets, N.W.
Washington, DC 20009
(202) 523-3000**

In addition to serving as a repository for U.S. records useful to
genealogical researchers—e.g.,
census records, military pen-
sions, East Coast ship-passenger
arrivals—the archives offers a
continuing program of courses
in genealogical research techniques. You may attend a basic
course, or one of the more specialized minicourses held several

times a year on Irish research.
The National Archives has several facilities across the country,
so ask which of these are near
you, and what courses they
offer. Write the National
Archives, Attn.: Genealogical
Research Courses, and ask to be
put on its mailing list for program announcements.

THE NEWBERRY LIBRARY
Local and Family History
  Division
60 West Walton Street
Chicago, IL 60610
(312) 943-9090

Houses a large collection of
genealogical data relating to
New England and the Midwest.

NEW ENGLAND HISTORIC
  GENEALOGICAL
  SOCIETY
101 Newbury Street
Boston, MA 02116
(617) 536-5740

NEHGS, the nation's oldest
membership organization for
genealogy, has built up an
extensive collection of genealogical records, particularly on
individuals and families who
immigrated to New England.
The society has a useful collection of Irish-related material.
Nonmembers may use the
library for a fee.

THE IRISH ANCESTRAL
  RESEARCH ASSOCIATION
  (TIARA)
P.O. Box 619
Sudbury, MA 01776

This nonprofit, nondenomina-
tional group offers Boston-area
residents a variety of educational
programs to aid them in pursuing Irish genealogical research:
talks by experts in the field;
workshops on the techniques of
genealogical research in general,
and Irish research in particular;
monthly group meetings; and a
quarterly newsletter that members use to exchange information, make inquiries, and so on.
Membership dues are $8.50/yr.
Nonmembers are welcome to
attend meetings, which are normally held at 7:30 p.m. on the
second Friday of each month
(except July and August) in
Room 307, Higgins Hall, Boston College, Newton, Mass.
Write for a schedule of forthcoming events.

NEW YORK PUBLIC
  LIBRARY
U.S. History, Local History
  and Genealogy Department
Fifth Avenue at 42nd Street
New York, NY 10018
(212) 930-0828

NYPL maintains a large collection useful in researching ances-

tors who lived in New York, and major ethnic collections, including Irish materials. Anyone may use the library at no charge.

GENEALOGICAL RESOURCES —PUBLICATIONS

IRISH ROOTS
2004 Kentmere Parkway
Wilmington, DE 19806-2014

Irish Roots, by Donn Devine, is a useful introduction for beginners interested in researching their Irish genealogies. Devine is a professional genealogist as well as genealogy columnist for *The Irish Edition,* Philadelphia. Send a $5 check or money order.

GENEALOGICAL PUBLISHING COMPANY
1001 North Calvert Street
Baltimore, MD 21202
(301) 837-8271

GPC offers several works invaluable for researching Irish roots. Two of them—Samuel Lewis, *A Topographical Dictionary of Ireland* (two volumes, $75) and *General Alphabetical Index to the Townlands and Towns, Parishes and Baronies of Ireland* ($45)—are reprints of works published in 1837 and

1861, respectively. They provide perhaps the best available surveys of both pre- and post-Famine Ireland. Another seven-book set, *The Famine Immigrants* ($45 each), gives data on over half a million people who left Ireland for America from 1846 to 1851: name, age, sex, family relationship (where noted), occupation, and when the person sailed, on what ship, and from which port.

GPC has also republished Margaret Dickson Falley's classic work, *Irish and Scotch-Irish Ancestral Research* (two volumes, $60), which was first issued in 1962. This is widely considered the best single tool for Irish genealogical research. Volume I "describes genealogical collections and indexes in all major Irish repositories, as well as published indexes, catalogs and source materials in Ireland and the United States." Volume II contains bibliographies of family histories, pedigrees and source data. *A New Genealogical Atlas of Ireland,* by Brian Mitchell (paper, $18.95) is particularly useful in conjunction with the topographical dictionary and the general alphabetical index. With orders, include $2.50 postage for the first book and $1 per additional volume. Request free catalog.

NEW ENGLAND HISTORIC GENEALOGICAL SOCIETY
101 Newbury Street
Boston, MA 02116
(617) 536-5740

Written by experts and pub-
lished by the Society in 1985,
The Irish in New England
includes chapters on the Irish-
American experience in
New England since im-
migration began; New
England sources for Irish-
American genealogical research;
and the genealogy of the
Kennedy family in New
England. For a copy, send
$3.95 (plus $2.50 postage).

NEW YORK IRISH HISTORY ROUNDTABLE
P.O. Box 2087
Church Street Station, NY 10008

This group (further described
under "Organizations, Irish-
American—Local, Selected") is
a useful resource for anyone
researching Irish-American forebears in the New York metro
area. In addition to meetings
each month or so, NYIHR
publishes an annual journal,
New York Irish History, and
issues a newsletter twice a
year.

THE GENEALOGICAL HELPER
Everton Publishers
P.O. Box 368
Logan, UT 84321
(801) 752-6022

This bimonthly magazine is
filled with articles, reviews,
course and meeting notices, and
advertisements for genealogical
books, materials, courses and
services. While only a fraction
of the contents deals specifically
with Irish and Irish-American
genealogy, *Genealogical Helper*
contains much information
useful to anyone researching
his or her roots, in Ireland or
elsewhere. Subscriptions:
$21/year.

ANCESTRY PUBLISHING
P.O. Box 476
Salt Lake City, UT 84110

Publishes *Irish Records: Sources
for Family and Local History,* by
James G. Ryan, Ph.D. (1988,
562 pages, index, $34.95). This
concise, informative introduction to record sources in Ireland
is arranged by county. It is especially useful for those beginning
Irish family research. Among
the categories of sources covered are: directories, wills and
administrations, family histories, gravestone inscriptions,

libraries, societies, newspapers, research services, journals, church registers and census records.

THE ALL-IRELAND HERITAGE
2255 Cedar Lane
Vienna, VA 22180
(703) 560-4496

Published quarterly, this genealogical journal is intended to give nonprofessionals information and research skills that will help them in tracing their Irish roots. A typical issue contains material in several of the following categories: county voter lists; extracts from wills probated in Ireland and the United States; extracts of births, marriages and deaths from old newspapers; unpublished source materials, such as church records and census data; articles on social and economic history; book review and problem-solving columns; a researcher's clearinghouse; and informative abstracts from letters sent home by emigrants to America.

The All-Ireland Heritage is edited by Donna Reid Hotaling, a nationally prominent genealogist who has been particularly active in practicing and promoting Irish genealogical research. Subscriptions: $24/volume (four

issues); $45/two volumes (eight issues).

GENEALOGISTS— PROFESSIONALS SPECIALIZING IN IRISH FAMILY RESEARCH

DONN DEVINE, C.G.I.
2004 Kentmore Parkway
Wilmington, DE 19806
(302) 656-7233

Devine writes a genealogy column for *The Irish Edition,* Philadelphia, in addition to consulting privately with individuals interested in their Irish or Irish-American roots. He does some research for clients, but prefers to help others plan their own research. Send a stamped, self-addressed envelope for information.

BOARD FOR CERTIFICATION OF GENEALOGISTS
P.O. Box 19165
Washington, DC 20036-0165

Although there are many experienced and competent genealogists who have never been officially certified, you may feel more confident using a professional who has taken and passed examinations to establish his or her competence. The Board certifies genealogists (C.G.), genealogical instructors (C.G.I.), and record searchers (C.G.R.S.). Send $2 for a directory of certified professionals in the United States. Listings include specialties, if any.

B-ANN MOORHOUSE, C.G.
222 Hicks Street
Brooklyn, NY 11202
(718) 858-9524

Moorhouse performs all phases of research involving Irish and Irish-American genealogy, with particular emphasis on families who entered the United States via the Port of New York.

SUZANNE McVETTY, C.G.
15 Titus Avenue
Carle Place, NY 11514
(516) 997-8393

Specializes in research on families whose Irish immigrant ancestors settled in the New York metropolitan area. Pursues the search back to Irish antecedents when applicable.

DONNA REID HOTALING
2255 Cedar Lane
Vienna, VA 22182
(703) 560-4496

Hotaling not only consults with individuals who wish to trace their Irish roots, but has organized several international congresses on genealogical and historical research in the 32 counties. She leads regular genealogical tours to Ireland and also publishes a helpful journal, *The All-Ireland Heritage. Note:* Hotaling has not been officially certified (see entry above) because she does most of her research in Irish records, and only specialists in U.S. research can be certified.

GOVERNMENT OFFICES—REPUBLIC OF IRELAND IN THE UNITED STATES
(See also "Exports, Irish—Information," "Industrial Development Opportunities, Ireland—Information" and "Travel—Information.")
Note: As we go to press, the Irish government is pursuing plans to consolidate all of its New York–based offices in a single building, to be called Ireland House. The plan may or may not ultimately come to pass.

CONSULATES GENERAL:

CONSULATE GENERAL OF
**   IRELAND**
655 Montgomery Street
San Francisco, CA 94111
(415) 392-4214

CONSULATE GENERAL OF
  IRELAND
400 North Michigan Avenue
Chicago, IL 60611
(312) 337-1868

CONSULATE GENERAL OF
  IRELAND
535 Boylston Street
Boston, MA 02116
(617) 267-9330

CONSULATE GENERAL OF
  IRELAND
515 Madison Avenue
New York, NY 10022
(212) 319-2555

EMBASSY:

EMBASSY OF IRELAND
2234 Massachusetts Avenue,
  N.W.
Washington, DC 20008
(202) 462-3939

UNITED NATIONS MISSION:

PERMANENT MISSION OF
  IRELAND TO THE
  UNITED NATIONS
1 Dag Hammarskjöld Plaza
Floor 2
885 Second Avenue
New York, NY 10017
(212) 421-6934

*GOVERNMENT OFFICES—
UNITED KINGDOM IN THE
UNITED STATES (FOR
BUSINESS RELATING TO
NORTHERN IRELAND)*

*CONSULATES GENERAL/
CONSULATES:*

U.K. CONSULATE
  GENERAL
Ahmanson Center, East
  Bldg.
Suite 312
3701 Wilshire Boulevard
Los Angeles, CA 90010
(213) 385-7381

U.K. CONSULATE
  GENERAL
Equitable Building, 9th Fl.
120 Montgomery Street
San Francisco, CA 94104
(415) 981-3030

U.K. CONSULATE
  GENERAL
225 Peachtree Street, N.E.
Suite 912
Atlanta, GA 30303
(404) 524-5856/5858

U.K. CONSULATE
  GENERAL
33 North Dearborn Street
Chicago, IL 60602
(312) 346-1810

U.K. CONSULATE
  GENERAL
Prudential Tower
Suite 4740
Boston, MA 02199
(617) 437-7160

U.K. CONSULATE
  GENERAL
845 Third Avenue
New York, NY 10022
(212) 752-8400

U.K. CONSULATE
  GENERAL
1650 Illuminating Building
55 Public Square
Cleveland, OH 44113
(216) 621-7674

U.K. CONSULATE
c/o Mather & Company
226 Walnut Street
Philadelphia, PA 19106
(215) 925-0118

U.K. CONSULATE
813 Stemmons Tower West
2730 Stemmons Freeway
Dallas, TX 75207
(214) 637-3600

U.K. CONSULATE
  GENERAL
Dresser Tower
Suite 2250
601 Jefferson
Houston, TX 77002
(713) 659-6270

U.K. CONSULATE
  GENERAL
820 First Interstate Center
999 Third Avenue
Seattle, WA 98104
(206) 622-9255

EMBASSY:

EMBASSY OF THE UNITED
  KINGDOM
3100 Massachusetts Avenue,
  N.W.
Washington, DC 20008
(202) 462-1340

UNITED NATIONS MISSION:

PERMANENT U.K. MISSION
  TO THE UNITED
  NATIONS
845 Third Avenue
New York, NY 10022
(212) 752-8400

INFORMATION OFFICE:

BRITISH INFORMATION
  SERVICES
845 Third Avenue
New York, NY 10022
(212) 752-8400

GREETING CARDS AND STATIONERY ITEMS

EIRE-MAIL
P.O. Box 56
Derby, CT 06418

Sells St. Patrick's Day and all-occasion cards designed and printed in Ireland. Cards come three to a set for $2.95 plus $.75 shipping and handling; matching envelopes are included.

GATEWAY
Box 403
Greenwich, CT 06830
(203) 531-7400

In addition to calendars and a variety of handcrafted Irish imports, Gateway carries Irish Christmas cards in season. Request free catalog.

MARY McSWEENEY
P.O. Box 971
Libertyville, IL 60048
(312) 816-7168

An Irish-born and -trained artist, McSweeney sells greeting cards and stationery she has "adapted from the Celtic tradition." Also, pen-and-ink prints (8½ inches by 11 inches) and notelets with illustrations taken from Irish life, scenery and culture. Request free catalog.

THE CELTIC CONNECTION
282 East 204th Street
Bronx, NY 10467
(212) 231-1210

Stocks bilingual Irish/English birthday and Christmas cards.

IRISH WOOL IMPORTS
P.O. Box 98093
Lubbock, TX 79499
(806) 793-0169; (800) 634-8554

Jim Fitzpatrick, a Dublin-born artist, has made a name for himself as an illustrator specializing in Irish and Celtic mythology. A number of his paintings have been incorporated into several series of greeting cards. They feature material drawn from the *Book of Kells,* Irish mythology, nature and Irish prehistory. Both Christmas cards—which must be ordered by November 10th—and all-occasion cards are available. Send $3 for color catalog and a sample card.

IMMIGRANTS, RECENT— CHURCH-SPONSORED PROGRAMS TO ASSIST

The programs that follow are sponsored by major Roman Catholic archdioceses serving the Boston and New York areas. Similar programs may exist elsewhere in the country at either the archdiocesan, diocesan or parish level, or may be in the planning stage. If you are a recent immigrant who needs assistance—and you don't live in Boston or New York—we suggest that you contact your local parish and/or diocese to see what help they may be able to provide.

**BOSTON IRISH PASTORAL
  CENTER
St. Mark's Parish
20 Roseland Street
Dorchester, MA 02124
(617) 282-9627 or 825-2852**

Situated in one of Boston's most heavily Irish communities, this center provides pastoral care for the Irish community in particular, including guidance for the newly arrived who need social services and general immigration advice. Phone for further details.

**PROJECT IRISH
  OUTREACH
Catholic Charities of the
  Archdiocese of New York
1011 First Avenue
11th Floor
New York, NY 10022
(212) 371-1000 ext. 2485**

Project Irish Outreach was established in 1987 to meet the specific needs of the tens of thousands of Irish young people who have recently emigrated to the New York area. It provides social services through programs directly sponsored by the Archdiocese and, indirectly, through its affiliated hospitals, child care agencies, counseling services and other agencies. In addition, it has established a network of four Irish-immigrant chaplains who live and work in areas with high concentrations of young Irish.

**THE IRISH APOSTOLATE
Archdiocese of Brooklyn and
  Queens
c/o Monsignor Dominic J.
  Finnerty
St. Theresa's Church
5020 45th Street
Woodside, NY 11377
(718) 784-2123**

Provides counseling on any of the wide range of problems that may confront young Irish immigrants in adjusting to life in Brooklyn and Queens, in particular, and the United States, in general. Where appropriate, the center refers individuals to other agencies for special assistance or services. Please avoid phoning after 9:00 p.m.

*IMMIGRANTS, RECENT—
INDEPENDENT PROGRAMS
TO ASSIST*

**IRISH IMMIGRATION
  REFORM MOVEMENT
National Headquarters
33-01 Greenpoint Avenue
Long Island City, NY 11101
(718) 478-5502/5503**

Founded in 1987, the IIRM has
worked to achieve three major
objectives relating to the recent
immigration of large numbers
of undocumented Irish young
people into the United States.
These objectives are (1) to
achieve legal status for all undocumented Irish people now in the
United States, (2) to secure
changes in the 1965 Immigration and Nationality Act so that
Irish immigrants can compete
for immigration visas on an
equitable basis with other
nationalities, and, (3) to address
the day-to-day needs of the
"new Irish community in
America." Since it was established in New York, IIRM has
added chapters in a growing
number of cities across the
United States (Boston, Chicago,
San Antonio, San Francisco, and
others), and more are being
added as local needs become
clear. In its efforts to lobby the
federal government for easing of
immigration restrictions and for
legalization of the undocumented, IIRM has received
considerable support from

other, older Irish-American
groups.

Assistance available to recent
immigrants includes (1) referral
to sympathetic sources of legal
advice, (2) advice on taxation
and financial matters, (3) referral
for job opportunities, (4) technical advice on immigration
matters, and, (5) advice, information and referral on social,
health and welfare problems.

If you live in the New York
area, phone the number(s) provided to receive the advice or
information you need, or to set
up an appointment. If you live
elsewhere, and don't know
whether there is a local IIRM
chapter in your area yet—or, if
there is, how to get in touch
with it—the national headquarters can tell you how to contact
your nearest IIRM chapter.
(*Note:* As we go to press, the
IIRM hot-line numbers are
staffed by volunteers on a
limited schedule: Tuesday,
Wednesday and Thursday evenings, 6:30 to 9:30 p.m., and
Saturday afternoons. By the last
quarter of 1989, however, the
IIRM headquarters expects to
have the center staffed on a full-
time basis.

*IMMIGRATION AND
NATURALIZATION—LEGAL
COUNSEL AND ASSISTANCE*

GEORGE A. FINNAN,
   ATTORNEY
20813 Stevens Creek
   Boulevard, #100
Cupertino, CA 95014
(415) 252-8800

JAMES M. BYRNE,
   ATTORNEY
785 Market Street
Suite 820
San Francisco, CA 94103
(415) 777-4444

PAUL SHEARMAN ALLEN,
   IMMIGRATION LAWYERS
1625 K Street, N.W.
Washington, DC 20006
(202) 638-2777

JAMES R. FINNERTY,
   ATTORNEY
168 North Michigan Avenue
Chicago, IL 60601
(312) 341-1636

MARY E. FRANKLIN &
   ASSOCIATES, INC.
Immigration and
   Naturalization Consultants
77 West Washington, #1519
Chicago, IL 60602
(312) 726-4053

ROY WATSON, JR.,
   ATTORNEY
262 Washington Street
Boston, MA 02108
(617) 227-0300

FREDERICK G. BARRY, JR.
   & WALTER L. GLEASON,
   JR., ATTORNEYS
372 Granite Avenue
East Milton Square
Milton, MA 02186
(617) 698-3770

BLANE & FRANK,
   ATTORNEYS
4808 Bergenline Avenue
Union City, NJ 07087
(201) 863-9000; (212) 947-8889
   in New York City

FREDERICK J. DENNEHY,
   ATTORNEY
90 Woodbridge Center Drive
Woodbridge, NJ 07095
(201) 636-8000

BURKE, BURKE & BURKE,
   ATTORNEYS
350 Fifth Avenue, #330
New York, NY 10118
(212) 629-8899

Offers Saturday consultations.

S. D. JEFFRIES, ATTORNEY
250 West 57th Street
Suite 2102
New York, NY 10107
(212) 315-0790

O'HARA & ASSOCIATES,
  ATTORNEYS
30 Vesey Street
Suite 803
New York, NY 10007
(212) 393-9600

JAMES A. O'MALLEY,
  ATTORNEY
299 Broadway
Suite 1400
New York, NY 10007
(212) 619-8387

JOHN L. PINNIX,
  ATTORNEY
Allen & Pinnix
P.O. Drawer 1270
Raleigh, NC 27602
(919) 755-0505

H. FRED FORD &
  ASSOCIATES, ATTORNEYS
Parkway Towers
Suite 1812
Nashville, TN 37219
(615) 244-3601

*IMPORTS—BUSINESSES
OFFERING A VARIED
SELECTION BY MAIL ONLY*

THE BLARNEY GIFT
  CATALOGUE
P.O. Box 160293
Irving, TX 75016
(800) 252-7639

Phone or send $2 for color cata-
log. Merchandise is shipped
from Ireland.

GAELIC DESIGN
7 Windsor Avenue
Auburn, MA 01501
(508) 832-3940

Phone or send $2 for color cata-
log. At least some merchandise
is shipped from Ireland.

GATEWAY TO IRELAND
Box 403
Greenwich, CT 06830-0403
(203) 531-7400

Request free catalog, *Best of Ireland.*

*IMPORTS, GENERAL—SHOPS
OFFERING A VARIED
SELECTION OF IRISH
PRODUCTS ON PREMISES*
(Most will also fill orders
by mail.)

Alaska

THE McMAC SHOPPE
183 West 25th Avenue
Anchorage, AK 99510
(907) 276-0585

THE IRISH SHOP OF
  JUNEAU
3199 Pioneer Avenue
Juneau, AK 99801
(907) 586-6055

Arizona

IRISH IMPORTS
   AT FLYNN'S
1710 Camelback
Phoenix, AZ 85015
(602) 242-8650

California

BALLYBRACK SHOP
916 South Baldwin Avenue
Arcadia, CA 91006
(818) 446-7545

FOUR GREEN FIELDS
   IRISH IMPORTS
1107 Burlingame Avenue
Burlingame, CA 94010
(415) 344-0372

HEART 'N HAND GIFT
   SHOP
1199 Broadway, Suite #3
Burlingame, CA 94010
(415) 343-2908

REDING'S HOUSE
   OF IRELAND
P.O. Box 755
Capitola, CA 95010
(408) 475-9393

CELTIC SHOPPE
21269 Stevens Creek
   Boulevard
Cupertino, CA 95014
(408) 252-3046

THE IRISH SHOP
334 2nd Street
Eureka, CA 95501
(707) 443-8343

THE IRISH IMPORT SHOP
738 North Vine Street
Hollywood, CA 90038
(213) 467-6714

IRISH WAY
1110 Prospect Street
La Jolla, CA 92037
(619) 454-4644

THE IRISH SHOP OF
   MENDOCINO
45050 Main Street
P.O. Box 1636
Mendocino, CA 95460
(707) 937-3133

SHAMROCK IMPORTS
7945 Laurel Canyon
   Boulevard
North Hollywood, CA 91605
(818) 764-3935

TIPPERARY FINE IRISH
   IMPORTS
5510 College Avenue
Oakland, CA 94618
(415) 428-9222

O'GRADY'S IRISH IMPORTS
123 North Palm Canyon
Palm Springs, CA 92262
(619) 327-2720

QUALITY IRISH IMPORTS
1021 R Street
Sacramento, CA 95814
(916) 446-1877

IRISH SHOP
3509 Fifth Avenue
San Diego, CA 92103
(619) 299-7812

HOUSE OF IRELAND
238 O'Farrell
San Francisco, CA 94102
(415) 781-1900

IRISH CASTLE GIFT SHOP
2123 Market Street
San Francisco, CA 94114
(415) 621-2200

IRISH DELIGHTS
77 West Portal Avenue
San Francisco, CA 94127
(415) 664-1250

IRISH IMPORTS
3244 Geary Boulevard
San Francisco, CA 94118
(415) 752-0961

THE KILKENNY SHOP
Ghirardelli Square
900 North Point
San Francisco, CA 94109
(415) 771-8984

IRISH GUILD HOUSE/
  "ALL THINGS IRISH"
1538 Altamont Avenue
San Jose, CA 95125
(408) 265-7512

SCOTTISH & IRISH
  IMPORTS
1413 Santa Monica Mall
Santa Monica, CA 90401
(213) 393-3321

JOYCE'S IRELAND
128 West Napa Street
Sonoma, CA 95476
(707) 935-3421

KELLY'S CARDS & GIFTS
330 El Camino Real
Tustin, CA 92680
(714) 832-0035

WEE BIT O' WOOL
6526 Washington Street
Yountville, CA 94599
(707) 944-8184

Colorado

SCOTTISH & IRISH
  REGALIA SHOP
741 Citadel Drive East
Colorado Springs, CO 80909
(303) 596-8515

THISTLE & SHAMROCK
1648 Welton
Denver, CO 80202
(303) 623-0089

LEPRECHAUN SHOPPE
943 Manitou Avenue
Manitou Springs, CO 80829
(719) 685-9213

Connecticut

THE IRISH CURRAGH
3 West Main Street
Mystic, CT 06355
(203) 536-6918

IRISH EYES
Old Mystic Village
Mystic, CT 06355
(203) 536-9960

LISSARD HOUSE
62 Main Street
New Canaan, CT 06840
(203) 972-3380

IRISH SENTIMENTS
127 Washington Street
Norwalk, CT 06854
(203) 838-2287

THE LIFE OF RILEY
1271 Boston Post Road
Old Saybrook, CT 06475
(203) 388-6002

TWIN IMPORTS/THE IRISH
SHOPPE
346 Ethan Allen Highway
(Route 7)
Ridgefield, CT 06877
(203) 431-6326

FIFTH PROVINCE IRISH
IMPORTS
Ridgeway Center
Upper Level
Stamford, CT 06905
(203) 348-9603

WOLFHOUND IMPORTS
934 High Ridge Road
Stamford, CT 06905
(203) 322-4349

TIPPERARY FINE IRISH
IMPORTS
Trumbull Shopping Park
Trumbull, CT 06611
(203) 372-1790

Delaware

THE CELTIC PAVILION
LTD.
113 Market Street
Lewes, DE 19958
(302) 645-4604

MOSTLY IRISH
47 Baltimore Street
Rehoboth, DE 19971
(302) 227-1266

IRISH IMPORTS &
ANTIQUES
16 Seagull Road
Selbyville, DE 19975
(302) 436-4721

CELTIC INC.
706 Delaware Avenue
Wilmington, DE 19801
(302) 654-9952

SHAMROCK IMPORT SHOP
429 Branmar Plaza
1812 Marsh Road at Silverside
Wilmington, DE 19810
(302) 475-7117

District of Columbia

THE EMERALD AISLE
50 Massachusetts Avenue,
   N.E.
Union Station
Washington, DC 20002
(202) 682-0563

THE IRISH CORNER/
   THREE-PENNY BIT
3122 M Street, N.W.
Washington, DC 20007
(202) 338-1338

Florida

HOUSE OF IRISH
   CRYSTAL, INC.
22191 Powerline Road
Suite 18B
Boca Raton, FL 33433
(407) 750-0890

IRISH IMPORTS GALORE
403 Golf View Drive
Boca Raton, FL 33432
(407) 392-2079

CELTIC CRAFTS
Sunset Gates Shopping
   Center
1553 Sunset Drive
Coral Gables, FL 33563
(813) 785-6163

MY IRISH COTTAGE
3302 N.E. 33rd Street
Fort Lauderdale, FL 33308
(305) 564-5542

HOUSE OF IRELAND
195 Space Coast Parkway
Ft. Walton Beach, FL 32548
(904) 243-6886

TIERNEY'S IRISH IMPORTS
9825-22 San Jose Boulevard
Jacksonville, FL 32217
(904) 268-0851

HOUSE OF IRELAND
5770 Orlo Bronson Highway
Kissimmee, FL 32816
(407) 396-6226

JOY OF IRELAND
Church Street Exchange
124 West Pine #142
Orlando, FL 32801
(407) 422-5814

CELTIC CRAFTS
6020 S.W. 81st Street
South Miami, FL 33143
(305) 666-6443

HOUSE OF IRELAND
139 St. George Street
St. Augustine, FL 32085
(904) 824-5040

HOLLAND HOUSE/
IRISH SHILLELAGH
520 Corey Avenue
St. Petersburg Beach, FL
33706
(813) 367-6907

O'CONNOR'S IRISH
VILLAGE
4615 Gulf Boulevard
Suite 108
St. Petersburg, FL 33706
(813) 360-2787

Georgia

TINKERS TWO
776 North Highland Avenue,
N.E.
Atlanta, GA 30306
(404) 892-5735

KENNEDY'S IRISH
COTTAGE
Old Street
P.O. Box 233
Helen, GA 30545
(404) 878-2489

CELTIC CONNECTION
1702 Huntingford Drive
Marietta, GA 30068
(404) 992-3890

POWERS IRISH IMPORTS
117 West River Street
Savannah, GA 31401
(912) 233-9626

Illinois

CELTIC CURRENT
O'Hare International Airport
Chicago, IL 60666
(312) 686-0392

DONEGAL IRISH
IMPORTS
5358 West Devon Avenue
Chicago, IL 60646
(312) 792-2377

ERINISLE
2246 North Clark Street
Chicago, IL 60614
(312) 975-6616

GAELIC IMPORTS
4736 North Austin
Chicago, IL 60630
(312) 545-6515

HOULIHAN'S IRISH
HUTCH
Ford City Mall
Chicago, IL 60652
(312) 581-8388

IRELAND HOUSE
132 East Delaware Place
Chicago, IL 60646
(312) 337-2711

IRISH IMPORTS
(TEAHAN'S)
2505 North Harlem Avenue
Chicago, IL 60635
(312) 637-3800

IRISH TREASURES &
IMPORTS
5536 South Pulaski Road
Chicago, IL 60629
(312) 581-5911

SHAMROCK IMPORTS
3150 North Laramie
Chicago, IL 60641
(312) 286-6866

SOUTHSIDE IRISH
IMPORTS
3234 West 111th Street
Chicago, IL 60655
(312) 881-8585

GRACE'S BIT OF IRELAND
605 West North Avenue
Elmhurst, IL 60126
(312) 279-5858

FINCARA
1701 Central Street
Evanston, IL 60201
(312) 328-0665

SHAMROCK IMPORTS
110 North Main Street
Galena, IL 61036
(815) 777-3600

HENNESSY'S IRISH
HOUSE
312 South 3rd Street
Geneva, IL 60134
(312) 208-9300

THE IRISH CONNOISSEUR
1232 Waukegan Road
Glenview, IL 60025
(312) 998-1988

HYNES IRISH COTTAGE,
LTD.
18218 Harwood Avenue
Homewood, IL 60430
(312) 957-5850

GALLO AND WARD
IMPORTS
Louis Joliet Mall
Joliet, IL 60435
(815) 439-1222

A TOUCH OF IRELAND &
EUROPE
140 La Grange Road
LaGrange, IL 60525
(312) 579-3473

THE IRISH BOUTIQUE
434 Coffin Road
Long Grove, IL 60047
(312) 634-3540

SHANNON IMPORTS
5726 West 95th Street
Oak Lawn, IL 60453
(312) 424-7055

**A TOUCH OF IRELAND &
  EUROPE**
Holiday Inn Arcade
4140 West 95th Street
Oak Lawn, IL 60453
(312) 422-3473

HYNES IRISH COTTAGE
15164 LaGrange Road
Orland Park, IL 60462
(312) 403-5888

INNISFREE SHOP
14240 South West Highway
Orland Park, IL 60462
(312) 349-4848

GAELIC GIFTS
115 North Longwood Street
Rockford, IL 61107
(312) 968-0022

FAILTE
Spring Hill Mall
W. Dundee, IL 60118
(312) 428-0303

BLARNEY IMPORTS
Hubbard Woods Plaza
83 Glencoe Road
Winnetka, IL 60093
(312) 835-3050

Indiana

KILLYBEGS LTD.
8702 Keystone Crossing
Indianapolis, IN 46240
(317) 846-9449

DEAVER'S DAUGHTERS
Ross Plaza
417C West 81st Avenue
  (Route 30)
Merrillville, IN 46410
(219) 736-LUCK

Iowa

ROCHE'S OF IRELAND
Duck Creek Mall
Bettendorf, IA 52722
(319) 359-1750

SHAMROCK IMPORTS
391 Bluff Street
Dubuque, IA 52001
(319) 583-5000

DUBLIN DOOR
207 Fifth Avenue
West Des Moines, IA 50265
(515) 277-2174

Kentucky

**HARP & SHAMROCK
  DESIGNS**
3715 Lexington Road
Louisville, KY 40207-3023
(800) 626-6381

IRISH WHITE HOUSE
933 Baxter Avenue
Louisville, KY 40204
(502) 451-7996

TWEED & TARTAN
4050 Westport Road
Louisville, KY 40207
(502) 897-1573

Louisiana

THE IRISH SHOP
723 Toulouse Street
New Orleans, LA 70130
(504) 523-6197

Maine

SIMON PEARCE
39 Main Street
Freeport, ME 04032
(207) 865-0464

PURPLE HEATHER
Lower Village
P.O. Box 244
Kennebunkport, ME 04046
(207) 967-8404

CELTIC DESIGNS LTD.
414 Fore Street
Portland, ME 04101
(207) 773-8372

IRELAND'S CRYSTAL &
   CRAFTS
10 Exchange Street
Portland, ME 04101
(207) 773-5832

Maryland

THE IRISH CENTRE
158 Main Street
Annapolis, MD 21401
(301) 267-9001

IRISH COUNTRY STORE
   LTD.
Harborplace
201 East Pratt Street
Baltimore, MD 21202
(301) 659-9304

SHEEP'S CLOTHING
1620 Shakespeare Street
Baltimore, MD 21231
(301) 327-2222

GRAND IRISH
6701 Democracy Boulevard,
   #300
Bethesda, MD 20817
(301) 571-9444

EIRINN ARTS
21B North Harrison Street
Easton, MD 21601
(301) 822-9303

THE IRISH SHOP/
   BRENDAN COLLECTION
6860 Route 108
Laytonsville, MD 20882
(301) 921-0928

Massachusetts

THE IRISH CONNECTION
139 Massachusetts Avenue
Arlington, MA 02174
(617) 641-3636

IRISH COTTAGE
21 Ledin Drive
Avon, MA 02322
(617) 583-2244

This is the buying office for
Irish Cottage shops in Braintree,
Hyannis, Worcester, Dedham,
Burlington and Peabody.

CELTIC WEAVERS
Faneuil Hall
   Marketplace
Boston, MA 02109
(617) 720-0750

McGURRINS'S GIFT SHOP
373 Washington Street
Brighton, MA 02135
(617) 254-3999

THE IRISH COTTAGE
1236 Burlington Mall
Burlington, MA 01803
(617) 272-1044

IRISH IMPORTS
1735 Massachusetts Avenue
Cambridge, MA 02138
(617) 354-2511

EMERALD ISLE
23 Drum Hill Road
Chelmsford, MA 01824
(617) 452-1614

THE IRISH CUPBOARD
38 Main Street
Concord, MA 01742
(508) 369-7037

IRISH ITEMS
821 Route 6A
P.O. Box 275
Dennis (Cape Cod), MA
   02638
(508) 385-9231

IRISH SPECIALTY SHOP
108 South Main Street
Fall River, MA 02721
(617) 678-4096

POT OF GOLD SHOPS
1481 Route 132
Hyannis, MA 02601
(508) 362-9437

IRISH JAUNTING CAR
   IMPORTS
89 South Broadway
Lawrence, MA 01843
(508) 683-9007

CELTIC ORIGINS
Walker Street
Lenox, MA 01240
(413) 637-1296

BOREEN IRISH IMPORTS
9 Boston Street
Lynn, MA 01904
(617) 598-9286

UPSTAIRS/DOWNSTAIRS
21 Main Street
Nantucket, MA 02554
(508) 228-4250

A CELTIC SOJOURN
18 Liberty Street, #4
Newburyport, MA 01950
(508) 465-2650

BRIDGETS—AN IRISH
   TRADITION
Cordage Park (Route 3A)
North Plymouth, MA 02360
(508) 747-2293

EMERALD ISLE EXPRESS
50 Billings Road
North Quincy, MA 02171
(617) 472-3214

OUT OF IRELAND
955 Washington Street
Norwood, MA 07062
(617) 769-8535

THE LUCKY LEPRECHAUN
170 Water Street
Plymouth, MA 02360
(508) 747-4030

PURPLE HEATHER
Pickering Wharf
Salem, MA 01970
(508) 744-6880

IRELAND CALLS
1683 Fall River Avenue
Seekonk, MA 02771
(508) 336-7830

HOUSE OF IRELAND
17 Crescent Street
Waltham, MA 02154
(617) 899-7733

ERIN'S OWN IRISH
   IMPORTS
118 Elm Street
Westfield, MA 01085
(413) 568-1707

MOLLY'S BARROW IRISH
   IMPORTS
P.O. Box 28
West Barnstable, MA 02668
(508) 362-2726

CAPE COD IRISH VILLAGE
512 Main Street
West Yarmouth, MA 02673
(617) 771-0100

IRISH COTTAGE IMPORT
   GIFT STORE
196 Apollo Road
Worcester, MA 01605
(617) 852-6532

Michigan

IRISH IMPORTS, INC.
13251 Michigan Avenue
Dearborn, MI 48126
(313) 584-1404

**DONOVAN'S IRISH
  COUNTRY**
33335 Grand River Avenue
Farmington, MI 48024
(313) 478-0668

KELTIC COTTAGE
8719 Gull Road
Richland, MI 49083
(616) 629-4077

**OLIVE BRANCH/THE
  IRISHMAN'S CORNER**
59 Courtland
Rockford, MI 49341
(616) 866-9761

IRISH WONDERS
221 East State Street
Traverse City, MI 49684
(616) 947-0302

Minnesota

THE DUBLIN WALK
1200 Nicollet Mall
Minneapolis, MN 55403
(612) 338-5203

Missouri

THE IRISH PEDDLER
2450 Grand, #142
Kansas City, MO 64108
(816) 421-4858

**SHEEHAN'S IRISH
  IMPORTS**
1412 Westport Road
Kansas City, MO 64111
(816) 561-4480

THE JOY OF IRELAND
#112 St. Louis Union Station
St. Louis, MO 63103
(314) 231-6398

KERRY COTTAGE
2117 South Big Bend
St. Louis, MO 63117
(314) 647-0166

THE SHANNON SHOP
13426 Clayton Road
St. Louis, MO 63131
(314) 434-8949

Nebraska

THE IRISH SHOP
214 Alpine Mall
Westroads
Omaha, NB 68114
(402) 391-2903

New Hampshire

SIMON PEARCE
P.O. Box 190
Francestown, NH 03043
(603) 547-2634

O'DONNELL'S IMPORTS
862 Lafayette Road (Route 7)
Hampton, NH 03842
(603) 926-2733

THE IRISH COTTAGE
Royal Ridge Mall
Nashua, NH 03060
(603) 888-4368

WOLFHOUND IMPORTS
P.O. Box 306
Waterville Valley, NH 03215
(603) 236-4681

New Jersey

ESSEX FELLS TRADING
Panther Valley Village
Route 517
Allamuchy, NJ 07820
(201) 850-4070

BALLYHUGH IRISH
  IMPORTS
235 South White Horse Pike
Audubon, NJ 08106
(609) 546-0946

COLONIAL HOUSE
9 West 25th Street
Bayonne, NJ 07002
(201) 436-8404

ESSEX FELLS TRADING
424 Hills Drive
Bedminster, NJ 07921
(201) 781-6100

BRIDGET'S IRISH
  COTTAGE II
Bridgewater Common Mall
Bridgewater, NJ 08807
(201) 563-0606

ALL IRISH
Carpenter Square
31 Perry Street
P.O. Box 599
Cape May, NJ 08204
(609) 884-4484

SHANNON IMPORTS
414 Washington Avenue
Elizabeth, NJ 07202
(201) 352-6161

KAREN'S IRISH COTTAGE
81 Main Street
Farmingdale, NJ 07727
(201) 938-6660

ECHOES OF ERIN
1 Klickityklack Depot
Flemington Depot
Flemington, NJ 08822
(201) 782-2427

GLENVEAGH GIFT SHOP
346 Valley Road
Gillette, NJ 07933
(201) 647-0423

CELTIC GALLERIES, INC./
  IRISH QUALITY SHOP
437 Kearny Avenue
Kearny, NJ 07032
(201) 997-3250

TARA IRISH GIFT SHOP
421 Kearny Avenue
Kearny, NJ 07032
(201) 998-7220

IRISH TINKER SHOP
59 West Front Street
Keyport, NJ 07735
(201) 888-8399

KILLEEN'S IRISH SHOP
11 North Main Street
Manahawkin, NJ 08050
(609) 597-4403

KATHLEEN'S OF
  MARLTON CROSSING
123 Route 73 South
Marlton, NJ 08053
(609) 985-0606

BRIDGET'S IRISH
  COTTAGE
1954 Washington Valley Road
Martinsville, NJ 08836
(201) 563-0606

KATHLEEN'S FESTIVAL AT
  HAMILTON
3954 East Black Horse Pike
Mays Landing, NJ 08330
(609) 625-7550

CROSS AND SHAMROCK
Clover Mall
3100 Quakerbridge Road
Mercerville, NJ 08619
(609) 586-9696

CLASSIC CREATIONS OF
  IRELAND
187-189 North Main Street
Milltown, NJ 08850
(201) 249-7460

GINTY'S IRISH GIFTS
2 De Hart Street
Morristown, NJ 07960
(201) 993-9788

McGETTIGAN'S IRISH
  IMPORTS
201 Tilton Road
North Field, NJ 08205
(609) 641-7833

SHAMROCK
406 Asbury Avenue
Ocean City, NJ 08226
(609) 398-1948

CELTIC COTTAGE
Plainsboro Town Center
10 Schalks Crossing Road
Plainsboro, NJ 08536
(609) 275-8484

FLANNERY'S IRISH MIST
651 Arnold Avenue
Point Pleasant Beach, NJ
  08742
(201) 899-8880

UNA'S IRISH HERITAGE
22 Prospect Street
Ridgewood, NJ 07450
(201) 447-3309

IRISH IMPORTS AT MY
  IRISH COTTAGE
452 Springfield Avenue
Summit, NJ 07901
(201) 522-1811

THE IRISH SHOP
139 Broad Street
Red Bank, NJ 07701
(201) 747-6181

GREEN ISLE IRISH
  IMPORTS
820 Kinderkamack Road
River Edge, NJ 07661
(201) 265-4984

QUEEN OF IRELAND
  IMPORT SHOP
4500 Landis Avenue
Sea Isle, NJ 08243
(609) 263-7883

KIELY'S EMERALD
  COTTAGE
Village Greene
Smithville, NJ 08201
(609) 652-0660

THE IRISH CENTRE
1120 Third Avenue
Spring Lake, NJ 07762
(201) 449-6650

IRISH PAVILLION OF
  STONE HARBOR
9825 Ocean Avenue
Stone Harbor, NJ 08247
(609) 368-1112

ST. FRANCIS GIFT SHOP
253 Knickerbocker Road
Tenafly, NJ 07670
(201) 568-0478

BIT O'ERIN IMPORTS
Dover Mall (Intersection of
  Routes 37 and 166)
Toms River, NJ 08753
(201) 240-1440

THE THATCHED COTTAGE
648 Bloomfield Avenue
Verona, NJ 07044
(201) 239-0858

New Mexico

RAINBOWS & SHAMROCKS
1331 Juan Tabo
Albuquerque, NM 87112
(505) 275-3549

New York

KILLARNEY COTTAGE
10 Ellen Street
Binghamton, NY 13901
(607) 648-4322

THE CELTIC CONNECTION
282 East 204th Street
Bronx, NY 10467
(212) 231-1210

SUTTON'S CACHE
60 Kraft Avenue
Bronxville, NY 10708
(914) 337-6077

ALL IRELAND IRISH
    IMPORTS
8515 Third Avenue
Brooklyn, NY 11209
(718) 748-9240

THE IRISH EXPERIENCE
8515 3rd Avenue
Brooklyn, NY 11209
(718) 748-9240

McGUINNESS' IRISH GIFT
    SHOP
3609 Avenue S
Brooklyn, NY 11234
(718) 627-0009

TARA GIFT SHOP
250 Abbot Road
Buffalo, NY 14220
(716) 825-6700

DUBLIN HOUSE OF FINE
    IRISH IMPORTS
10633 Main Street
Clarence, NY 14031
(716) 759-7068

IRISH IMPORTS & THINGS
73 Main Street
Cold Spring, NY 10516
(914) 265-4570

GUARANTEED IRISH
Route 145
East Durham, NY 12423
(518) 786-1588

THE IRISH ALLEY
7 Green Street
Huntington, NY 11743
(516) 427-0298

LITTLE SHOP OF
    SHAMROCKS
572 Main Street
Islip, NY 11751
(516) 224-4311

GIBBON'S IRISH IMPORTS
72-12 Broadway
Jackson Heights, NY 11372
(718) 476-0633

THE CLADDAGH SHOP
252-24 Northern Boulevard
Little Neck, NY 11363
(718) 224-3500

TRADITIONS CELTIC
    IMPORTS
125 Dolson Avenue
Middletown, NY 10940
(914) 343-5736

IRISH COUNTRY LOFT
LTD.
P.O. Box 230
Gossmans Dock
Montauk, NY 11954
(516) 668-4964

MATTIE HASKINS
SHAMROCK IMPORTS
205 East 75th Street
New York, NY 10021
(212) 288-3918

PEARCE & VANCE
285 Bleecker Street
New York, NY 10014
(212) 924-1142

TARA IRISH SHOP
609 West 207th Street
New York, NY 10034
(212) 569-8644

WILLIAMSON'S IRISH
IMPORTS
6 Fulton Street
South Street Seaport
New York, NY 10038
(212) 425-4331

SOMETHING IRISH
P.O. Box 1046
Falls Station
Niagara Falls, NY 14303
(716) 285-0227

KILKELLY COTTAGE
7 Camp Avenue
North Merrick, NY 11566
(516) 223-0390

THE IRISH COTTAGE
20 South Main Street
Pearl River, NY 10965
(914) 735-9505

VIGREN &
O'SHAUGHNESSY
39 South Main Street
Pittsford, NY 14534
(716) 248-8346

EMERALD COTTAGE
101 West Broadway
Port Jefferson, NY 11777
(516) 331-9531

EMERALD COTTAGE
1145 Route 1
Port Jefferson Station, NY
11776
(516) 473-5243

IRISH IMPORT SHOP
3821 Ridge Road West
Rochester, NY 14626
(716) 225-1050

KATHLEEN'S OF
DONEGAL
10 North Park Avenue
Rockville Centre, NY 11570
(516) 536-9616

IRISH TREASURES
100 South Main Street
Sayville, NY 11782
(516) 567-4286

IRISH ELEGANCE
17 Singer Lane
Smithtown, NY 11787
(516) 265-9306

THE CLADDAGH SHOP
605 Forest Avenue
Staten Island, NY 10310
(718) 422-6400

QUAKER GIFT SHOP
770 Castleton Avenue
Staten Island, NY 10310
(718) 442-6200

CASHEL HOUSE
224 Tompkins Street
Syracuse, NY 13204
(315) 472-4438

BROWNE'S IRISH IMPORTS
642 Willis Avenue
Williston Park, NY 11596
(516) 248-6342

CELTIC CRAFTS
54-02 Roosevelt Avenue
Store #3
Woodside, NY 11377
(718) 397-7645

SHAMROCK GIFT SHOP
916 McLean Avenue
Yonkers, NY 10704
(914) 237-3223

IRISH IMPORT SHOP
334 Underhill Avenue
Yorktown Heights, NY 10598
(914) 962-7231

North Carolina

THE GAELIC SHOP
Route 1
Box 292-16
Banner Elk, NC 28604
(704) 898-9501

THE CELTIC TRADER
2400 Park Road
Charlotte, NC 28203
(704) 332-2358

DUBLIN DOOR
301 Over Street Mall
Charlotte, NC 28202
(704) 334-2070

IRISH IMPORT SHOP
1247 Georgia Highway
Franklin, NC 28734
(704) 369-7275

Ohio

GAELIC IMPORTS
3830 Pearl Road
Cleveland, OH 44109
(216) 398-1548

IRISH IMPORTS
  INTERNATIONAL
400 North High Street
Columbus, OH 43215
(614) 461-0346

FITZGERALD'S IRISH
  IMPORTS
28 West Third Street
Arcade Square
Dayton, OH 45402
(513) 461-3258

HA'PENNY BRIDGE
  IMPORTS
75 South High Street
Dublin, OH 43017
(614) 889-9615

EMERALD UNLIMITED
199 East 228th Street
Euclid, OH 44123
(216) 261-2207

EMERALD IRISH IMPORTS
14722 Detroit Avenue
Lakewood, OH 44107
(216) 221-3378

CASEY'S IRISH IMPORTS
19626 Center Ridge Road
Rocky River, OH 44116
(216) 333-8383

O'RODDY'S IRISH
  BOUTIQUE
31 North State Street
Westerville, OH 43081
(614) 895-1138

Oregon

THE IRISH WAY
P.O. Box 102 (Highway 101)
Depoe Bay, OR 97341
(503) 765-2330

FALCARRAGH IRISH
  IMPORTS
P.O. Box 303
Eugene, OR 97401
(503) 485-3882

KATHLEEN CONNOLLY'S
  IRISH SHOP
725 S.W. 10th Avenue
Portland, OR 97205
(503) 228-4482

MRS. QUINN'S COTTAGE
Sun River Mall
Sun River, OR 97707
(503) 593-2675

Pennsylvania

CLARKE'S CARDS & GIFTS
62 North Main Street
Ashley, PA 18706
(717) 823-9217

THE BLACKTHORN STICK
630 North New Street
Bethlehem, PA 18018
(215) 865-0289

DONEGAL SQUARE
523 Main Street
Bethlehem, PA 18018
(215) 866-3244

TINKERS CART IRISH
  SHOP
6810 North Radcliffe Street
Bristol, PA 19007
(215) 943-1769

THE IRISH SHOP
824 Lancaster Avenue
Bryn Mawr, PA 19010
(215) 527-1312

TIPPERARY WEST
4206 Peach Street
Erie, PA 16509
(814) 864-6102

THE IRISH SHOP
279 Keswick Avenue
Glenside, PA 19038
(215) 576-5770

IRISH ARTIST LTD.
603 Mercer Street
Box 2449—RD 2
Harrisville, PA 16038
(412) 735-2820

TREASURE SHOP
44 Broadway
Jim Thorpe, PA 18229
(717) 325-8380

IRELAND'S OWN GIFT
   SHOPS
King of Prussia Plaza
King of Prussia, PA 19406
(215) 962-0101

DONEGAL BAY COMPANY
Peddlers Village, Shop #8
Route 202
Lahaska, PA 18931
(215) 794-3418

GAELIC SHOP OF
   LIGONIER
209 East Main Street
Ligonier, PA 15658
(412) 238-4371

THE GAELIC SHOP OF
   NEW HOPE
25 North Main Street
P.O. Box 6
New Hope, PA 18938
(215) 862-9285

OXFORD HALL
106 Lincolnway West
New Oxford, PA 17350
(717) 624-2337

IRELAND'S OWN GIFT
   SHOPS
34 West Winona Avenue
Norwood, PA 19074
(215) 461-8825

DANNY BOY'S IRISH SHOP
R.D. 2, Route 29—Box 56
Perkiomenville, PA 18074
(215) 234-8416

TULLYCROSS
602 South Hancock Street
Philadelphia, PA 19147
(215) 925-1995

IRISH DESIGN CENTER
303 South Craig
Pittsburgh, PA 15213
(412) 682-6125

ST. BRENDAN'S CROSSING
Station Square Shops, #7
Pittsburgh, PA 15219
(412) 471-0700

THE TARA SHOP
30 Grant Avenue
Pittsburgh, PA 15223
(412) 781-1666

DENNA IRISH IMPORTS
130 Almshouse Road
Richboro, PA 18954
(215) 357-7441

CRONIN'S IRISH COTTAGE
1326 North Keyser Avenue
Scranton, PA 18504
(717) 342-4448

IRELAND'S OWN GIFT
  SHOPS
Route 420 and Baltimore
  Pike
Springfield, PA 19064
(215) 543-1200

ABBEY GREEN IRISH
  SHOP
1036 Wilmington Pike
West Chester, PA 19382
(215) 692-3310

Rhode Island

IRISH SHOP
Water Street
Block Island, RI 02807
(401) 466-2309

IRISH IMPORTS
Bowen's Wharf
Newport, RI 02840
(401) 847-3331

Tennessee

IRISH CREATIONS
102 Harbour Ferry
Collierville, TN 38017
(901) 853-6314

Texas

IRISH IMPORT BOUTIQUE
13614 Highway 71 West
Austin, TX 78733
(512) 263-2147

JOY OF IRELAND
602 Munger, Box 1
Dallas, TX 75202
(214) 720-3956

Vermont

CELTIC COTTAGE LTD.
5 Burlington Square
Burlington, VT 05401
(802) 863-5524

IRISH HOUSE
P.O. Box 917
Manchester, VT 05254-0917
(802) 362-4004

CAROL BROWN'S
P.O. Box C-100
Putney, VT 05346
(802) 387-5875

Virginia

THE IRISH WALK
Tavern Square
415 King Street
Alexandria, VA 22314
(703) 548-0118

IRISH EYES
725 Caroline Street
Fredericksburg, VA 22401
(703) 373-0703

IRISH COTTAGE
Cottage Row
P.O. Box 136
Hot Springs, VA 24445
(703) 839-5835

BANTRY'S OF IRELAND
11 Loudon Street, S.W.
Leesburg, VA 22075
(703) 777-1388

IRISH GOODS UNLIMITED
13345 Midlothian Turnpike
P.O. Box 285
Midlothian, VA 23113
(804) 379-4260

ERIN'S TREASURES
333 Waterside Drive
Norfolk, VA 23510
(804) 622-5136

Washington

**KENNEDY'S IRISH
  IMPORTS**
610 First Street
La Conner, WA 98257
(206) 466-3322

IRISH WAYS
1013 Water Street
Port Townsend, WA 98368
(206) 385-1935

GALWAY TRADERS
7518 15th Avenue, N.W.
Seattle, WA 98117
(206) 784-9343

THE HARP & SHAMROCK
2704 North Proctor
Tacoma, WA 98407
(206) 752-5012

Wisconsin

TRALEE IMPORTS
17125-E West Bluemound
  Road
Brookfield, WI 53005
(414) 797-8100

IRISH HOUSE
Box 302
Highway 42
Fish Creek, WI 54212
(414) 868-3528

ERIN ISLE
830 Main Street
Lake Geneva, WI 53147
(414) 248-4433

FLEMINGS LTD.
771 Main Street
Lake Geneva, WI 53147
(414) 248-4637

INDUSTRIAL & ECONOMIC DEVELOPMENT IN IRELAND —PROGRAMS TO ASSIST

THE IRISH AMERICAN
  PARTNERSHIP
Attn. Mr. Joseph Leary
4th Floor
Faneuil Hall Marketplace
Boston, MA 02109
(617) 723-2707

This nonpolitical, nonsectarian Irish-American organization was established with the encouragement of the Irish government in 1985. It aims to assist in the economic development of Ireland—all 32 counties —by raising money for new enterprises that will create jobs, and by arranging programs that will offer management training in the United States for Irish young people who will return and apply their talents in Ireland. The partnership has about 2,500 members, who belong to chapters in Chicago, Detroit, Boston, Philadelphia, New York, and Washington, D.C., with the establishment of new chapters anticipated in other cities. The Partnership has boards of directors in both the United States and Ireland, and raised about $600,000 in 1988 to further its objectives. Contact for further information.

INDUSTRIAL OPPORTUNITIES IN IRELAND—CONSULTANTS

PAN ATLANTIC
  CONSULTANTS, INC.
148 Middle Street
Portland, ME 04101
(207) 871-8622

Ireland offers business advantages for manufacturing firms of all types. But no firm would want to invest large sums to open a plant anywhere before knowing all the pros and cons. Pan Atlantic, headed by Irish-born David Miley, has prepared feasibility, strategy and market research studies for several leading U.S. firms interested in Irish operations. Pan Atlantic Consultants says opportunities are particularly good for small to medium-size firms. Contact David Miley for information on their services and fees.

INDUSTRIAL OPPORTUNITIES IN IRELAND—INFORMATION

Some 350 American companies now have plants in Ireland, among them such well-known names as IBM, Wang, Apple, Digital Equipment, Pfizer, Microsoft, Memorex and Land O' Lakes. The advantages they cite for their decisions to manufacture in Ireland include low taxes, generous government grants, and a young, technologically oriented labor force. (Ireland produces more college graduates per capita in computer science than the United States.) If you'd like more information about the general advantages of operating in Ireland, and the specific locations best suited to your company's needs, contact one of the U.S. offices of the Industrial Development Authority of Ireland, as follows:

IDA IRELAND
3000 Sand Hill Road
Building 1, Suite 100
Menlo Park, CA 94025
(415) 854-1800

IDA IRELAND
1821 Wilshire Boulevard
Suite 317
Santa Monica, CA 90403
(213) 829-0081

IDA IRELAND
P.O. Box 11727
Atlanta, GA 30355
(404) 351-8474

IDA IRELAND
75 East Wacker Drive
Suite 600
Chicago, IL 60601
(312) 236-0222

IDA IRELAND
Two Center Plaza
Boston, MA 02108
(617) 367-8225

IDA IRELAND
Two Grand Central Tower
140 East 45th Street
New York, NY 10017
(212) 972-1000

INDUSTRIAL AND INVESTMENT OPPORTUNITIES, INFORMATION ON— REPUBLIC OF IRELAND AND NORTHERN IRELAND

PRICE WATERHOUSE AND
COMPANY
153 East 53rd Street
New York, NY 10022
(212) 527-7886

The Center for International Taxation at this major international public accounting firm publishes an informative booklet, *Doing Business in the Republic of Ireland* (Information Guide Series), to help promote the consulting services it offers firms interested in possible ventures in Ireland. Also available are publications entitled, *Ireland: A Guide for U.S. Investors* and *Doing Business in Northern Ireland.* You may request copies by contacting the firm.

INDUSTRIAL OPPORTUNITIES IN NORTHERN IRELAND— INFORMATION

INDUSTRIAL DEVELOPMENT BOARD FOR NORTHERN IRELAND
845 Third Avenue
New York, NY 10022
(212) 593-2258

INTERIOR DESIGN, CELTIC-STYLE—HOME, OFFICE OR BUSINESS

CELTIC IMAGE
14A Marine Road
South Boston, MA 02127
(617) 268-6702

Using traditional Celtic styles and patterns, Richard Coit spe-

cializes in wall ornamentation and mural painting. He undertakes both business and residential assignments. Contact for information and photocopies showing his work.

INTERNATIONAL DELIVERY— EXPRESS LETTER AND PARCEL SERVICE TO IRELAND

The following services offer express delivery of letters and packages from the United States to Ireland, and vice versa. Depending on where the delivery originates, and where it is to be made, delivery may require as little as one or two days—or as many as four. Check with each service separately for rates, restrictions and other details. Make sure that the service has a facility near you, and that it offers delivery to the specific place in Ireland you need.

DHL WORLDWIDE COURIER EXPRESS
(800) 225-5345

EXPRESS MAIL INTERNATIONAL SERVICE
United States Postal Service
(Contact your local post office.)

FEDERAL EXPRESS
(800) 238-5355

EMERY & PUROLATOR
   COURIER
(800) 645-3333

UNITED PARCEL SERVICE
Phone directory assistance or
   consult your telephone
   directory

IRISH STUDIES—RESOURCES
(See also "Books,"
"Directories," "Language
Study—Gaelic," "Magazines
and Journals—Irish-American"
and "Organizations—Irish-
American.")

GREENWOOD PRESS
88 Post Road West
P.O. Box 5007
Westport, CT 06881
(203) 226-3571

GP has published *Irish Research:
A Guide to Collections in North
America, Ireland and Great Britain,* by DeeGee Lester. Request
price, details.

UNIVERSITY PRESS OF
   AMERICA
Box 19101
Washington, DC 20036
(301) 459-3366

*The Irish-American Experience: A
Guide to the Literature,* edited by

Seamus Metress and published
in 1981 by UPA, is perhaps the
best survey available of books
and articles dealing with the
Irish-American community in
all its aspects, historical and current. This 226-page work may
be ordered in paperback for $14,
or, with a library binding, for
$29.75. Request free descriptive
brochure.

AMERICAN CONFERENCE
   FOR IRISH STUDIES
   (ACIS)
Attn.: Dr. Maureen
   O'R. Murphy
Dean of Students
Hofstra University
1000 Fulton Avenue
Hempstead, NY 11550
(516) 560-6913

ACIS publishes *A Guide to Irish
Studies in the United States,*
which is revised at intervals; the
most recent edition was issued
in 1988. This excellent directory
surveys, state by state and institution by institution, courses
currently taught in various
aspects of Irish studies. It covers
both public and private colleges
and universities. Most courses
come under such disciplines as
history, political science, languages, literature, folklore and
sociology; some are interdisci-
plinary. Single copies of the

Guide are available to nonmembers of ACIS either free or at a nominal charge, depending on whether a particular edition has been subsidized by a grant-making organization. Contact Dean Murphy for current information.

JEWELRY—TRADITIONAL DESIGNS (See also "Crafts—Traditional.")

CELTIC JEWELRY IMPORTS
P.O. Box 852
West Covina, CA 91793
(818) 338-7400

Claddagh rings and pendants; Celtic cross items. Available in 9- and 14-carat gold as well as silver. Request free brochure.

ALL THINGS IRISH
P.O. Box 94
Glenview, IL 60025
(312) 998-4510

Imports Claddagh jewelry and other Irish items in Sterling silver and 9- and 14-carat gold. Many items feature Connemara marble and marcasites. Sells at both wholesale and retail. Request free color catalog.

T. G. MURPHY JEWELRY
619 East Broadway
South Boston, MA 02127
(617) 268-0033

Claddagh rings in 10- and 14-carat gold. Also: Claddagh pendants and earrings, Celtic cross pendants. Request free brochure.

KENNY JEWELERS
308 Main Street
Avon-by-the-Sea, NJ 07717
(201) 775-3336

Offers a wide choice of gold and silver jewelry in traditional Irish designs, including Claddagh items, St. Brigid's and Celtic crosses, Tara brooches, and harps. Request free brochure.

QUEENS IRISH IMPORTS
72-12 Broadway
Jackson Heights, NY 11372
(718) 476-0633

Claddagh rings, pendants and earrings, Celtic crosses, and St. Brigid's crosses. Available in 9- and 14-carat gold or Sterling silver.

TULLYCROSS
602 South Hancock Street
Philadelphia, PA 19147
(215) 925-1995

Handcrafted and -finished jewelry, including Claddagh items,

Celtic and St. Brigid's crosses, and pieces modeled after *Book of Kells* designs. Free catalog.

LACE—IRISH

IRISH VENTURES
P.O. Box 426
New York, NY 10024
(212) 947-9320

Irish Ventures is the sole American representative for new Carrickmacross lace. Available items, which include a keepsake ($14) and a bridal veil ($280), are all made by hand following techniques developed in Ireland during the nineteenth century. Write for free catalog.

LANGUAGE STUDY, IRISH—INSTRUCTION OFFERED BY COLLEGES AND ORGANIZATIONS

If you're learning Irish for the first time, a teacher will normally be more effective than a recorded course. Hundreds of colleges and universities throughout the United States offer Irish (Gaelic) instruction. If you live in a large metropolitan area, you might try calling various local institutions of higher learning. The American Confer-

ence for Irish Studies publishes a comprehensive directory of such courses. (See "Irish Studies—Resources.") Instruction is also available through many local Irish-American organizations and private teachers. Consult announcements in Irish-American newspapers serving your area, or contact local organizations.

LANGUAGE STUDY, IRISH—MATERIALS FOR SELF-INSTRUCTION

EDUCATIONAL SERVICES, INC.
1725 K Street, N.W., #408
Washington, DC 20006
(202) 298-8424

Sells a course in Irish prepared and recorded by native-speaker Coilin Owens, a teacher at George Mason University. Two cassettes provide 1½ hours of lessons and guided practice in commonly used words and phrases. Topics covered include traditional music, dances, pub culture, seasonal greetings, festivals, religion, theater, sports and pastimes. The course comes in a vinyl album with a phrase dictionary.
Price: $14.95.

CONVERSA-PHONE INSTITUTE, INC.
1 Commack Loop
Ronkonkoma, NY 11779
(516) 467-0600

Offers a one-record introductory course in Irish, including 20 lessons with an instruction manual. Also available on audiocassette. Price: $9.98 plus $2.50 shipping and handling. Request free brochure.

LIBRARIES AND RESEARCH FACILITIES (See also "Irish Studies—Resources.")

The following are some of the more important Irish research collections in the United States. If you're doing serious research as a student, scholar or journalist, you will normally receive permission to use a collection by writing the chief librarian or the librarian in charge of special collections.

SAMFORD UNIVERSITY
Harwell G. Davis Library
800 Lakeshore Drive
Birmingham, AL 35209

Nineteenth- and twentieth-century materials on Ireland.

UNITED IRISH CULTURAL CENTER OF SAN FRANCISCO
2700 45th Avenue
San Francisco, CA 94116
(415) 661-2700

Several thousand volumes covering Irish history, drama, poetry and other literature, folklore, genealogy, and the 32 counties. Irish and Irish-American newspapers and periodicals are also available.

UNIVERSITY OF CHICAGO
The University Library—
  Department of Special
  Collections
1100 East 57 Street
Chicago, IL 60637
(312) 753-4308

Social and cultural history of Ireland from the seventeenth through nineteenth centuries.

COLBY COLLEGE
Library, Special Collections
Waterville, ME 04901
(207) 873-1131

Literary manuscripts and other papers of nineteenth- and twentieth-century Irish authors, including Shaw.

BOSTON COLLEGE
Bapst Library—Irish
  Collection
Chestnut Hill, MA 02167
(617) 969-0100

Contains 7,500 books and several dozen journals and serials. The collection covers Irish political and social history, art, archaeology, education, government, and literature—Gaelic and Anglo-Irish.

COLLEGE OF ST. THOMAS
The Celtic Collection
Box 4268
c/o The Library
St. Paul, MN 55105

Collection includes nearly 5,000 items covering history, literature, folklore and philology.

SETON HALL UNIVERSITY
The McManus Collection
McLaughlin Library
405 South Orange Avenue
South Orange, NJ 07079
(201) 762-9000

Contains 4,000 volumes on Irish literature, history and politics—particularly the Home Rule question. Also: autographs, clippings and correspondence.

AMERICAN IRISH
  HISTORICAL SOCIETY
991 Fifth avenue
New York, NY 10028
(212) 228-2263

Holdings include a large book collection as well as manuscript collections and archives dealing with Irish individuals, families and organizations, mainly from the nineteenth and twentieth centuries.

ELIZABETH SETON
  COLLEGE
The Library
1061 North Broadway
Yonkers, NY 10701
(914) 969-4000

Irish music manuscripts.

IRISH CULTURAL LIBRARY
Gwynedd-Mercy College
7032 Loretto Avenue
Philadelphia, PA 19111
(215) 745-6000

LIFE INSURANCE—
FRATERNAL

HIBERNIAN LIFE
  INSURANCE
790 South Cleveland Avenue
Suite 221
St. Paul, MN 55116
(612) 690-3888

Originally founded by the Minnesota Ladies' Auxiliary,

Ancient Order of Hibernians (AOH), Hibernian Life now administers all life insurance programs offered by AOH units throughout the United States. The company offers three types of whole-life policies, which are available to any or all family members: (1) whole-life policies requiring premium payments until age 85, (2) policies requiring a single, lump-sum premium payment, and (3) 20-pay whole-life policies, whose total premiums are paid over a 20-year period. HLI is licensed to sell policies by mail to residents of all 50 states, and also sells to Chicago-area residents through a local agency. Contact HLI for details on eligibility requirements and insurance application forms. (Hibernian Life also funds two scholarship programs of special interest to Irish-Americans. See "Scholarships.")

LINEN—IMPORTED

GUARANTEED IRISH
Route 145
East Durham, NY 12423
(518) 786-1588

U.S. distributor for Fingal Irish Linen products. Imports pure linen tea towels in about 50 colorfast designs, including traditional blessings, recipes, maps, calendars and pictures. The towels also make attractive wall hangings. Also distributes Irish linen damask tablecloths in various sizes and designs. These items are commonly carried by import shops (see "Import Shops—General"). Guaranteed Irish sells these linen items through its own shop and will be pleased to refer you to a dealer near you that also handles them.

ULSTER WEAVING COMPANY, LTD.
148 Madison Avenue
New York, NY 10016
(212) 684-5534

Importer and wholesale distributor of household linens and piece goods made in Ireland by its parent company. These include large selections of table linen, with many items incorporating Celtic designs: linen damask tablecloths, mats and napkins. Also: printed tea towels, including maps of Ireland, stories of Irish traditions, Irish verse and blessings; guest towels; and men's and women's handkerchiefs, including many hand-embroidered and lace-edged items. Ulster Weaving will give you the names of stores in your area that stock its products. Request free catalog.

*MAGAZINES AND JOURNALS
—IRISH-AMERICAN* (See also
"Newspapers—Irish-American"
and "Newspapers and
Magazines, Imported—U.S.
Subscription Agents.")

AN GAEL
**c/o The Irish Arts Center
553 West 51st Street
New York, NY 10019
(212) 757-3318**

An illustrated quarterly devoted
to traditional Irish culture and
its perpetuation and revival in
America. Subscriptions: $10/yr.;
$11 in Canada; $12 elsewhere.

DUCAS
**c/o The Irish American
  Cultural Institute
2115 Summit Avenue
College of St. Thomas
St. Paul, MN 55105
(612) 647-5678**

A newsletter devoted to brief
items on Irish and Irish-American history, culture and miscel-
lany as well as IACI news.
Issued eight times a year, in
months when *Eire-Ireland* (see
following entry) is not published. A subscription is
included with membership in
the IACI, which starts at
$25/yr. (tax deductible).

EIRE-IRELAND
**c/o Irish American Cultural
  Institute
2115 Summit Avenue
College of St. Thomas
St. Paul, MN 55105
(612) 647-5678**

A learned journal of Irish studies
covering history, music, literature, traditional Irish culture,
folklore, etc. A four-issue subscription—plus eight issues of
Ducas (see previous entry)—
comes with membership in
IACI, starting at $25/yr. (tax
deductible).

FOLK HARP JOURNAL
**c/o International Society of
  Folk Harpers and
  Craftsmen, Inc.
4718 Maychelle Drive
Anaheim, CA 92807-3040
(714) 998-5717**

A quarterly journal covering all
aspects of this traditional Irish
and Celtic instrument: its history and evolution, its construction, playing techniques, music
written for it, and contemporary use throughout the world.
Subscriptions: $12/yr. (libraries
only, on calendar-year basis).
For others, subscriptions are
available without additional
charge through membership in
the ISFHC, which requires a
donation to the Society of at

least $15 (U.S.). Outside the United States, a postage surcharge must be added, as follows: Canada and Mexico, $2; all other countries—$2 for surface mail, $5 for air. Membership is on a calendar-year basis.

**IRISH AMERICA
P.O. Box 5141
Grand Central Station
New York, NY 10163
(212) 725-2993/2994**

This attractive monthly is the first magazine in the United States devoted to regular news coverage and features of Irish-American interest. Subscriptions: $20/yr.; $36/two yrs. Many newsstands and Irish import shops also carry this publication.

**THE RECORDER
c/o American Irish Historical
  Society
991 Fifth Avenue
New York, NY 10028
(212) 288-2263**

The official journal of the AIHS, *The Recorder* publishes articles on Irish and Irish-American history, literature, sociology, literary criticism and other disciplines, mostly written by scholars. Formerly available only to members, it is now available to all. Subscriptions to

this annual publication are $22.50 for individuals, and $34 for libraries and institutions. Outside the United States, add $2 for foreign surface mail and $9 for airmail.

**IRISH LITERARY
  SUPPLEMENT
Attn.: Robert G. Lowery,
  Editor
114 Paula Boulevard
Selden, NY 11784
(516) 698-8243**

Published twice yearly, ILS contains literary criticism and reviews of recent works of Irish and Irish-American history, poetry, drama, fiction, literature and literary criticism. Covers about 75 books per issue from Irish, American and British publishers. Also publishes news of the Irish literary world and of happenings of interest to readers of Irish literature. Subscriptions: $5/yr. for two issues.

**JAMES JOYCE QUARTERLY
The University of Tulsa
Tulsa, OK 74104
(918) 631-2501**

Publishes critical essays on the works of Joyce and other major Irish writers as well as notes, book reviews and checklists.

Individual subscriptions (United States): $12/yr., $23.50/two yrs.; for institutions, $13/yr., $25.50/two yrs.

MAILING LISTS—
IRISH-AMERICAN

DIRECT
  COMMUNICATIONS
Attn.: Jerry Henkel
75 Main Street
Fair Haven, VT 05743
(802) 265-8144

This firm brokers a variety of lists, including U.S. subscriber lists for *Irish Life, Ireland of the Welcomes, Irish America,* and *The Irish Echo,* and mail-order customer lists for such businesses as Gateway to Ireland, Genuine Irish, and Rego Irish Records & Tapes. Most lists require a minimum order of 5,000 names, and rental is subject to approval by the owner or its representative. Request details on available lists, formats, and prices.

AMERICAN CONFERENCE
  FOR IRISH STUDIES
  (ACIS)
Attn.: Michael Gillespie,
  Secretary
c/o Department of English
Marquette University
Milwaukee, WI 53233
(414) 224-3472

The ACIS membership list contains over 1,400 names, a high proportion of whom are teachers and scholars in the humanities and social sciences. Members share a common interest and specialty: Ireland and/or Irish America. Rental of list is subject to ACIS approval. Contact for rates and other details.

MAPS—ANTIQUE

GEORGE RITZLIN BOOKS
  & MAPS
P.O. Box 6060
Evanston, IL 60204
(312) 328-1966

Rare maps, atlases and books. Mrs. Ritzlin is a McMichael by birth, so her husband tries to keep old Irish items in stock, but finds that they sell quickly.

ERIN RARE COIN CO., INC.
P.O. Box 170
Merrick, NY 11566
(516) 868-8828

Stocks antique maps of Ireland, as available.

THE ARGOSY BOOK
  STORE
116 East 59th Street
New York, NY 10022
(212) PL3-4455

Stocks a good selection of maps of Ireland (and parts of Ireland) published between the sixteenth and nineteenth centuries. Will send items on approval: you send payment for what you keep, if anything, and return the rest, undamaged, without obligation.

MAPS & TRAVEL GUIDES— CURRENT

PHILEAS FOGG'S BOOKS AND MAPS FOR THE TRAVELER
540 University Avenue
Palo Alto, CA
(415) 327-1754

Maps and travel guides of Ireland.

RAND McNALLY MAP STORE
595 Market Street at 2nd
San Francisco, CA 94105
(415) 777-3131

RAND McNALLY MAP STORE
23 East Madison
Chicago, IL 60602
(312) 267-6868

AMERICAN MAP CORPORATION
46-35 54th Road
Maspeth, NY 11378
(718) 784-0055

Request free 35-page catalog.

RAND McNALLY MAP STORE
150 East 52nd Street
New York, NY 10022
(212) 758-7488

WIDE WORLD BOOKS & MAPS
401 N.E. 45th Street
Seattle, WA 98105
(206) 634-3453

Travel books, guides, and maps of Ireland including the Ordnance Survey maps, which show topographical features and are ideal for hikers. Also, atlases of Ireland and roadmaps published by Bartholomew's, Michelin and Geographia. Contact for further details.

MARINE SHIPPING SERVICES —BETWEEN IRELAND & THE UNITED STATES

The following marine transport firms provide containership service between U.S. ports and the Irish ports of Cork and/or Dublin:

ATLANTIC CONTAINER LINE
(800) 526-6802

DART CONTAINER LINE
(212) 432-9050

HAPAG-LLOYD
(800) 522-1720

SEA-LAND SERVICE
(800) 732-5263

TRANS FREIGHT LINES, INC.
(800) 835-2665

MONUMENTS (See "Cemetery Monuments, Traditional Designs—Imported.")

MOVERS, OVERSEAS— SPECIALISTS IN SHIPMENTS BETWEEN THE UNITED STATES AND IRELAND, INCLUDING HOUSEHOLD OR OFFICE RELOCATIONS

AIR-SEA-PAC
2300 East Higgins Road
Elk Grove, IL 60007
(312) 640-8033

MOVERS INTERNATIONAL
1549 Ardmore
Itasca, IL 60143
(312) 773-3772

NORTH AMERICAN VAN LINES, INC.
5001 U.S. Highway 30 West
P.O. Box 988
Fort Wayne, IN 46801-0988
(800) 348-2111

Contact customer service at the number above for the location of your nearest NAVL agency.

OMEGA SHIPPING COMPANY
172-70 Baisley Boulevard
Jamaica, NY 11434
(718) 978-9000; (800) 232-0037 outside NY State

LIFFEY MOVERS
229 East 120th Street
New York, NY 10035
(212) 410-3500

OVERSEAS MOVING SPECIALISTS, INC.
1285 Avenue of the Americas
35th Floor
New York, NY 10019
(212) 233-3332; (800) 631-4911 outside New York State

LYNCH INTERNATIONAL, INC.
34-37 65th Street
P.O. Box 1112
Woodside, NY 11377
(718) 672-8900; (800) 672-7266

Serves the Boston and Philadelphia areas as well as Greater New York.

MUSEUMS

THE HOUSE OF IRELAND
Balboa Park
San Diego, CA 92101
(619) 466-7654

This authentic replica of a rural Irish cottage dates from the 1930s. Open Sundays from 1:30 to 4:30 p.m., the cottage is the focus of instrumental music and song, art, dance and other activities designed to preserve and promote an appreciation of Ireland's traditional culture. Tea and soda bread are served to visitors in the Kennedy Kitchen.

UNITED IRISH CULTURAL
CENTER OF SAN
FRANCISCO
2700 45th Avenue
San Francisco, CA 94116
(415) 661-2700

The center's impressive All-Irish Library, which houses several thousand books, periodicals and other items, also maintains a minimuseum that displays Irish artifacts and paintings.

MUSEUM OF FINE ARTS
465 Huntington Avenue
Boston, MA 02115
(617) 267-9300

MFA exhibits items representing various aspects and periods of Irish culture. On display are ancient Celtic ornaments; Irish silver; portraits by John Singleton Copley, who became an expatriate in London but had been born in Boston of Irish descent; paintings by Jack Yeats, W.B's brother; Irish Chippendale furniture; and a Waterford crystal chandelier.

DETROIT INSTITUTE OF
ARTS
5200 Woodward Avenue
Detroit, MI 48202
(313) 833-7900

Among the institute's many excellent exhibits is perhaps North America's largest collection of ancient Irish gold jewelry from the pre-Celtic Bronze Age (2000 B.C. to 200 B.C.). The museum is closed Mondays.

NEW YORK STATE IRISH
AMERICAN HISTORY
MUSEUM
Route 145
East Durham, NY 12324
(518) 432-6598

Founded in 1986 with a state grant, this new museum is co-located in East Durham, and in Albany, at the College of St. Rose. From Memorial Day through October, the East Durham museum offers exhibits and programs relating to the Irish-American experience. The College of St. Rose provides a home for the research center, which is devoted to collecting books, periodicals and other documents on the Irish-American experience, and to making them available to students, scholars and the public. We suggest you phone before visiting to see whether the museum or library have the specific types of exhibits or research material you're looking for.

THE IRISH CLASSROOM
The Cathedral of Learning
University of Pittsburgh
Pittsburgh, PA 15213

One of 18 "international classrooms" grouped around the Commons Room of the Cathedral of Learning, the Irish Classroom—the only stone room—features elements from both northern and southern Ireland. It has the shape, size and materials of a sixth-century Irish oratory, or small chapel. The vestibule entrance is copied from Killeshin Chapel, County Laois.

MUSICAL INSTRUMENTS, TRADITIONAL IRISH— INSTRUCTION

Instruction in various traditional Irish instruments is available throughout the United States. You will generally be able to locate suitable instructors through advertisements in Irish-American newspapers (see "Newspapers—Irish-American") and through local Irish centers and societies, including chapters of Comhaltas Ceoltoiri Eireann, the Traditional Irish Musicians Association. (See "Organizations, Irish-American —National.")

MUSICAL INSTRUMENTS, TRADITIONAL IRISH— SOURCES

LARK IN THE MORNING
Box 1176
Mendocino, CA 95460
(707) 964-5569

Sells Irish harps, uillean and other bagpipes, bodhrans, concertinas, Irish-style flutes, and hammered dulcimers. Send $2.50 for catalog.

**DRAGONWHISPERS BY
  BETTY R. TRUITT**
P.O. Box 211
Sunrise Highway
Mt. Laguna, CA 92048
(619) 473-9010

Handcrafted folk harps, including Irish, neo-Irish and Celtic styles in sizes from 3 to 5 feet high. Harps may be custom-carved, -painted and -decorated to your specifications. Also sells harp stands, strings, and electronic tuners. You may visit the workshop by appointment. Request free product literature.

ROBINSON'S HARP SHOP
33908 Mount Laguna Drive
P.O. Box 161
Mt. Laguna, CA 92048
(619) 473-8556

This shop, operated by Roland Robinson, sells strings, components and other accessories for harps. Robinson's also publishes plans for building harps, and sells instructional videos and books as well as audio recordings and harp music. Roland Robinson was one of the founders of the Society of Folk Harpers and Craftsmen and the *Folk Harp Journal* (Robinson is the source to contact for *back issues*). Request free brochure covering harps, books, record-

ings (tapes, LPs, CDs and videocassettes), and other items.

IRISH IMPORTS
3244 Geary Boulevard
San Francisco, CA 94118
(415) 752-0961

Harps handmade by Brian McGirr, a highly regarded craftsman in County Tyrone; accordions; bodhrans; and tin whistles. Also: instruction books and instrumental music collections.

TRIPLETT HARPS
220 Suburban Road
San Luis Obispo, CA 93401
(805) 544-2777

Manufactures and repairs folk harps. Also offers kits, assembled kits that require finishing, books, records, and tapes. Request free catalog.

FOLK MOTE MUSIC
1034 Santa Barbara Street
Santa Barbara, CA 93101
(805) 962-0830

Specialists in traditional Irish instruments, including bodhrans, harps, bouzoukis, tin whistles and hammered dulcimers. Also: books of traditional Irish music, and records and tapes. Harp lessons available. Request free catalog.

HOBGOBLIN MUSIC
P.O. Box 5311
South San Francisco, CA
   94080
(415) 991-4040

Stocks traditional musical instruments and supplies, including fiddles, uillean pipes, bodhrans, harps and harp kits, accordions, melodeons, and bones. Also carries a limited selection of recordings, song and tune books, and used instruments. Request free catalog.

LYON & HEALY HARPS
168 North Ogden Avenue
Chicago, IL 60607
(312) 786-1881; (800) 621-3881

Manufactures and sells the Lyon & Healy folk harp, a Celtic-style instrument. Also: harp music, strings, and other accessories. Request free catalog.

HOUSE OF MUSICAL
   TRADITIONS
7040 Carroll Avenue
Takoma Park, MD 20912
(301) 270-9090

Traditional Celtic and Irish instruments, including Folkcraft and Dusty Strings harps, Irish and Scottish bagpipes, bodhrans, tin whistles, bouzoukis, tenor banjos, and Irish flutes

and fifes. Also: books and recordings. Send $2 for catalog.

BOSTON MUSIC COMPANY
116 Boylston Street
Boston, MA 02116
(617) 426-5100

Sells the Lyon & Healy troubador harp, tin whistles, and other instruments. Contact for further information.

SANDY'S RECORD SHOP
896A Massachusetts Avenue
Cambridge, MA 02139
(617) 491-2812

Sells tenor banjos, mandolins, bones, bodhrans, accordions, and Celtic harps (occasionally).

WALTON MUSIC
   CORPORATION
P.O. Box 1505
Westfield, MA 01085
(413) 562-0223; (800) 541-5004

This is the U.S. headquarters of Ireland's largest music publishers, and sells printed music, recordings and instruments. Instruments include a full range of tin whistles, including whistles for beginners as well as experienced players, bodhrans, and several Irish- and Celtic-style harps. Also: strings for harps and other instruments; song and music books, including collections of tunes by O'Carolan and Moore; and cassette/music book combinations with music for various Irish instruments as well as groups. Wholesale inquiries welcome. Individuals may also request free copies of the Walton catalog as well as the location of their nearest Walton dealer.

**CASTIGLIONE ACCORDION
  COMPANY**
P.O. Box 05367
12644 East Seven Mile Road
Detroit, MI 48205
(313) 527-1595

Shamrock accordions and other brands. Irish musette tuning. Write or call collect for catalog.

IMBUSCH HARPS
c/o Kevin Imbusch
86 West 12th Street
New York, NY 10011
(212) 691-7486

For decades, some of the world's finest folk harps were made by George Imbusch, who died in his native Limerick in 1985. His son, Nial, learned the craft from his father, and now carries on the family tradition. The Imbusch harp stands 3 feet 11 inches high, has a range of 4½ octaves and a frame completely handcrafted from

mahogany. To acquire one—or obtain more information—contact Kevin Imbusch.

MANDOLIN BROTHERS
629 Forest Avenue
Staten Island, NY 10310
(718) 981-3226

Offers a variety of Irish mandolins, mandolas, octave mandolins, mando-cellos, bouzoukis, tenor banjos, guitars, cases, accessories, instructional books, and tapes. Request free catalog.

MARKWOOD HARPS
1250 N.E. 5th Street
Bend, OR 97701
(503) 389-6775

Makes Celtic and Irish folk harps. Request free catalog.

THE MUSIC BARN
490 Easton Road
Horsham, PA 19044
(215) 674-5505

Irish and Celtic folk harps.

**BUCKS COUNTY FOLK
  MUSIC SHOP**
40 Sand Road
New Britain, PA 18901
(215) 345-0616

Sells bodhrans, rosewood Irish whistles, Irish bouzoukis, penny whistles, mandolins, concertinas, rosewood and maplewood fifes, and books and recordings of traditional Irish music.

NEEDLE ARTS— TRADITIONAL IRISH TECHNIQUES OR DESIGNS
(See also "Crafts & Craftspeople—Traditional.")

IRISH CROCHET TREASURES
P.O. Box 1625
562 Milk Street
Fitchburg, MA 01420
(617) 342-1152

Imports woolen cushion covers embroidered with designs from the famous *Book of Kells.* Contact for sizes, prices and other information.

NEWSPAPERS & MAGAZINES, IMPORTED—NEWS DEALERS

HAROLD'S HOMETOWN NEWSSTAND
599 Post
San Francisco, CA 94102
(415) 441-2665

IRISH IMPORTS
3157 Geary Boulevard
San Francisco, CA 94118
(415) 752-0961

DONEGAL IMPORTS
5358 West Devon Avenue
Chicago, IL 60646
(312) 792-2377

SHANNON IMPORTS
5726 West 95th Street
Chicago, IL 60453
(312) 424-7055

OUT OF TOWN NEWS
Zero Harvard Square
Cambridge, MA 02138
(617) 354-7777

National and county newspapers—and selected magazines —flown in regularly from Ireland.

JEANNIE CAMPBELL'S IRISH STORE
508 Broadway
New York, NY 10034
(212) 567-9029

National and county newspapers from Ireland.

HOTALINGS NEWS AGENCY, INC.
Foreign News Depot
142 West 42nd Street
New York, NY 10036
(212) 840-1868

National and county newspapers flown in every Tuesday morning.

NEWSPAPERS AND
MAGAZINES, IMPORTED—
U.S. SUBSCRIPTION AGENTS

IRELAND OF THE
WELCOMES
Subscription Forwarding
P.O. Box 54138
Boulder, CO 80321-4138

This bimonthly publication,
published by the Irish Tourist
Board, is a travel magazine—
and more. Through color and
black-and-white photos and
informative articles, it provides
an all-around entrée to Irish culture today—and the heritage of
Ireland's past.

Ireland of the Welcomes covers
virtually any subject of interest
dealing with Ireland and those
of Irish heritage. Recent issues,
for example, have contained
stories on such diverse subjects
as the renaissance of Irish quilt-
ing; contemporary buildings
and town planning in Ireland;
Irish emigration to Australia
during the age of sail; the rocks
and geological formations of
Ireland; the master stonecarvers
of Durrow, County Laois, who
carry on the tradition started
with the great high crosses; the
many attractions of Fota Island,
County Cork; the story of the
Gaelic Athletic Association; and
Graninne Ui Mhaille (Grace

O'Malley), the legendary sixteenth-century chieftainess who
built a kingdom on the west
coast of Ireland based on trade
and piracy.

You may order a one-year
subscription—at a special
rate—by sending a check or
money order for $9.95 to the
address provided here. Individual issues may also be pur-
chased at many Irish book and
import shops.

IRISH LIFE
Subscription Forwarding
P.O. Box 53286
Boulder, CO 80322-3086

This new four-color bimonthly,
published in Ireland, includes
photo essays; travel features;
articles on food, sports, art,
music and other aspects of Irish
culture; articles by celebrity
authors; a current events
column; and calendars of upcoming events in Ireland. Subscriptions: $19.95/yr., six issues;
$34.95/two yrs.; $46.95/three
yrs.

IRELAND'S NEWSPAPERS
Attn.: Stanley Plitt
230 East 44th Street
New York, NY 10017
(212) 661-9320

Offers "fast mail delivery" of newspapers from the 26 counties in the Republic, and of the major daily and Sunday Dublin newspapers—over 60 different newspapers in all. Sells in bulk to retailers, and takes subscription orders from individuals (subscription copies are mailed from New York). Request free brochure and catalog.

NEWSPAPERS—IRISH-AMERICAN (See also "Events, Calendars of—Irish-American" and "Magazines and Journals —Irish-American.")

THE IRISH AMERICAN PRESS
2554 Lincoln Boulevard, #236
Marina del Rey, CA 90291
(213) 391-1858 or 827-0243

Monthly. Covers "things Irish in California and in Ireland," including cultural affairs, business and economics, sports, religion and politics. Subscriptions: $18/yr. in the United States; $25/yr. in Canada.

THE IRISH HERALD
2123 Market Street
San Francisco, CA 94114
(415) 621-2200

Monthly. Subscriptions: $10/yr.

THE IRISHMAN
P.O. Box 11278
San Francisco, CA 94101
(415) 665-2838

Monthly. Concentrates on covering the California Irish-American community and its activities. Subscriptions: $14/yr.

IRISH AMERICAN NEWS
2400 Hassell Road
Suite 350
Hoffman Estates, IL 60195
(312) 882-4410

Monthly. Covers not only Chicago, but most of mid-America, through a network of correspondents in cities from Ohio to Texas. Subscriptions: $13/yr. in the United States; $20/yr. in Canada, and in other countries via surface mail; $50/yr. in other countries via airmail.

SOUTH BOSTON TRIBUNE
395 West Broadway
Boston, MA 02127
(617) 268-4747

Formerly called *The Irish Star*. Weekly. Subscriptions: $10/yr.

BOSTON IRISH NEWS
14 Franconia Street
Dorchester, MA 02122
(617) 825-1400

Monthly. Subscriptions: $10/yr.

THE IRISH ADVOCATE
15 Park Row
New York, NY 10038
(212) 233-4672

Weekly. Subscriptions: $10/yr.

THE IRISH ECHO
309 Fifth Avenue
New York, NY 10016
(212) 686-1266

Weekly. Covers Irish-related
news and activities across the
United States, through correspondents in major cities. The
Boston edition, previously
issued separately, has been
incorporated into the national
edition. Subscriptions: $20/yr.

THE IRISH VOICE
432 Park Avenue South
New York, NY 10016
(212) 725-2993/2994

Weekly. Offers news from Ireland as well as national coverage
of the Irish-American political,
social and business scenes and
other topics. Subscriptions:
$20/yr.; $38/two yrs.

THE NATIONAL
** HIBERNIAN DIGEST**
c/o James Brennan
Advertising Director
207 North Zane Highway
Martin's Ferry, OH 43935

Bimonthly. Subscriptions are
normally available only to
members of the Ancient Order
of Hibernians, and are included
with membership. (See "Organizations, Irish-American—
National.") Advertising space is
available in the *Digest,* however,
and sample copies and rate
information are available by
writing to the address provided
here.

THE IRISH EDITION
P.O. Box 44102
Philadelphia, PA 19144
(215) 849-4404/4405

Monthly. Covers Philadelphia
and the mid-Atlantic states.
Subscriptions: $13/yr. (domes-
tic); $20/yr. (foreign via surface
mail); $25/yr. (Canada via air-
mail, and domestic via first-
class mail); and $35/yr. (foreign
via airmail).

ORGANIZATIONS, IRISH-
AMERICAN—IRISH CENTERS

UNITED IRISH CULTURAL
** CENTER OF SAN**
** FRANCISCO**
2700 45th Avenue
San Francisco, CA 94116
(415) 661-2700

This modern center offers a ballroom that can accommodate 1,000; modern kitchen and bar; a cocktail lounge with a stage for floor-show entertainment, a dancing area, seating for 300 and a dining area; rooms for meetings and receptions held by clubs and private parties; a large library of Irish materials; and recreational facilities.

IRISH AMERICAN HERITAGE CENTER
4626 North Knox Avenue
Chicago, IL 60630
(312) 282-7035

Housed in a former junior college building and renovated at a cost of $3 million, this center serves the Chicago Irish-American community with a variety of facilities. Rooms are available for organizational meetings, and an auditorium seats 900 for large meetings and performances. There is a full-service kitchen on premises, and plans call for adding a library, a museum, a chapel and an Irish-American Hall of Fame in the near future. The Heritage Center is located in the near northwest section of Chicago, convenient to major highways and public transit.

IRISH CULTURAL SOCIETY OF NEW ORLEANS
3600 Chestnut Street
3rd Floor
New Orleans, LA 70115
(504) 488-3338

Founded several years ago, this group now has limited permanent facilities in a private home. These include a meeting room and a library. Activities held here or elsewhere, as needed, include ceilis, Irish dancing instruction, a genealogy club, Irish history lectures, Gaelic classes, evening discussions of Irish literature and poetry, and performances of traditional music.

GAELIC LEAGUE & IRISH AMERICAN CLUB OF DETROIT
2068 Michigan Avenue
Detroit, MI 48216
(313) 964-8700

Opened in 1920, this center features banquet facilities for 300, a library, and meeting rooms of various sizes.

IRISH AMERICAN CENTER
297 Willis Avenue
Mineola, NY 11501
(516) 746-9392

This facility serves its own membership as well as renting

rooms to other Irish-American groups. The center has banquet facilities that seat 300 people, and the largest "Irish" library on Long Island. Classes are offered in the Irish language, bagpiping, and other subjects.

THE IRISH CENTER/ COMMODORE BARRY CLUB
6815 Emlen Street
Philadelphia, PA 19119
(215) 843-8051

Located in Philadelphia's Mt. Airy section, the Irish Center/ Commodore Barry Club is the main focus of Irish-American activities in the city. The organization is housed in a large, older building whose facilities include one of the city's largest ballrooms, many smaller rooms for meetings and other functions, a bar/lounge with a dancing area, a kitchen for catering, and a library. Many independent Irish-American groups make their home here, and the regular activities schedule includes: classes in step dancing, Irish language, Irish harp and other instruments; evening ceilis; performances of Irish drama; and meetings of the local Gaelic Athletic Association and other societies.

IRISH CENTRE OF PITTSBURGH
6886 Forward Avenue
Pittsburgh, PA 15217
(412) 521-9712

Set on a 4½-acre site, the Pittsburgh Centre contains an extensive library; a large hall with stage for dancing, concerts, exhibitions and lectures; as well as offices and a kitchen for catering. There's even an outdoor swimming pool. The activities schedule, equally impressive, includes an Irish choral group; step dancing and Irish music classes; speakers; and special events, including an annual feis. The Centre's focus is educational, cultural and social, with a large family membership.

ORGANIZATIONS, IRISH-AMERICAN—LOCAL, SELECTED (See also "Organizations, Irish-American —Irish Centers.")

Note: There are thousands of local Irish-American organizations—and chapters of national organizations—throughout the United States. Those listed here are merely a handful of the more prominent. To find out about the activities of organizations in your area—and how to contact them—consult appro-

priate Irish-American newspapers (see "Newspapers—
Irish-American") and calendars
of events (see "Events, Calendars of—Irish-American"). For
most of the Midwestern and
Rocky Mountain states, and
those in between, the best single
source is the monthly calendar
published in *The Irish American
News,* Chicago.

**EIRE SOCIETY OF BOSTON
c/o George Ryan
49 Franklin Street
Boston, MA 02110
(617) 482-4316**

Since it began in 1937, the Eire
Society has been working to
promote the "knowledge of
Irish culture through the
encouragement of study in the
arts, sciences, literature, language and history of Ireland."
One means it uses is an excellent
bulletin, which contains fascinating articles on Irish and Irish-
American culture and history.
The society also sponsors
monthly lectures from October
through April. It awards a gold
medal each year to a prominent
individual. Recipients have
included Fianna Fail leader
Charles Haughey, journalist
Bob Considine, film director
John Ford, U.S. House of Representatives Speakers John W.
McCormack and Thomas J.

"Tip" O'Neill, and Archbishop
of Boston Richard Cardinal
Cushing. Eire Society dues are
$30/yr., including the bulletin.

**THE CHARITABLE IRISH
SOCIETY
32 Fremont Street
Needham, MA 02194
(617) 449-4949**

This group merits mention if
only because it is the oldest Irish
organization in the United
States, founded in 1737. While
the exodus to the suburbs has
helped bring membership down
to 500 or so, the CIS still carries
on one of its original aims: helping to assist the poor in Ireland,
the United States and elsewhere.
The society holds quarterly
meetings, as well as a gala dinner each March at Boston's
Copley Hotel. Over the years, it
has hosted speeches by such
noted Irish-Americans as John
F. Kennedy (a member) and
Babe Ruth. Senator Edward
Kennedy, John Boyle O'Reilly
and former Mayor of Boston
Patrick Collins have also been
members.

**NEW YORK IRISH
HISTORY ROUNDTABLE
P.O. Box 2087
Church Street Station, NY
10008**

Founded in 1984, this organization works to promote study of

Irish-American history in New York City and surrounding areas. It also helps provide its members—scholars and laypeople alike—with information on source materials available in local libraries, archives and other institutions.

The Roundtable publishes an annual journal, *The New York Irish,* and a twice-yearly newsletter. Meetings are held twice a year, and other activities include (1) occasional field trips of historic interest, (2) a Graduate Scholarship Fund, (3) an oral history project, and, (4) preparation of an index encompassing all issues of *The Irish Echo* since it began publication some 50-odd years ago.

Membership dues are $15/yr. for residents of the New York metropolitan area, and $10 elsewhere. To join, write to the address provided here, enclosing payment, or send $1 for a sample copy of *The New York Irish.*

THE IRISH ARTS CENTER/ AN CLAIDHEAMH SOLUIS
553 West 51st Street
New York, NY 10019
(212) 757-3318

This organization conducts most of its activities in New York, but it's more than a local New York institution. This is due in large part to its excellent quarterly magazine, *An Gael: Irish Traditional Culture Alive in America Today* (see "Magazines & Journals—Irish-American").

Newly renovated, the Center's three-story quarters bustle with a continuous round of activities. There are classes in Irish music, dance, history and language, and first-rate theatrical performances by the Irish Arts Centre Theatre, its resident company, and other groups.

Elsewhere in the city, the center sponsors regular ceilis as well as an annual festival of traditional Irish music and dance. National membership ($20/yr.) includes a subscription to *An Gael,* free courses, and 20-percent discounts on plays, ceilis and other cultural events. Sponsor ($50) and Patron ($100) memberships bring you these and additional benefits. Request a free sample issue of the center's bimonthly newsletter, *Litr Nuacht.*

ORGANIZATIONS, IRISH-AMERICAN—NATIONAL

AMERICAN IRISH HISTORICAL SOCIETY
991 Fifth Avenue
New York, NY 10028
(212) 288-2263

A nonsectarian, nonpolitical organization that works to promote a better appreciation of the Irish role in American history and society. AIHS maintains a library of 25,000 volumes, chiefly covering Irish and Irish-American history and genealogy. It also sponsors a series of regular entertainment and educational programs, including performances by Irish musicians, poetry readings, and lectures by scholars and by Irish leaders in various fields. The society also publishes a twice-yearly journal, *The Recorder,* sent without charge to members. Membership dues are $25/yr. for students, $100 for others. Write for membership information and an application form.

AMERICAN CONFERENCE FOR IRISH STUDIES (ACIS)
Attn.: James Donnelly, President
c/o Department of History
University of Wisconsin
Madison, WI 53706
(608) 263-1971

This nationwide organization, with a membership of 1,500-plus scholars and others, works to foster scholarship on Ireland and Irish America in such varied disciplines as history, literature, political science, folklore, economics, archaeology, art, sociology and linguistics. Members present papers at a spring national conference and at regional conferences in the fall.

ACIS publishes a thrice-yearly newsletter, and *A Guide to Irish Studies in the United States,* a directory to courses offered at institutions across the country. Members also receive the *Irish Literary Supplement.* Dues for calendar-year membership are $11.50 for students and retirees, $15 for U.S. residents, and $18 for those outside the United States and Canada.

ANCIENT ORDER OF HIBERNIANS IN AMERICA (AOH)
National Office
13002 Fork Road
Baldwin, MD 21013
(301) 591-9345

Founded in 1836, AOH is the nation's largest Irish-American organization, with a reported 91,000 members affiliated with divisions and chapters throughout the United States. AOH traces its roots to an Irish society founded in the sixteenth century. Membership is currently restricted to Roman Catholic men of Irish heritage. There is a parallel ladies' auxiliary, the Ladies Ancient Order of Hibernians (LAOH). There

has been at least one attempt—
so far unsuccessful—to accept
Irish-American men of non-
Catholic heritage.

Nationally and locally, AOH
works to promote awareness
and action on Irish-related public issues, provides social and
fraternal activities for members,
sponsors scholarships and other
awards, and offers members
reasonably priced fraternal life
insurance (see "Life Insurance—
Fraternal"). Members receive a
bimonthly newspaper, *National
Hibernian Digest*.

**COMHALTAS CEOLTOIRI
  EIREANN
Traditional Irish Musicians
  Association
c/o Bill McEvoy, North
  American Coordinator
928 Hawkins Avenue
Lake Grove, NY 11755
(516) 588-3709**

This international society, head-
quartered in Ireland, has 30 local
chapters—and over 4,000 members—in North America. Its
goals are to preserve traditional
Irish music in all its forms—
instrumental, song and dance—
and to promote a better appreciation of the Irish language.
Local chapters usually hold
monthly functions open to both
members and nonmembers.

Annual dues are $12, and
include a subscription to the
quarterly magazine, *Treoir*
("The Message"). To find out
where your nearest chapter is
located, call or write Mr.
McEvoy.

**EMERALD SOCIETIES
(Independent societies are
  located in various cities).**

Unique among Irish-American
groups, the Emerald Societies
are organized along occupa-
tional lines. They are generally
open to those of Irish birth or
heritage who share a common,
often governmental, employer;
for example, a police department, fire department, board of
education, sanitation department or other agency.

Emerald Societies offer members an opportunity to meet
other Irish-Americans in the
same trade or profession. They
also work to foster appreciation
of Irish culture and traditions,
and pursue charitable and
nationalist objectives. Emerald
Society pipe bands are a fixture
in many St. Patrick's Day
parades; there are about 10 such
bands in New York alone.

The first Emerald Society was
established in New York City in
the early 1950s, and similar
groups have followed in Bos-

ton, Chicago and other cities. The tri-state (New York/New Jersey/Connecticut) area alone now claims over 40 Emerald Societies coordinated by a Grand Council.

THE GAELIC LEAGUE
(Independent chapters are located in several U.S. cities.)

The American units of this prestigious international society, each chartered independently by the Irish parent organization, seek to promote the goals put forth in 1893 by their Irish founders, Douglas Hyde (a leading Gaelic scholar and the first President of Ireland) and historian Eoin MacNeill, later chief of staff of the Irish Volunteers. These goals were to keep the Gaelic language alive where it was still spoken and to promote wider study and appreciation of the language as well as the music, dance and other cultural activities associated with it.

The League was instrumental in persuading the Irish government to require Gaelic instruction in schools, but neither it nor the government has been able to make Gaelic the everyday language of Ireland's people. It is among Irish-Americans, in particular, that Gaelic is becoming an increasingly popular subject of study, and Gaelic League chapters in several U.S. cities do a worthy job of promoting language instruction and wider cultural activities.

The organization is nonsectarian in membership and outlook. You may find out whether or not there is a chapter near you by contacting the Irish American Cultural Institute (see next entry). *Note:* We refer here to the "Gaelic" language. It is, however, increasingly popular to use the term *Irish* when referring to the indigenous language spoken in Ireland, since another form of Gaelic is spoken in parts of Scotland.

IRISH AMERICAN CULTURAL INSTITUTE
Mail 5026
2115 Summit Avenue
College of St. Thomas
St. Paul, MN 55105
(612) 647–5678

This international foundation is devoted to promoting the cultural heritage of Ireland and Irish America, and has no religious, political, social or fraternal objectives in the usual sense.

The Institute carries out its aims through a variety of activities and programs, which include (1) publication of *Eire-Ireland,* a highly regarded quarterly journal of Irish studies, and *Ducas,* an informative newsletter published in months when *Eire-Ireland* is not; (2) annual awards of $10,000 to Irish writers and artists; (3) an endowed research fund to support scholarly study of the Irish-American experience; (4) bringing dramatic and musical productions and art exhibits to the United States from Ireland; (5) sponsorship of Irish Perceptions, a program that brings leading Irish writers, scholars and artists to lecture and perform in several U.S. cities six times a year; (6) sponsorship of local chapters in over a dozen U.S. cities (IACI has members in all 50 states); (7) The Irish Way program, which offers summer experiences in Ireland for U.S. high school students; (8) Trees for Ireland, a program to help promote the reforestation of Ireland; and (9) the production of 53 half-hour television programs and 13 half-hour films on various aspects of Irish culture.

IACI depends for its funds on memberships (Member, $25/yr.; Sponsor, $50/ yr.; and Patron, $150/yr.) as well as on gifts from individuals, companies and foundations. Donations are tax-deductible. Request literature.

THE IRISH GEORGIAN SOCIETY
7-13 Washington Square North
New York, NY 10003
(212) 254-4862

As the American arm of the IGS, this organization works to help preserve, maintain and restore the architectural and artistic treasures created in Ireland from the late seventeenth through the early nineteenth century. There are 22 local chapters throughout the United States. Membership benefits include (1) lectures on aspects of Irish Georgian culture and arts, (2) an annual newsletter, and (3) chapter tours to Ireland, which include visits to great houses and art collections not open to the general public. Regular membership dues are $25/yr.; contributing membership, $150/yr.; and life membership, $1,000.

PEAT (TURF)—BRIQUETTES IMPORTED FROM IRELAND

ERIN LAND IMPORTS LTD.
5105 Gladstone Avenue
Minneapolis, MN 55419
(612) 823-6518

Stocks gift packages of "Irish Heartland" turf briquettes.

CLARK & WILKINS INDUSTRIES, INC.
1871 Park Avenue
New York, NY 10035
(212) 534-5110

Imports and sells genuine Irish turf, the fuel used for centuries for heating Irish homes and for cooking. The turf comes in compressed briquettes: a 28-pound box costs $30, including delivery by UPS. May only be available in the eastern United States.

PHOTOGRAPHS—IRELAND

CELTIC IMAGES
P.O. Box 6755
Towson, MD 21285-6755
(301) 527-0965

This firm specializes in original scenic photography—in color—of Irish landscapes and people, especially in the West of Ireland. All photos are hand printed and are available in matted format, or framed. CI also accepts commissions to do specific photographic assignments during regular visits to Ireland. Request free brochure.

POSTCARDS

OLD WINDSOR ANTIQUES
345 Bethlehem Road
New Windsor, NY 12550
(914) 564-6775

Stocks a large selection of old Irish postcards. You may order cards on approval, paying for those you keep and returning the rest undamaged. Suitable for framing, gifts or collecting. Request details.

POSTMARKS, UNITED STATES—"IRISH"

Whether you're doing a mailing to customers of your Irish-related business, members of your Irish-American organization, or just sending St. Patrick's Day or other greetings to special friends or relatives, you can add a memorable touch by having your mail postmarked in any of several U.S. communities with special Irish names.

Enclose your stamped envelope(s) in a larger envelope addressed to: U.S. Post Office, Attn.: Postmaster, (town or city of your choice, with zip code, from the list that follows). Enclose a brief note asking that the stamps on the enclosed envelopes be canceled with the local postmark and mailed. If you're doing a large mailing, you should write or phone the post office first for instructions.

Erin, NY 14838

Erin, TN 37061

Hibernia, NJ 07842

Ireland, IN 47545

Ireland, TX 76536

Shamrock, NC 28205

Shamrock, OK 74068

Shamrock, TX 79079

Shamrock Station, PA 19552

If there's an Irish place with special meaning for you, check the list under "Irish Names upon Our Land" in *The Irish-American Almanac* section of this book to see whether or not there's a place of the same name in the United States. If so, you can ask your local post office for the correct zip code, and follow the procedure previously described.

POTTERY & CERAMICS— IMPORTED

CELTIC FOLKWORKS
RD #4
Box 210
Willow Grove Road
Newfield, NJ 08344
(609) 691-5968

Hand-thrown pottery with hand-painted Celtic designs, made in Ireland at the Orchard Pottery, County Limerick. Items include vases, tankards and teapots. Send $1 for catalog.

PEARCE & VANCE
385 Bleecker Street
New York, NY 10014
(212) 924-1142

Sells traditional dinnerware and pottery items handmade at the Philip Pearce and Stephen Pearce potteries in Shanagarry, County Cork. Made from Blackwater River clay and fired (in the case of Stephen Pearce Pottery) in turf-burning kilns, the line includes plates, bowls, mugs, pitchers, servers and other dinnerware and kitchen items. The shop also stocks traditional hand-blown lead glassware from the Simon Pearce Glass Mill, Quechee, VT. (See "Crafts and Craftspeople—Traditional.") Send $2 for catalog.

WILD GEESE
INTERNATIONAL
217 West 16th Street
New York, NY 10011
(212) 989-7853

U.S. importer of products from the Sligo Craft Pottery. Contact for product information and locations of stores near you that stock items in which you are interested.

PRINTS—ANTIQUE

ARGOSY BOOK STORE
116 East 59th Street
New York, NY 10022
(212) PL3-4455

Offers a variety of old Irish prints—typically hand-colored engravings—portraying such subject matter as noted Irish people, town and city plans, and scenic views. No catalog is available, but Argosy will send items to you on approval: you keep what you like, forwarding payment, and return the rest, undamaged, without further obligation.

PUBS—IRISH-AMERICAN

If you're fond of the camaraderie and good drink that characterize the typical Irish-American pub, you probably already have your own favorite(s). In any event, there are thousands of pubs across the country—simply too many to begin to list here. If you'd like to shop around, however, many pubs run ads in various Irish-American newspapers. In addition, each issue of *Irish America* magazine contains a guide to selected pubs in New York City and Boston.

RADIO—IRISH-AMERICAN PROGRAMS

There are probably hundreds of radio programs broadcast locally throughout the United States for Irish-American audiences. Their formats generally emphasize music, news and commentary about Ireland, news and announcements of local Irish-American activities, or some combination of these. We haven't attempted to list these programs or stations here. Some—such as Dorothy Hayden Cudahy's program and "The Adrian Flannery Show" in New York—have been on for decades. A fair percentage of them come and go rather quickly, however, or at least change their time slots. In any case, there are simply too many to list. To find out which programs can be heard where you live, check the current radio schedules published in the Irish-American newspapers serving your area. (See "Newspapers—Irish-American.")

RADIO—IRISH-LANGUAGE PROGRAMS

**BLAS MEIRICEANACH/
  ACCENT AMERICAN
Attn.: Paul Murphy
WFDU-FM Radio
Fairleigh Dickinson
  University
Teaneck, NJ 07666
(201) 692-2806**

This one-hour program, which recently debuted as "the first Irish-language radio talk show" in the United States (and perhaps Ireland as well), airs each Saturday from 3:00 to 4:00 P.M. The first half hour is called "Best of Irish" and is devoted to language instruction. The remainder offers commentary and discussion in Irish. WFDU-FM can be found at 89.1 on the FM dial and can be heard within about a 50-mile radius of Teaneck.

*REAL ESTATE, IRISH—
FOR RENT*

House and cottage owners throughout Ireland welcome vacationers who'd like to rent their homes instead of staying in the usual hotel. Irish-American newspapers—especially *The Irish Echo,* New York, and *The Irishman,* San Francisco—regularly run advertisements for such rentals. U.S. consular offices can refer you to appropriate real estate agents in either the Republic or Northern Ireland. (See "Government Offices —Republic of Ireland" and "Government Offices—United Kingdom.")

The Irish Tourist Board also has two helpful free booklets you may wish to request: *Rent an Irish Cottage* and *Self-Catering Accommodation.* (See "Travel— Information" for the address of its main U.S. office.)

Shannon Development Company serves as agent for a number of rental-cottage developments in the south and west of Ireland. Your travel agent may obtain information or make reservations for you by calling, toll free, one of the wholesale tour operators listed in this directory under "Travel, Ireland—Wholesale Tour Brokers and Operators."

*REAL ESTATE, IRISH—
FOR SALE*

You needn't be an Irish citizen to own property in Ireland. For current listings, check for classified and display advertisements in various Irish-American newspapers, especially *The Echo* and

The Irishman. (See "Newspapers —Irish-American.")

You may also contact the nearest Irish or British consulate —depending on the county of interest—and request the names and addresses of local real estate agents. (See "Government Offices—Republic of Ireland in the United States" or "Government Offices—United Kingdom in the United States.")

RECORDINGS—IRISH MUSIC

As you probably know, the recording industry is going through a period of dramatic change. Compact discs (CDs) are becoming more popular— though they still run second to cassette tapes—while few new long-playing records are being issued and inventories of LPs already issued are quite small in many stores. Most of the companies listed here are responding, to one degree or another, to these changes. Because the market has not yet stabilized, however, we will not specify the formats of recordings published or stocked by each. Call them or request their catalogs for current information.

THE EVEREST RECORD GROUP
Box 699
Beverly Hills, CA 90212
(213) 557-0309

Request free catalog describing Everest's Irish recordings, which include performances by prominent Irish musicians and groups.

DOWN HOME MUSIC
10341 San Pablo Avenue
El Cerrito, CA 94530
(415) 525-1494

Features one of the largest selections available of Irish traditional and folk music. Also available: books of Irish tunes and song lyrics, and instrumental instruction books. Sells through its own retail store as well as by mail and phone. Ask to receive their bimonthly newsletter, which describes new Irish recordings.

IRISH IMPORT SHOP
738 North Vine Street
Hollywood, CA 90004
(213) 467-6714

Carries a wide selection of traditional Irish music in various recording formats. Contact for details.

IRISH IMPORT SHOP
3244 Geary Boulevard
San Francisco, CA 94118
(415) 752-0961

Recordings of traditional Irish musical groups, show bands, ceili music, and leading Irish singers, past and present: "One of the most extensive collections of Irish music available in the United States."

GREEN LINNET RECORDS
70 Turner Hill Road
New Canaan, CT 06840
(203) 966-0864

Green Linnet's free catalog of traditional and folk music recordings serves up a generous helping of Irish fare. Each recording is described in detail. All formats available. Sells at retail (to individuals) and wholesale. Mail orders only.

IRISH RECORDS
INTERNATIONAL
Box 196
Accord, MA 02018
(617) 878-7936; (800) 338-1757

Stocks a good selection of albums by the leading Irish recording artists, including the Clancy Brothers, the Irish Rovers, the Dubliners and James Galway. Serves mail-order and wholesale customers. Request free catalog.

BRIGGS AND BRIGGS, INC.
1270 Massachusetts Avenue
Cambridge, MA 02138
(617) 547-2007

Stocks a variety of Irish recordings, including many hard-to-find imported traditional items.

SANDY'S RECORD SHOP
896A Massachusetts Avenue
Cambridge, MA 02139
(617) 491-2812

Offers a wide selection of Irish traditional and folk music. Fills mail orders.

WALTON MUSIC
CORPORATION
P.O. Box 1505
Westfield, MA 01086
(413) 562-0223; (800) 541-5004

See listing under "Musical Instruments, Irish—Traditional."

SHANACHIE RECORDS
37 East Clinton Street
Newton, NJ 07860
(201) 579-7763

One of the largest sources in the United States for recordings of traditional Irish music. Also: books of traditional Irish music for various instruments. Sells at both retail and wholesale. Request free catalog.

THE CELTIC CONNECTION
282 East 204th Street
Bronx, NY 10467
(212) 231-1210

Stocks about 400 Irish record and tape titles as well as recordings from other Celtic nations.

REGO IRISH RECORDS & TAPES, INC.
64 New Hyde Park Road
Garden City, NY 11530
(800) 854-ERIN;
(516) 328-7800 in New York State

Sells a large selection of recordings by Irish popular singers and musicians as well as traditional groups. Request free catalog, which also includes several videos.

FIESTA RECORD COMPANY
251 Broadway
Lynbrook, NY 11563
(516) 599-5522

Request free catalog of international recordings, including over 25 Irish selections.

RELEASE RECORDS
225 Washington Street
Mount Vernon, NY 10550
(914) 667-8900; (800) 922-TUNE

Imports or produces and distributes "the largest collection of Irish traditional and ballad material." Sells both at retail and wholesale. Mail orders only. Request free catalog.

ALCAZAR PRODUCTIONS, INC.
Box 429
Waterbury, VT 05676
(802) 244-5178

Sells by mail recordings on about 350 different labels, including a wide variety of Irish selections. Request free catalog, which lists Irish items under "British Isles." Also sells at wholesale under the name Silo, Inc.

RELIGIOUS GOODS & BOOKS

ST. PAUL BOOKS & MEDIA CENTER
172 North Michigan Avenue
Chicago, IL 60601
(312) 346-4228

THOMAS P. EGAN & SONS
518 Gallivan Boulevard
Dorchester, MA 02122
(617) 436-4360; (800) 442-2099 in Massachusetts; (800) 235-0003 in other states

Religious articles and church supplies, including statues, rosary beads, religious pictures and memorials.

M. J. CURLEY COMPANY
1360 Hancock Street
Quincy, MA 02169
(617) 770-1205

Religious articles, including rosaries and medals, books, church supplies, recordings, candles and memorials. Request free catalog.

RESORTS—IRISH-AMERICAN

New York's Catskill Mountains may be better known for their "Borscht Belt," a mecca for vacationing Jewish-Americans, but two communities to the northeast—East Durham and Cairo—are the Irish-American equivalent. Whether for a weekend or longer, these resorts offer Irish-style food, gift shopping, entertainment, and hotels for every budget. For information on attractions and accommodations, contact:

**EAST DURHAM
  VACATIONLAND
Box 67
East Durham, NY 12423
(518) 622-3243**

Though no other resorts rival these Catskill communities, several other Northeastern resorts have hotels and establishments catering primarily to Irish-Americans. Among these are the New Jersey seaside towns of Atlantic City, Ocean City and Cape May, and several Cape Cod communities. For details on these, check ads in Irish-American newspapers serving New York, Philadelphia and Boston. (See "Newspapers—Irish-American.")

SCHOLARSHIPS

COMHALTAS CEOLTOIRI EIREANN/THE TRADITIONAL IRISH MUSICIANS ASSOCIATION

This international group works to preserve traditional Irish music through performances, teaching and other means. Local chapters generally offer scholarships to permit talented young performers to pursue formal music studies. (See "Organizations, Irish-American—National" for contact information.)

**HIBERNIAN LIFE
  INSURANCE
790 South Cleveland Avenue
Suite 221
St. Paul, MN 55116
(612) 690-3888**

HLI funds several scholarships each year, under two programs: (1) nonpublic high school scholarships, and (2) scholarships for The Irish Way, which support summer study under a program operated by the Irish American Cultural Institute, St. Paul, Minn. (See "Travel, Ireland— Student Travel" and "Travel/ Study Programs.") For details on scholarship eligibility and application forms, contact HLI.

NEW YORK IRISH HISTORY ROUNDTABLE
P.O. Box 2087
Church Street Station
New York, NY 10008

This group offers financial aid to graduate and postgraduate students engaged in research involving Irish-American his- tory, especially subjects with a New York connection. Write for details and application form.

THE DERMOT HARRIS FOUNDATION
University of Scranton
Scranton, PA 18510

The Irish-born screen actor Sir Richard Harris recently estab- lished this fund—in memory of his late brother—to provide complete scholarship support for study at the University of Scranton for promising young Irish men and women of all faiths. The Dermot Harris Scholarships may be used for study in any of the 42 major fields offered by the University.

Write for application forms and other details. The Foundation also welcomes donations, which are tax-deductible.

SOUVENIR ITEMS, WHOLESALE AND RETAIL— FOR FUNDRAISING, FESTIVALS, PROMOTIONS, ETC.

ERIN INTERNATIONAL COMPANY
15 Denmark Avenue
Milton, MA 02186
(617) 696-1470

Sells a variety of "Irish" items, including Claddagh, shamrock and U.S.A./Ireland flag pins; keychains; jewelry; brass door knockers; caps; T-shirts; and stick-ons. Request free catalog.

SPEAKERS—SOURCES

IRISH PERSPECTIVES
c/o Irish American Cultural Institute
Mail 5026
2115 Summit Avenue
College of St. Thomas
St. Paul, MN 55105
(612) 647-5678

Each year, Irish Perspectives brings several public figures, scholars, writers, artists and others from Ireland to speak before members of the dozen or so IACI chapters across the United States. Sometimes, arrangements can be made for these individuals to speak before other groups, perhaps including yours. In such cases, additional fees and expenses are, of course, the responsibility of your organization. Write Irish Perspectives at the address provided, asking to be put on their mailing list for schedules of upcoming speakers, and for details on how to arrange a program for your group.

SPORTS, GAELIC—IN THE UNITED STATES

Since its founding at Thurles, County Tipperary, in 1884, the Gaelic Athletic Association (GAA) has worked to foster traditional Irish sports as part of a broader effort to preserve traditional Irish culture. Hurling and Gaelic football have been the mainstays of GAA competition from the beginning; handball, a centuries-old Gaelic sport, and camogie, a women's version of hurling, have joined the GAA repertoire more recently.

In the United States, officially sanctioned Gaelic sports competition comes under the auspices of two separate and mutually exclusive bodies: the GAA of New York governs local teams and competition in New York, southern Connecticut and northern New Jersey; all other states come under the jurisdiction of the GAA/North American Board.

Each spring, before the start of its regular season, the New York GAA hosts exhibition matches at Gaelic Park, The Bronx, against all-star hurling and football teams from Ireland. U.S. GAA teams also make annual playing visits to Ireland. Now that the Central Division of the GAA/North American Board has moved into its splendid new stadium in the Chicago suburbs, we may expect more exchanges of this type involving teams outside New York. Most New York GAA games are played at:

GAELIC PARK
4000 Corlear Avenue
Bronx, NY 10463
(212) 548-9568

Schedules for New York GAA events are published in the *Irish Echo* at least two weeks in advance. Games under the GAA/North American Board are held at facilities throughout the country, including the Chicago area's new Gaelic sports park:

GAELIC PARK
6119 West 147th Street
Tinley Park, IL 60477
(312) 687-9323

The latest annual schedule of games under the GAA/North American Board is available from:

GAELIC ATHLETIC ASSOCIATION
North American Board
9145 South Central Park
Evergreen Park, IL 60642
(312) 636-8560

SPORTS—LIVE BROADCASTS FROM IRELAND

NORBERT HENNESSY
5824 Broadway
Bronx, NY 10463
(212) 601-3833

Hennessy, who runs the Irish Sports Results telephone line and distributes videocassettes of Irish sports matches through Irish Video, can also arrange for your group to hear live radio broadcasts of football, hurling and other Irish sports matches via transatlantic connection.

SPORTS—ORGANIZATIONS
(See also "Sports, Gaelic—in the United States.")

NORTH AMERICAN CURRACH ASSOCIATION
Attn.: James Gallagher,
Secretary
351 Boston Post Road
East Lyme, CT 06333
(203) 739-8216

This group works to revive and foster the traditional craft of building *currachs,* small boats used for centuries along the western coast of Ireland. It also sponsors races among crews from currach clubs in various cities, which include New London, Conn.; Annapolis, Md.; City Island, N.Y.; New York, N.Y.; and Pittsburgh, Pa. The races are usually held as part of festivals designed to keep alive the broader Irish cultural traditions associated with currach building.

SPORTS—RESULTS FROM IRELAND

IRISH SPORTS RESULTS LINE
(212) 601-3800

A three-minute recording that reports the latest team sports scores from Ireland. A new tape goes on-line each Sunday at about 2:00 p.m. This free service—you pay only for the phone call—maintains over 20 lines to handle incoming calls.

STAMPS, IRISH POSTAGE— ORGANIZATIONS

EIRE PHILATELIC ASSOCIATION
Attn.: Robert C. Jones, Secretary
Eight Beach Street
Brockton, MA 02402
(508) 587-6382

Affiliated with an Irish parent organization, the Eire Philatelic Association is open to adults interested in Irish stamps and other philatelic items, especially as collectors. EPA currently has 10 chapters across the United States with about 800 members. It holds informal meetings coordinated with major U.S. stamp expositions, conducts mail auctions of Irish stamps and related materials, publishes an informative quarterly, *The Revealer,* and holds an annual meeting, sometimes irregularly. Dues are $10/yr. Write for membership kit.

TELEVISION PROGRAMS— IRISH-AMERICAN

IRISH TELEVISION/ CHICAGO
Cablecom/Abbey Productions
3825 North Elston Avenue
Chicago, IL 60618
(312) 539-6000

A weekly one-hour program in "magazine" format. Typical programs include local and national Irish-American news; news from Ireland; feature stories (which have dealt with golfing in Ireland, shark fishing off Achill Island, and climbing Croagh Patrick, a place of pilgrimage associated with St. Patrick); performances of Irish song, dance and music, both traditional and popular; and sports coverage. The producers hope to "go national" with the program before long. Meanwhile, it can be seen in Chicago on Group W Cable, Chicago Cable and on systems serving about 30 suburban communities. For the time and station, check your cable program guide or phone the number provided here.

IRELAND ON THE MOVE
Box 583
Hyde Park, NY 02136
(617) 364-3041

A one-hour program covering news of Irish-American activities in the Greater Boston area, including sports, politics, festivals and personalities. Each program also offers a feature segment and an interview with an author, entertainer, businessperson or other personality of Irish-American interest. New programs air every two weeks. Can be seen in the Boston area on Cable Channel A3 (BNN, Public Access) Fridays at 8:00 p.m. The same show repeats the following week. In some other parts of the state, the show may be seen on other cable systems.

IRISH CIRCLE NEWS
MAGAZINE
Attn.: Larry McEvoy
c/o Celtic Productions
527 Third Avenue
New York, NY 10016
(212) 689-4853

A typical program includes coverage of Irish and Irish-American news, a cultural feature, a guest editorial, and a brief Irish-language lesson. Telecast on Manhattan Cable TV and Paragon Cable TV, Channel 16, each Tuesday from 6:00 to 6:30

p.m. The producers are currently trying to secure a regularly scheduled slot on Brooklyn/Queens Cable TV, Channel 35 (Public Access).

TRAVEL—IRELAND—
BOOKINGS—RETAIL TRAVEL
AGENTS

Nearly any travel agency can handle the arrangements you need for a trip to Ireland. Those we list are agencies owned and/or operated by Irish-Americans, many of them Irish-born. They are likely to have more specialized Ireland-related experience than the average agency, and be better able to help you plan a satisfying visit.

IRELAND TRAVEL
HEADQUARTERS
3355 Mount Diablo
Boulevard
Lafayette, CA 94549
(415) 283-7521

O'CALLAGHAN TRAVEL
1527 Wilshire Boulevard
Los Angeles, CA 90017
(213) 413-2525

LOPEZ TRAVEL
Attn.: Mrs. Pat Foley
303 A Street
San Diego, CA 92101
(619) 232-2128

HIBERNIA
  INTERNATIONAL
  TRAVEL SERVICE/IRISH
  AIR AGENCY
2123 Market Street
San Francisco, CA 94114
(415) 863-1126

IRELAND TRAVEL
  CONSULTANTS/
  KIVLEHAN TRAVEL
3150 California
San Francisco, CA 94115
(415) 567-2882

IRELAND TRAVEL
  HEADQUARTERS
680 Beach
San Francisco, CA 94109
(415) 885-5563

IRISH TRAVEL SERVICE
3157 Geary Boulevard
San Francisco, CA 94118
(415) 752-0961

TARA TRAVEL, INC.
681 Market Street
San Francisco, CA 94105
(415) 777-4555

ROUND TOWER TRAVEL
6754 Diversey Street
Chicago, IL 60635
(312) 889-7533; (800) 621-7442

GAFFNEY TRAVEL
  SERVICE
4604 West 103rd Street
Oak Lawn, IL 60453
(312) 636-1683

ROUND TOWER TRAVEL
11700 Old Columbia Pike
Silver Spring, MD 20904
(301) 421-9042; (800) 225-9988

HOLIDAIR TRAVEL
210 Boylston Street
Chestnut Hill, MA 02167
(617) 969-4650

JULIA'S TRAVEL SERVICE
126 Alden Street
Dedham, MA 02026
(617) 326-0388

ROUND TOWER TRAVEL
18 Central Street
Norwood, MA 02062
(617) 762-9090

ABBEY TRAVEL SERVICE
657 Adams Street
Quincy, MA 02169
(617) 479-7990

IRELAND-AMERICAN
  FLIGHTS & TOURS/
  IRELAND TRAVEL
  CENTER
15 Crescent
Waltham, MA 02154
(617) 899-7733

IRISH TRAVEL
  SPECIALISTS
1896 Centre
West Roxbury, MA 02132
(617) 327-1300

TARA TRAVEL
389 Highway 35
Middletown, NJ 07701
(201) 530-2020

GRIMES TRAVEL AGENCY
95 Madison Avenue
Morristown, NJ 07960
(201) 539-6674

CELTIC INTERNATIONAL
  TOURS
161 Central Avenue
Albany, NY 12206
(518) 463-5511

DONOGHUE HEALY
  O'SULLIVAN TRAVEL
22 East Kingsbridge Road
Bronx, NY 10468
(212) 733-4600

MURPHY & BROWN
  TRAVEL
25 East Bedford Park
  Boulevard
Bronx, NY 10468
(212) 584-2224

SHAMROCK WORLDWIDE
  TRAVEL SERVICE
6045 Riverdale Avenue
Bronx, NY 10471
(212) 549-8898

TARA TRAVEL
265 West 231st Street
Bronx, NY 10463
(212) 548-6500

GLENWOOD TRAVEL
1485 Flatbush Avenue
Brooklyn, NY 11210
(718) 434-4344

BRENDAN WARD TRAVEL
86–16 Queens Boulevard
Elmhurst, NY 11373
(718) 651-6161; (800) 251-6161

BRIAN MAY TRAVEL
37–12 82nd Street
Jackson Heights, NY 11372
(718) 458-0030

SHANNON TRAVEL
  SERVICE
76–11 37th Avenue
Jackson Heights, NY 11372
(718) 639-0667

DILLON'S TRAVEL, INC.
One East 42nd Street
New York, NY 10017
(212) 490-3510

GRIMES TRAVEL AGENCY
250 West 57th Street
New York, NY 10019
(212) 307-7797

HEALY O'SULLIVAN
  TRAVEL
22 South Main Street
Pearl River, NY 10965
(914) 735-9500

ROCKAWAY TRAVEL
100–02 Rockaway Beach
  Boulevard
Rockaway, NY 11694
(718) 747-8200

GRIMES TRAVEL AGENCY
54 Mamaroneck Avenue
White Plains, NY 10601
(914) 761-4550

PAT LYNCH'S WOODSIDE
  TRAVEL
60–25 Roosevelt Avenue
Woodside, NY 11377
(718) 478-9016

ROUND TOWER TRAVEL
3016 Township Line Road
Drexel Hill, PA 19026
(215) 853-3050; (800) 225-9988

DURKIN WORLD TRAVELS
156 West Chelten Avenue
Philadelphia, PA 19144
(215) 843-4800

*TRAVEL—IRELAND—
INFORMATION*

The Irish Tourist Board operates several U.S. offices. Its
New York office, however, is
best equipped to serve individuals. For general information
and literature; brochures on
attractions, accommodations,
car rentals and escorted tours; or
answers to more specific questions, contact:

IRISH TOURIST BOARD
757 Third Avenue
New York, NY 10017
(212) 418-0800; (800) 223-6470

For similar assistance involving
Northern Ireland, contact:

NORTHERN IRELAND
  TOURIST BOARD
40 East 57th Street
New York, NY 10019
(212) 581-4700

*TRAVEL—IRELAND—RAIL
SERVICE INFORMATION*

IARNROD EIREANN/IRISH
  RAIL
(212) 697-3914; (800) 243-7687
  outside New York

Irish Rail features "Europe's
most modern railway," with

air-conditioned rail cars, on-
board food service and special
bargain-priced rail passes. A
Rail Rambler ticket entitles you
to unlimited rail travel for 8 or
15 days. You may also wish to
ask about Student Youth Rambler tickets and Dublin Explorer
tickets. The latter give you four
days of unlimited train and bus
travel in and around Dublin,
including use of the Dublin
Area Rapid Transit (DART).

TRAVEL—IRELAND— SPECIAL-INTEREST PROGRAMS

IRISH TOURIST BOARD
9th Floor
757 Third Avenue
New York, NY 10017
(212) 418-0800

ITB publishes a series of Information Sheets on various special-interest activities that
visitors to Ireland may enjoy.
They include, to give but a few
examples, pony trekking, fishing (salt- and fresh-water),
genealogical research, visits to
traditional places of pilgrimage,
golf, sailing, fox hunting, and
visits to great houses. They will
be pleased to send you information they may have on your particular interest.

TRAVEL—IRELAND— STUDENT TRAVEL & TRAVEL/STUDY PROGRAMS

PROGRAM IN IRISH SOCIETY & POLITICS
c/o Department of Politics
Catholic University of
America
620 Michigan Avenue, N.E.
Washington, DC 20017
(202) 635-5488

U.S. college students accepted
for this one-semester program
work in Dublin as research
assistants to members of the
Irish parliament. Request details
and application forms.

THE IRISH WAY PROGRAM
c/o The Irish American
Cultural Institute
Mail 5026
2115 Summit Avenue
College of St. Thomas
St. Paul, MN 55105
(612) 647-5678

This summer program is
designed to give American
high-school students a five-
week Irish experience that
includes educational, cultural,
recreational and social aspects.
Based at Gormanston College, a
superbly equipped campus
north of Dublin, participants

spend five weeks in planned activities, including (1) non-graded classes and field trips dealing with Irish history, current affairs, literature, language, sports, music, song and dance; (2) horseback riding, golf, tennis, swimming and other sports; (3) evening activities such as movies, ceilis, discos, group talent shows and the like. Each teenager also spends several days as the guest of a selected Irish family.

Program costs are $1,650 per student, plus airfare and money for personal expenses such as gifts, souvenirs, postage, snacks, horseback riding and some local transportation. A limited number of scholarships —generally covering part of the costs—are funded by various Irish and Irish-American organizations. For further information, application forms and (if desired) a scholarship application, contact the program administrator at the address above. Applications should be submitted as soon as possible after January 1 of the year in which the student wishes to participate.

ENCOUNTER IRELAND
c/o Council on International
Educational Exchange
(CIEE)

205 East 42nd Street
New York, NY 10017
(212) 661-1414

CIEE, in cooperation with the Union of Students in Ireland—Travel (USIT), offers this five-week summer travel/study program for U.S. college students. The program is based at historic Trinity College, Dublin (TCD), where participants attend lectures and seminars on Irish culture and history. This academic segment, for which academic credit may be arranged, is supplemented by a home stay with an Irish family and an opportunity for independent travel around Ireland. Program costs are between $2,100 and $2,650, depending largely on the cost of airfare between the student's home city and Ireland. For more information and application forms, contact CIEE.

IRISH TOURIST BOARD
757 Third Avenue
New York, NY 10017
(212) 418-0800

ITB publishes an informative booklet, *Live and Learn,* which describes a wide range of programs throughout Ireland for young people. Among them are experiences involving travel, study, voluntary service, summer camp, hostelling and home stays. The booklet also covers programs in bird-watching, golf, hang-gliding, inland cruising and many other special interests. Copies are free, subject to availability. Other helpful ITB publications include Information Sheet #39, *Youth Hostels*.

**U.S. IRISH STUDENT
TRAVEL SERVICE**
356 West 34th Street
New York, NY 10001
(212) 239-4247

This is the U.S. office of the Union of Students in Ireland—Travel (USIT), and operates to help further a cultural exchange agreement designed to help college students in both countries enjoy unique educational and cultural experiences on both sides of the Atlantic. USISTS offers American students discount travel arrangements within Ireland. It also cosponsors the Irish Studies program at Trinity College, Dublin (see previous entry).

*TRAVEL—IRELAND—
WHOLESALE TOUR BROKERS
& OPERATORS—
COMMERCIAL*

BRENDAN TOURS
15137 Califa Street
Van Nuys, CA 91411
(818) 785-9696; (800) 421-8446
  in California; (800) 421-8446
  outside California

**CELTIC INTERNATIONAL
  TOURS**
161 Central Avenue
Albany, NY 12206
(518) 463-5511; (800) 833-4373
  outside New York State

LISMORE TOURS
106 East 31st Street
New York, NY 10016
(212) 685-0100; (800)
  LISMORE outside New
  York City

LYNOTT TOURS
350 Fifth Avenue
New York, NY 10118
(212) 760-0101; (800) 537-7575
  in New York State; (800)
  221-2474 outside New York
  State

EMERALD TOURS
5249 Duke Street
Suite B
Alexandria, VA 22304
(703) 684-2129 from metro
  DC; (800) 368-3267
  nationwide

TRAVEL—IRELAND—
WHOLESALE TOUR BROKERS
& OPERATORS—OFFICIAL

C.I.E. TOURS
  INTERNATIONAL
122 East 42nd Street
New York, NY 10168
(212) 972-5600; (800) 522-5258
  in New York State; (800)
  CIE-TOUR from other
  states nationwide

This is Ireland's official transportation authority, which specializes in booking wholesale
travel arrangements involving
Ireland, the United Kingdom
and/or the Continent. (The Irish
Tourist Board, by contrast, is
responsible for promoting travel
to Ireland by providing information and other services.)
C.I.E. operates the most modern fleet of tour buses in
Europe, and says it stresses
quality in booking arrangements, whether in cottage rentals, self-drive tours, guided
tours, or whatever. In addition
to the 64-page brochure it mails
to thousands of U.S. travel
agents each year, C.I.E. publishes a 128-page *Irish Touring
Guide,* which is given without
charge to individual travel customers when they arrive in Ireland.

VIDEO—RECORDINGS (See
also "Films—Documentary.")

IRISH VIDEO
5824 Broadway (at 238th
  Street)
Bronx, NY 10463
(212) 601-3833 or 549-9698

Distributes recordings of recent
Irish sports matches in hurling,
rugby, Gaelic football and soccer. Tapes are normally available one or two days after an
event, and are supplied on
American-standard (NTSC) cassettes in VHS (and perhaps
Beta) format. Request details.

REGO IRISH RECORDS,
  TAPES & VIDEO, INC.
64 New Hyde Park Road
Garden City, NY 11530
(516) 328-7800

Write or call for free catalog.

CELTIC PRODUCTIONS
527 Third Avenue
New York, NY 10016
(212) 689-4853

Request free *Videos of Ireland*
catalog, which describes about
30 tapes, including Irish travelogues, educational programs,
musical performances, and so
on.

TRIBUNE FILMS
303 Fifth Avenue
New York, NY 10016
(212) 689-3180/3181

Sells several video programs about Ireland, including *Destination Donegal, Lovely Leitrim, Reflections—Ireland, The Magic of Ireland* and *Ireland—Bird's Eye View*. Prices range from $14 to $20, plus $2 postage and handling per tape. Available only in VHS. Request free descriptive price list.

VIDEO—STANDARDS
CONVERSION SERVICES

Important Note: It *seems* simple. Aunt Brigid in Cork sends you a videocassette of, let's say, your cousin's first communion. Her videocassette recorder (VCR) is VHS-format, like yours, so you pop the cassette into your machine and settle back for . . . static! The problem is, European and American VCRs may *look* the same, and the same cassettes fit both, but unless the tape was recorded using the *electronic* format your machine uses, it won't play back.

Irish VCRs use the so-called PAL standard, while their American counterparts are designed to record and play back in NTSC, a different standard. (We're not referring to video format—for example, VHS, Beta or 3/4-inch U-Matic. The standards problem affects all three alike.) So, if you're sending a tape to Ireland —or receiving one from someone there—make sure it's converted to the correct standard before expecting it to play back. The following are services equipped to convert your tapes:

VIDEO RECORDS
  PRODUCTIONS
3 Bayview Drive
San Carlos, CA 94070
(415) 593-4617

PAL VIDEO
19061 Tina Place
Tarzana, CA 91356
(818) 344-1603

GLOBAL VIDEO
  COMMUNICATIONS
  CORPORATION
774 West Church Street
Orlando, FL 32805
(305) 423-8299

IRISH VIDEO
5824 Broadway
Bronx, NY 10463
(212) 549-9698 or 601-3833

A.N.S. INTERNATIONAL
   VIDEO, LTD.
396 Fifth Avenue
New York, NY 10018
(212) 736-1007

DEVLIN PRODUCTIONS,
   INC.
150 West 55th Street
New York, NY 10019
(212) 582-5572

GLOBAL VIDEO
   COMMUNICATIONS
   CORPORATION
333 West 52nd Street
New York, NY 10019
(212) 581-7543

*WATER, IRISH SPRING—
IMPORTED*

If you can't find one of the following Irish bottled spring
waters in your area, contact the
following importers for the
location of dealers near you.

ANHEUSER BUSCH, INC.
One Busch Place
St. Louis, MO 63118
(314) 577-2000

Ballygowan spring water.

IRISH SPRING BEVERAGE
   CO., INC.
P.O. Box 516
Nashua, NH 03061
(603) 673-4936

Irish Spring water.

EMERALD ISLE IMPORTS,
   INC.
P.O. Box 253
Northvale, NJ 07647
(914) 735-9300

Glenpatrick spring water.

WATERS OF IRELAND
351 North Broadway
Suite 1B
Yonkers, NY 10701
(914) 476-2003

Tipperary Irish spring water.

WOOLEN PRODUCTS (See
also "Fashions—Imported.")
Most general Irish import
stores (see "Imports") also
stock at least some imported
wool items.

CELTIC WEAVERS
1 Civic Center Plaza
Hartford, CT 06103
(203) 522-6566

Sells hand-knit Aran and other
sweaters, handwoven throws
and blankets, coats, capes,
shawls, caps, hats, ties and
scarves.

IRISH CROCHET
   TREASURES
P.O. Box 1625
562 Milk Street
Fitchburg, MA 01420
(617) 342-1152

Sells sweaters hand-knit in County Sligo: Aran fishermen's sweaters in cardigan and pullover styles, Icelandic-design pullovers, and mohair pullovers for women. Custom orders welcomed. Request free price list.

WILLIAMSON'S IRISH IMPORTS
6 Fulton Street
South Street Seaport
New York, NY 10038
(212) 425-4331

Stocks traditional and designer items for men and women, including sweaters, capes, women's jackets, tweed hats and scarves.

MRS. McKENNA'S
10 Anderson Avenue
Ardmore, PA 19003
(215) 642-8110

Sells imported hand-knit fishermen's sweaters, scarves, mittens, and hats.

IRISH DESIGN CENTER
303 South Craig Street
Pittsburgh, PA 15213
(412) 682-6125

Handwoven pure wool shawls, 54 inches square, made by Avoca Handweavers, Ireland's oldest handweaving mill, dating from 1723.

YARN—IMPORTED

IRISH IMPORTS LTD.
1735 Massachusetts Avenue
Cambridge, MA 02138
(617) 354-2511

Stocks three-ply knitting yarns from the Kerry Woolen Mills, Beaufort, County Kerry. These are well-suited for knitting Irish sweaters, scarves, hats, afghans, mittens, etc. Eight-ounce skeins are $9.60 each, and are available in 10 colors, including creamy white, slate blue and Kelly green.

Index

*(Page numbers in **boldface** indicate listings in The Green Pages.)*

About the Author

BRIAN E. COOPER, a professional writer, book packager, and communications consultant, conceived and edited the first edition of *The Irish-American Almanac & Green Pages,* which was published in 1986. Mr. Cooper is a member of the American Conference for Irish Studies and the American Irish Historical Society, reflecting his interest in history and in his Irish heritage, in particular.

Mr. Cooper has held managerial and writing positions in corporate and agency public relations and advertising/marketing. He has worked at Hill and Knowlton, the world's largest public relations firm, and at St. Regis Paper Company, Harcourt Brace Jovanovich, Treadway Inns & Resorts, and The Port Authority of New York and New Jersey.

Brian Cooper holds degrees in history from Princeton University (B.A. magna cum laude) and the University of Michigan (M.A.). He currently lives in Chapel Hill, N.C.